Palgrave Global Media Policy and Business

The *Palgrave Global Media Policy and Business Series* has published over 22 books since its launch in 2012. Concentrating on the social, cultural, political, political-economic, institutional, and technological changes arising from the globalization and digitization of media and communications industries, the series considers the impact of these changes on business practice, regulation and policy, and social outcomes. The policy side encompasses the challenge of conceiving policy-making as a reiterative process that recurrently addresses such key challenges as inclusiveness, participation, industrial-labor relations, universal access, digital discrimination, and the growing implications of AI in an increasingly globalized world, as well as local challenges to global media business and culture. The business side encompasses a political economy approach that looks at the power of transnational corporations in specific contexts — and the controversies associated with these global conglomerates. The business side considers as well the emergence of small and medium media enterprises, and the role played by nation-states in promoting particular firms and industries.

Based on a multi-disciplinary approach, the series tackles four key questions:

- To what extent do new developments in platforms, and approaches to personal data require radical change in regulatory philosophy and objectives towards the media?
- To what extent do technologies, datafication and transforming media consumption require fundamental changes in business practices and models?
- To what extent do privatisation, datification, globalisation, and commercialisation alter the creative freedom, cultural and political diversity, values and public accountability of media enterprises?
- To what extent does the structure of global communications contribute to (in)equality within the Global South?

Preeti Raghunath
Editor

Critical Political Economy and Southern Approaches to AI

A Dialogue

palgrave
macmillan

Editor
Preeti Raghunath
Lecturer in Digital Media and Society
School of Sociological Studies
University of Sheffield
Sheffield, UK

ISSN 2634-6192 ISSN 2634-6206 (electronic)
Palgrave Global Media Policy and Business
ISBN 978-3-032-14089-0 ISBN 978-3-032-14090-6 (eBook)
https://doi.org/10.1007/978-3-032-14090-6

This Palgrave Macmillan imprint is published by the registered company Springer Nature Switzerland AG.
The registered company address is: Gewerbestrasse 11, 6330 Cham, Switzerland

To those who have and continue to lead 'frontier lives'.
I am grateful to the authors in this edited collection for their work and commitment to this endeavour, and to the editors at Palgrave Macmillan for their patience and professionalism.

Contents

Notes on Contributors

Deepak Prince is an anthropologist with an interest in the sociality of technology (specifically, screen-based computational technologies) and in practices of imagination. Other interests include political anthropology, violence and public art. Deepak was founding sociology faculty at GITAM, Hyderabad. He has also taught at Shiv Nadar University and at IIT Jodhpur. He has an MA in Economics from the Delhi School of Economics and a PhD in Sociology (Anthropology) from Shiv Nadar. He is on the editorial board of the STS journal, *Tecnoscienza*. Deepak co-founded openstudio, an art collective taking an ethnographic approach to public art projects produced collaboratively with local communities.

Preeti Raghunath is Lecturer in Digital Media and Society at the University of Sheffield, UK. Over the past decade, she has traversed academic landscapes in India, Malaysia, and the UK. Her research interests have broadly explored global communication, with a focus on policies, infrastructures, and people. She conducted an expansive policy ethnography on community radio in South Asia, which was published as *Community Radio Policies in South Asia: A Deliberative Policy Ecology Approach* (Palgrave Macmillan, 2020). Her current theoretical and empirical research is on the global AI and data economy, especially as they play out in the Global South. Preeti has served as a research consultant with the United Nations University, Macau on research projects on AI and its policies in Southeast Asia, and digital transformation and sustainability.

Sananda Sahoo is a University Fellow at the University of North Carolina, Asheville, USA. Sananda worked as a journalist and reporter for many years before pursuing a PhD at the University of Western Ontario, where she worked on media representation of violence. Around the same time, she developed an interest in the usage of artificial intelligence in governance and journalism. For the past few years, she has worked on a research project on automated decision-making systems using a multi-technique approach, including mapping, interviews, and document analysis. Her areas of interest span critical data studies, journalism, media studies, and technology law.

Gabrielle Bezerra Sales Sarlet is a professor of the undergraduate course and PPGD at PUCRS—Pontifical Catholic University of Rio Grande do Sul and Coordinator of the specialization course in Digital Law at PUCRS. She is a lawyer and holds a PhD in Law from the University of Augsburg—Germany with a thesis validated by the PPGD—UFGRS, and a Master's degree in Law from the Federal University of Ceará—UFC. She holds a postdoctorate in Law from the University of Hamburg—Germany and also from PUCRS. She is a visiting researcher and scholarship holder at the Max-Planck-Institut für ausländisches und internationales Privatrecht—Hamburg—Germany (2018).

Nishanshi Shukla is a PhD candidate in Arts, Technology, and Emerging Communication at the University of Texas at Dallas. She is an interdisciplinary scholar working in the field of critical digital media studies and digital humanities, specifically critical data and code studies. Her research investigates power and politics of AI by studying caste-based discrimination in India AI systems through a feminist and post-colonial lens.

Lucas Reckziegel Weschenfelder is a doctoral student in Law at the Pontifical Catholic University of Rio Grande do Sul, and a PhD International Researcher at Goethe Universität. Lucas holds a Law degree.

Suci Lestari Yuana is a lecturer at Universitas Gadjah Mada specializing in digital platforms, ridesharing, sustainability transitions, circular economy, and innovation in the Global South. She earned her PhD from Utrecht University and leads the STAIR Community Indonesia. Yuana's research includes Mundane Circular Economy and AI Colonialism, and she serves as managing editor of Global South Review. She has won Best Paper Awards in International Sustainability Transition Conferences 2020.

List of Figures

CHAPTER 1

Conversing Across Incommensurables?: Critical Political Economy and Southern Approaches to Artificial Intelligence

Preeti Raghunath

Sheela is a young graduate with a Bachelor of Sciences degree from one of the colleges in a district of Telangana, India. She initially wanted to pursue a Bachelor of Education (BEd) degree after her education in the sciences, to become a school teacher. Schools that she knew could employ her were at least 20 kilometres away in the town. Her house was in one of the villages and transportation was not the easiest to come by. One day, a friend informed Sheela of a "computer company" setting up shop in their village and looking to recruit bright young women with Bachelor's degrees. Excited and curious, Sheela went and found out more, attended interviews and landed a job at what was a data labelling and annotation firm that had come up in their village. She would now clean datasets, label and tag images and texts, and segregate data. What's more, she would not have to travel to the town for a job. This was happening right in the vicinity of her house!.

P. Raghunath (✉)
University of Sheffield, Sheffield, UK
e-mail: p.raghunath@sheffield.ac.uk

P. Raghunath (ed.), *Critical Political Economy and Southern Approaches to AI*, Palgrave Global Media Policy and Business, https://doi.org/10.1007/978-3-032-14090-6_1

Young women like Sheela form the backbone of the USD 807.0 million (figures as per 2022) international data annotation industry, only poised to grow rapidly at a CAGR of almost 30% over the next few years. These data annotation firms cater to the rapidly expanding artificial intelligence and cloud computing markets, catering directly to their data training needs. Data annotation firms form part of the global value supply chain of the 'data industries'. As I have written elsewhere,

> Data industries are enterprise ventures of diverse proportions, from big technology corporations and platforms to small annotation firms located in the Global South that serve as conduits to a workforce that then work on outsourced data labelling jobs. They further include massive data centres built as part of cloud infrastructures as well as data analytics firms. The phrase 'data industries' allows us to trace, locate and bring the lens onto these varied enterprise ventures that have and continue to be deeply implicated in different ways in the business of datafication. These data industries exercise a huge influence, impacting lives and livelihoods, informing governance and framing regulation. (Raghunath 2023a)

Even as the setting up of these firms in countries in the Global South points to opportunities for social mobility as well as altering the gendered nature of the IT job market, the reality is a lot more complex. Human labour is a big part of what is seen as an automated, self-learning industry (Chandhiramowuli and Chaudhuri 2023). News reportage on the deployment of cheap labour at firms housed in Asia, Africa, and Latin America to clean and feed datasets for the training of these AI systems is steadily streaming in (Williams et al. 2022). These include reports on the low-paid Kenyan workers behind ChatGPT who earn less than $2 an hour. Time Magazine's report (Perrigo 2023) highlights the precarious and difficult conditions of work faced by data enrichment workers behind the Generative AI application that has had an impact across sectors and spheres of work and life. Sama brands itself as an ethical AI company uplifting thousands of data workers by providing them employment opportunities and takes on outsourced data labelling and content moderation contracts from big technology corporations. Kenyan data workers recently petitioned the country's National Assembly, calling for an investigation into the work conditions at companies like Sama. The world of content moderation has been rife with dark stories of excruciating and exploitative work conditions for a few years now. The documentary, *The Cleaners*, sheds light on these conditions and practices in countries like the Philippines. Big Tech corporations are now slowly being implicated in ensuring that their content moderators are provided mental health support.

All of these realities on ground make it imperative that academia takes cognisance of work and employment in the transnational data industries, as also the hierarchical nature of the global distribution of this work. These instances, though new in the context of the technology in question, are still not without precedent. Such global patterns of the extraction of transnational labour and distribution of resources are quite entrenched. They have been studied in the context of the outsourcing of technology and business processes (Chandrasekhar 2005), content moderation services (Gillespie 2018), and ghost work (Gray and Suri 2019). Research in recent years has showcased how machine learning (ML) and artificial intelligence (AI) technologies are prone to accentuating inequities already existing in societies, through black-box training of datasets laden with biases that reflect such societal imbalances (Buolamwini and Gebru 2018). Evidently, taking cognisance of this global division of labour would not offer a full picture without taking into account the internal colonisation within societies, which gets compounded and amplified in the face of geopolitical inequities. This must be addressed by any effort aimed at mitigating these inequities that are premised, as the above authors among others, on extant disparities along patriarchal, racialised, eugenicist, casteist, regional, economic and ableist lines that then get amplified by selective design and implementation of these technologies.

This introductory chapter aims to address the premise of this edited collection—locating these "localised" marginal experiences in the larger context, by placing in conversation the frameworks of Critical Political Economy (CPE) and experiences of Southernness. While Critical Political Economy (Cox 1981, 1987) has been useful in delineating and critiquing structural conditions that give rise to marginalisation and powerlessness, Southern theorising and approaches have been able to dislodge the universalist assumptions of Western theoretical traditions to focus on experiences of the South. Both sets of frameworks have come under criticism—CPE for not accounting for agency and focusing on a critique of macro-structural factors, and Southern Theory for risking being particularistic as well as charges of determinism. Certainly, both theoretical traditions are complex and successfully offer explication and accounts of structural and situated experiences from their own vantage points. This chapter is an effort in placing these two supposedly incommensurable theoretical endeavours in conversation, in a bid to piece together the AI story. While the task appears to be daunting, this chapter draws inspiration from and joins recent efforts being made in a similar vein.

For instance, Chiumbu and Radebe (2020) present the possibilities for a decolonial critical political economy approach to media with a focus on the African continent, where they draw on Marxist theory and decolonial thought to identify strands of common concern. They talk about how Marxist political economy has been critiqued for presenting a linear teleology of development, reducing its main concerns to issues of class alone, for being Eurocentric and not explicitly addressing colonialism. The authors talk about how "… 'stretching' Marxism to foreground explicitly issues of race, empire, and coloniality become imperative" (ibid, 2021, 9). They then go on to retheorise ownership, ideology, and production of media texts from a decolonial critical political economy perspective. From a different arena, Jessop et al. (2012) has written about a cultural political economy approach, seeking to place what is perceived as a "soft" cultural approach rooted in constructivism to a "hard" political economy approach that focuses on materialism more directly. Grosfoguel (2009) draws on the epistemic perspective of border thinking, among others, to shed both dominant and marginal fundamentalisms, in writing about a decolonial approach to political economy. Finally, in my recent writing, I have tried to place in dialogue critical theory and a Southern Standpoint as proposed by Go (2016), with the latter drawing on feminist standpoint theory and perspectival realism, in order to present a situated, historicised, relational, and reflexive approach to data governance (Raghunath 2023b). All of these efforts are useful in my continued endeavour to address questions of power and conflict in the starkly unequal global distribution of technological know-how, quality of access and work. This leads us to explore a dialogue between critical and Southern approaches to technology, broadly speaking, and to AI, specifically. The key contribution of this chapter that sets the tone for this edited collection, is this novel integration of the Critical Political Economy framework and Southern approaches to technology. This chapter synthesises four key principles from this dialogue and cross-pollination, elaborated towards the end.

The first section following this introductory setting of the scene presents the Critical Political Economy framework, criticisms levied against the framework, and its approach to technology. The second section draws out the various definitions of what it means to be talking about the 'South', and engages with scholarship on Southernness. It then explores criticisms of Southern theorising, and presents Southern approaches to technology. The third section places the two frameworks discussed thus far in dialogue, and attempts to tease out commonalities and incompatibilities. The section then explores some common conceptual frames, before moving on to present a set of principles to draw on towards an emancipatory project of technology. It does so by thinking through the possibilities of engaging with *geosocial* location as a standpoint to the global as seen in the case of AI technologies and associated businesses. The chapter then weaves together the contributions presented in this collection as themes.

Critical Political Economy as a Framework

Critical Political Economy (CPE) grew to become a strand under the broader umbrella of Political Economy. While having been specifically rooted in Marxist and the Frankfurt School of Critical Theory, in particular, the framework has encompassed other kinds of critical theorising, including feminism, anti-racism, and anti-casteism. The common concerns that tie together these critical theories are their critique of situated and entrenched power structures, commodification of human labour, extraction of value from labour and its consolidation by corporations, and similar ideas that are particularly rooted in critiques of capitalism and neoliberal economic policies and practices. What is characteristic of CPE is its focus on presenting a materialist critique of such conditions. Robert Cox (1987, p. 1), arguably one of the first proponents of Critical International Political Economy, wrote about how production "creates the material basis for all forms of social existence, and the ways in which human efforts are combined in productive processes affect all other aspects of social life". The focus on materialism is a central tenet of CPE. Importantly, CPE provides us the vocabulary and strategy to study inequalities and how they are produced and reproduced across institutional and non-institutional settings. However, critique is not the only thing that CPE offers. In presenting a critique of unequal societal conditions, CPE also strives to produce knowledge that contributes to the emancipatory project. What follows is an engagement with some scholarship on CPE and how the framework has been approached in the context of technology.

The 'Critical' in CPE

Scholars have been looking at the political economy of international systems in varied ways. International Political Economy (IPE) as a field has involved an empirical study of actors and their practices in the international system. However, at least since the 1970s, there have been divides along the approach to the study of the international system. The Latin American Dependency School had its influence in providing a core-periphery framing of the world system, which provided a global view of the distribution and deployment of capital and labour. Cox wrote about the divide incisively as the distinction between International Political Economy's 'problem-solving' and positivist approach and Critical International Political Economy's focus on emancipation and post-positivism (1981). The divide became pronounced under monikers of the 'American' School championing the problem-solving and empiricist approach, and the 'British' School that espoused a social and post-positivist lens (Shields et al. 2011). While both sides have provided justifications and critiques of themselves and each other, the popularity of Critical Political Economy became more pronounced after the 2008 global financial crisis. Scholars on the 'critical' side of the divide pointed to IPE's inability to predict the crisis and offer any solutions. They were able to develop their critique of the capitalist economy further and raise questions around inequity, extraction of surplus value and accumulation, all central to CPE. In the context of massive concerns around wars and the global climate crisis, it becomes even more imperative for us to adequately engage with these questions of power, resource extraction, and redistribution. As Shields et al. (ibid.) who drew on Worth (2011) suggest, CPE does not merely dismantle existing frameworks. Instead, there must be an understanding of how things could change in favour of equity, dignity, and rights.

In writing about Global Political Economy, Wigger (2022) provides reasons for a critical political economy approach to its study. She emphasises that the usage of 'critical' has now become more of a fad, and must not be understood as solely critiquing or criticising. Drawing on Cox (1996), she argues that criticality does not end at critique, but in sharing alternative visions of how things could be. While criticism is usually understood as negative judgement, critique is an inquiry into truth claims, how they get naturalised and how they may be unsettled. Wigger talks about the unification of theory and practice as central to critical scholarship and work, where ideas of building theory from praxis and to influence praxis are engaged with. She also makes an important point on the idea of neutrality, and how critical is seen as normative, while other forms of positivist research are seen as objective, neutral, and not normative when in fact they are just as value-laden. The myth of neutrality plaguing our understanding of objectivity is something she contests.

Jäger (2022) writes about dialectical and historical materialist methodology as central to CPE. The author quotes Marx (2012), in writing that, "The concrete is concrete because it is the concentration of many determinations, hence unity of the diverse. It appears in the process of thinking, therefore, as a process of concentration, as a result, not as a point of departure, even though it is the point of departure in reality and hence also the point of departure for observation and conception." While this may be useful for the CPE project, it has oftentimes come under scathing criticism—for obscuring what are seen as "particularist" or "localised" experiences—from imperialism to discrimination along gender, caste, and racial lines. Further and more generally, CPE has come under criticism for its overt and almost conflated reliance on Gramscian and in turn, Marxian thought, mainly due to Cox's engagement with them and his influence on CPE. However, CPE spans many disciplines and strands of critical theory. The criticisms only highlight and necessitate dialogic and deliberative intellectual engagement with other approaches and ways of thinking, not with the intent to integrate but in the vein of seeking common ground and staying attuned to lived realities even in catering to a so-called intellectual project. Section "Critical Political Economy Contra Southernness?: A Dialogue" of this chapter engages with these predicaments further.

Critical Political Economy and Media Technology

This subsection looks at interdisciplinary scholarship pertaining to a critical political economy approach to digital media technologies, before engaging with some concepts that have been influential in such an endeavour. A glaring aspect of much work on presenting a critique of media and capitalism, broadly put, is that they focus on "political economy", which falls under a centre-right tent in the spectrum of economic policies. Some scholars have presented a critique of such confusing conflation of political economy, which Marx critiqued, with left-wing tendencies. Some others continue to use the terminology to indicate a critical political economy perspective. Mosco (2009) presents a political economy of communication, writing extensively on media concentration and commodification.

Media scholar Nick Garnham (1979) situates the political economy of media in a wider social framing of cultural production and reproduction. Hardy (2014) writes that scholars have underscored democratic and participatory processes as being relinquished in the face of capture of private capital in media institutions (McChesney 2012; Murdock and Golding 2005) and instead espouse equity and fairness. Fuchs' works have presented a critical theory of communication and media, broadly speaking (2016).

With the doubling up of Big Tech corporations as media entities and the influx of what are seen as emerging technologies, recent scholarship in this realm has focused on digital technologies. Rieder (2022) presents a political economy of technical systems by presenting the case of Google. The author does so by zeroing in on specific technologies that Google works in, proposing the idea of 'data amalgams' to interrogate the manner in which Google operates as a technical system. In doing so, we are acquainted with a materialist critical of specific technologies built and deployed by technical systems. Next, Verdegem presents a good overview of a critical political economy of AI capitalism. Towards this, the author recasts and elaborates on concerns that are key to a CPE framework by looking at data capture, extraction and commodification, the concentration of technological as well as socio-political power in the hands of Big Tech corporations from the Silicon Valley, and AI and compute capacity drawing on ideas of rentier capitalism. Verdegem then moves into presenting an alternative vision by proposing a Commons approach. Most recent work by Lindgren (2023) draws up a Critical Theory of AI and argues for a sociological imagination in approaching AI. The author looks at ideology, social construction of technology, and discursive practices that AI systems perpetuate.

Drawing from the above slice of scholarship, some ideas that are crucial and tied into current conversations to do with a CPE of AI are those of platform and AI capitalism (Srnicek 2016; Verdegem 2022) and the social construction of technologies like AI. One can perhaps suggest that this body of work that is being developed in the context of large-scale policy measures and investments being made into AI, and in the midst of conversations and programmatic agendas on security of AI systems under different nomenclature, all belong under the umbrella of Critical AI Studies. The next section engages with Southernness in its many definitions, and draws attention to work that approaches technology from a Southern perspective.

Southernness as an Axis of Inquiry

When one talks of a possible 'South', 'Southern' or 'Southernness', one risks the word being used in a manner that obscures any other framings of the word. 'South' as an idea, political subjecthood, an experience, a location and more are all important in developing a Southern axis of inquiry. The "South" accrued formal meaning at the Non-Aligned Movement's Bandung conference in 1955, where conversations on South-South cooperation were mentioned by countries who had endured centuries of European colonial rule. Drawing from this, the South may refer to the Global South, but may also be much more. Perspectives and experiences of political subjecthood, subjectivities, shared and peripheral lived experiences of oppression across geographies are important and deemed to underscore Southernness. I would add experiences of internal colonisation within societies as an important element of approaching Southernness, in the mix. Societies in the Global South (as also in the Global North) are deeply divided, with a number of factors rendering many people more marginalised than others. Given the intersecting influences of multiple axes of structures of violence, it becomes important to recognise Southernness as a marginalised, peripheral lived experience across societies, rendered thus due to a multiplier effect of violence. It then becomes clear that any reification of the 'South' as an essentialist category is not a useful exercise in helping us get acquainted with the nuances of lived experience. Having said that, the South is caught between metaphoric allusion and an assertion rooted in praxis. This calls for engagement with scholarship that uses the many meanings attributed to the South.

Engaging with Southernness: Metaphor and Praxis

In scholarship, Raewyn Connell's classic *Southern Theory* (2007) offers an exploration of the contours of Southern Theorising, though it is by no means the first such effort. Scholars like Fanon (1968) and Said (2003) have paved the way to dislodge the stronghold of Eurocentrism. Connell writes about how the discipline of sociology is constructed as being founded on the scholarship of theorists from the Global North, who dominate how the discipline is studied. This obscures earlier work in the discipline by thinkers from non-European backgrounds. Linda Tuhiwai-Smith's much-cited *Decolonizing Methodologies* (2012) critiques European colonialism and imperialism tied to the practice of dominant research. The author presents an approach to research drawing on Kaupapa Maori principles and methods. Sujata Patel (2023), in her masterful overview of the field of global social theory and anti-colonial thought, presents its trajectory in two phases: from 1940s to 1980s, and 1980s to the present day. What follows is a very short sketch of some key scholarship that has contributed to engagement with Southernness. It is by no means an indication of the expanse of scholarship on Southernness, and instead serves as a sampling of such work from Latin America, Asia, and Africa.

Latin American engagement with decolonial thought offers excellent ground to understand the experiences behind concepts like the modernity/coloniality matrix (Quijano 2007; Mignolo 2007), the pluriverse (Escobar 2017), transmodernity (Dussel and Fornazzari 2002), and praxis (Freire 2017). The scholars who have proposed these concepts allow us to engage with histories of colonialism, and its interlinkages with modernity and the erasure of what is seen as "unmodern". Quijano and Mignolo allow us to examine this epistemic violence, not just in non-European contexts but also in the West. Next, the idea of Escobar's Pluriverse emanates from self-governance practices of the Zapatistas in Mexico. In documenting autonomous design practices prevalent among communities in Latin America, Escobar allows us to engage with the concept to collectively develop an anti-capitalist envisioning of a just and sustainable world. Enrique Dussel's tryst with liberation theology/philosophy has been widely influential in presenting a critique of colonialism, imperialism, modernism and postmodernism, through the lens of transmodernism. The transmodern offers a way to integrate plural cultural standpoints as a way to engage with the modern. Here, European modernity is part of the larger puzzle, only not the dominant one. Dussel proposes a plurilectic way to move towards this meta-framework of the transmodern, questioning grand projects that entail totalising narratives and hegemonic power. Paolo Friere develops critical education and praxis as central to his pedagogy. Education is proposed as a means to achieve critical consciousness towards embracing and utilising one's human agency and freedom. Freirian pedagogy was hugely influential on the Latin American liberation philosophy movement of the 1970s.

Similarly, anti-colonial struggles and the development of postcolonial, subaltern, anti-caste, anti-racial and decolonial schools of thought (all of which may overlap or be at odds with each other) from Asia and Africa can be seen as engagement with Southernness. Malaysian intellectual Syed Hussein Alatas (1972) wrote about the "captive mind" in the Asian context, as one that was uncritical, unimaginative, and imitative of Western modes of thinking without any engagement with practices and organic intellectualism existent in one's own context. The concept has since travelled to other parts of the former formally colonised world, helping interrogate knowledge practices. A recent reader on Alatas' thought explores the life of the concept (Byrd and Miri 2022). Bhambra's scholarship on connected sociologies (2012) and global social theory (Bhambra et al. 2019) are useful in helping address Eurocentric underpinnings of much teaching on social theory. She proposes connectedness as a way to unearth and reiterate linkages between European colonialism and the experiences of former colonised nations, thereby bringing explicit recognition to the former. Julian Go has written about postcolonial thought and social theory (2016), manifestations and patterns of empire (2008, 2011, 2023) and most interestingly, on a Southern Standpoint (2016). The sociologist brings feminist standpoint theory, subaltern studies, critical/perspectival realism to bear on questions of empire and modern colonialism. Further, Patel's scholarship on social theory and anti-colonial thought has engaged critically with frames of methodological nationalism (2023). She helps us understand why methodological nationalism, while having some problems, was deemed necessary after formal decolonisation of former colonised nations, in order for them to retrieve, develop, build, and articulate bodies of knowledge rooted in their own experiences. She recognises, at the same time, the need for provincialising Eurocentric scholarship and decolonising nationalist knowledge-building.

Ngũgĩ wa Thiong'o's work on decolonising the mind (1986) focuses on language and its constructive role in developing an identity and consciousness in one's own linguistic background and history. The book presents a critique of imperialism from a linguistic perspective, drawing on language as culture and communication and offers it a preeminent role in human consciousness. Hountondji's view on endogenous knowledge (1997) seeks to unearth knowledge systems and thought rendered obscure by colonialism. The philosopher has been critical of the use of the term "indigenous" as being pejorative and of ethnophilosophy as having no disciplinary basis. Hountondji also highlights the lack of material facilities in the African continent to facilitate the retrieval, exploration, compilation, and development of knowledge in academic centres (2009). Mbembe's writing on the postcolony (2001) and conceptualisation of necropolitics (2019) have been influential in offering direction when Afro-Marxist perspectives were on a wane in the continent. Mbembe's writing on the postcolony dealt with an exposition, using philosophical frameworks, of the complexities of African life after formal decolonisation. His work on necropolitics has allowed for an exploration of the interplay of violence and racism. Ndlovu-Gatsheni's extensive work on coloniality (2013b), decolonisation (with Siphamandla Zondi) (2016) and African subjectivity (2013a) has been fundamental to our understanding of modes of coloniality—coloniality of power, coloniality of knowledge, and coloniality of being. The scholar draws on Latin American exposition of the modernity/coloniality matrix in the development of this threefold understanding. Nkrumah's (1965) writing on neocolonialism has drawn attention to continuities in coloniality, where economic and trade relations continue to shape the African continent in the name of development.

The above snapshot, as reiterated, just scratches the surface of the rich wealth of scholarship that constitutes engagement with Southernness. This is amplified by work on internal colonialism (Casanova 2002), which looks at intellectual colonialism and how it is a disservice to understanding complex lines of social inequities in former colonies. The framework of internal colonisation (Turner 2018) brings into conversation empire, race, and liberal governance. These frameworks are explored further in the next section, where Southern approaches are placed in dialogue with critical political economy. At this juncture, it is noteworthy that much of the fillip that these perspectives received was at the end of the Cold War, when Marxian thought was deemed to be on the wane.

Criticisms of Southern Theorising

Southern theorising has come under criticism from scholars for possibly being essentialist in its approach. In other words, charges of essentialising cultural difference and its alleged rootedness in epistemic relativism have been levied against these perspectives (Biegel 2016). Further, due to the emergence of the postcolonial nation-state after formal decolonisation and its imperative for nation-building, a number of scholarly traditions in the former colonised parts of the world have been hinged on methodological nationalism. Criticisms of this approach and the need to overcome it have also been central to decolonial thought (Rogers et al. 2021). Further, ideas and policies of multiculturalism in what are considered the metropoles, have again been rooted in difference, thereby inviting criticisms for accentuating rigidities and offering ground for the elite from former colonies to exert their influence further. This ties into work on the role of premodern intellectuals in colonial knowledge production (Wagoner 2003), who were seen as enabling colonial administrators in taking forward their mission to colonise by aiding the translation and creation of native knowledge that was conducive to the continuation of retaining power in their respective societies. Further, Collins (2013) identifies two problematic strands in Southern theory, where 'Northern' or Western social theory is seen as a goalpost and Southern theory is offered as critiqued, thereby inadvertently centring Western theory as the standard. The next is that of presenting a list of Southern thinkers and theorists to bring legitimacy to the Southern canon, which replicates knowledge practices of the North.

The above criticisms offer ground to reexamine and clarify the stances and arguments presented under the umbrella of Southern theorising and approaches. Irrespective of this, the continued importance of theorising from the rootedness of peripheral experiences, drawing from gendered, racialised and caste-laden realities of the global majority cannot be overstated.

Southern Approaches to Media Technology

In order to explore Southern approaches to AI, it becomes imperative for us to understand larger and longer histories of technology. At the international level, technologies like the radio and telegraph were part of efforts to deepen colonial governance and were deployed for propaganda during World War 2 and the Cold War. At the national level, after formal decolonisation, the former colonies saw in technology an impetus to aid national development and growth. International and intergovernmental organisations like UNESCO and UNDP aided these efforts in the so-called developing world then. This was coupled with the use of technology to enable a national approach to reviving cultures. In the post-Cold War era, globalisation and liberation impacted national economic policies. In parallel, the Silicon Valley of the 1980s and 1990s saw the establishment of software companies that grew rapidly to set up offices globally as multinational corporations. Today, they are known by the moniker of Big Tech corporations and have a huge influence on national governments world over. Big Tech corporations include social media companies, internet advertising giants, digital infrastructure corporations, among others. Algorithms and machine learning technologies have been developed and deployed by these corporations as part of their business models.

In recent years, scholarship on tech imperialism and digital colonialism, particularly focused on United States-based Big Tech corporations, has abounded. These include work on data colonialism which explore the extractive practices around data and how it is reminiscent of imperial pasts (Couldry and Mejias 2019a, b), technocolonialism as seen in the humanitarian sector's usage of technology (Madianou 2019) and on data's colonial history (Gray 2023). Writings on AI colonialism (MIT Technology Review, 2022), AI and digital colonialism (Browne 2023), gig economy and labour practices in the Global South (Krishna 2020; Heeks et al. 2020) are constantly hitting headlines and newsletters. In response to these developments, national governments in the Global South have responded in diverse ways. These include developing their national AI strategies and data policies, investing in homegrown Big Tech and also replicating Silicon Valley start-up environments by enacting business-friendly economic and taxation policies, among other things. This is seen as an effort in asserting digital sovereignty (Derivry 2023), where national governments in the Global South seek to harness and harvest their population's data as well as deploy biometric, algorithmic, and machine learning technologies in service delivery (Carnegie Endowment for International Peace 2019, 2023).

It is here that the many facets of Southernness can be understood. National regimes in the Global South have sought to replicate colonial practices in the name of digital sovereignty, seeing any criticism as anti-national (Prasad 2021). This obscures practices that could be termed as truly decolonial and/or Southern. It is imperative then, to go beyond national frames and explore horizontal, cross- and trans-regional dialogic flows of tech knowledge and practice. Scholars like Moyo (2020) write about the decolonial turn in media studies in Africa and the Global South. Among other things, Moyo writes that media (technology) studies lie at the heart of Euro-American modernity and is a bastion of the coloniality of knowledge. The author calls for trans-epistemic dialogue between the North and South. Further, inspiring practices of indigenous data governance (Kukutai and Taylor 2016) offer lessons and serve as great cases of Southern approaches to media technology. Seen as a practice of self-determination, indigenous communities in Canada and Aotearoa New Zealand have initiated and developed ways of retaining sovereignty over their own data. This has been deemed important to influence how indigenous peoples are represented in data and to serve as a corrective to being seen as a "problem variable". First Nations communities in Canada have developed what are called the OCAP principles—ownership, control, access and possession—to safeguard the manner in which their data is accessed, used, erased, or showcased (FNIGC 2014). CARE principles—Collective Benefit, Authority to Control, Responsibility, Ethics—proposed by the Global Indigenous Data Alliance (GIDA) is another such framework (Carroll et al. 2020). Numerous grassroots and community collectives and initiatives are beginning to address the AI question, especially to address problems arising from racialised training and deployment of algorithms and AI technologies, the latter now well-documented in scholarship (Noble 2018; Benjamin 2019).

The heterogeneity of Southern approaches to technology has been outlined above. The next section attempts to place key tenets of Critical Political Economy and Southern approaches in dialogue in a bid to tease out congruences and incompatibilities, and to explore the possibilities of presenting a common set of concerns. These concerns are then brought to bear on the AI question.

Critical Political Economy Contra Southernness?: A Dialogue

This section seeks to explore some key underpinnings of Critical Political Economy and Southern Approaches in a dialogic exercise. Critical Political Economy, as drawn out in Section "Critical Political Economy as a Framework", has tended to focus on structures of domination and the manifestations of power that produce social inequities. Similarly, diverse Southern Approaches have emphasised metaphoric and praxeological stances by operating from a peripheral location. Concerns that surface immediately when one thinks of a dialogic exercise between the two, are ideas of principles, location, scale, and levels of analyses.

Totalism versus *Localism*: In making a case for CPE, scholars have spoken about the framework offering a full explication of how power and its concentration, and its effect towards commodification and extraction of surplus value operate. In her writing, Wigger (2022) suggests: "Based on ... integrated understanding of the realm of politics, society, the state and economic production, Critical Political Economy is ontologically equipped to analyse the totality of social life and to ask the big questions, without losing sight of concrete and detailed phenomena." While the author is quick to emphasise internal plurality of CPE by drawing on Gill (2012, p. 519), who suggests that "critical thought can neither be singular, nor imprisoned by practices of theoretical closure", one is left wondering if beyond critique, CPE incorporates a dialecticism that is self-perpetuating. This instantiates Moyo's contention with Hegelian dialectics that he sees as constant (re)production of knowledge (Moyo 2020). In other words, the self-perpetuating thesis-antithesis-synthesis method of knowledge production is seen as producing "new" knowledge time and again, obfuscating existing and plural knowledge systems. In synthesising negation into its fold, CPE may perhaps not allow us to understand and engage with the rootedness and situatedness of a multiplicity of peripheral experiences. On the other hand, Southernness has been conflated with localism time and again. By perceiving situated experiences as "local", one disallows any large-scale transformative abilities they may contain. In other words, Southern approaches are seen as championing essentialism and particularism, and can often boil down to identity-based profiling (Go 2016).

Thinking about Modernity: One of the key criticisms levied against CPE is its over-reliance on Marxian frameworks and European modernity. Latin American decolonial thought takes on the phenomenon of modernity/coloniality directly, as illustrated in Section "Southernness as an Axis of Inquiry". McArthur (2022) explores the relevance of critical theory in a decolonial age, by drawing on May's call for Western critical theorists to be self-aware and not perpetuate Charles Taylor's phrasing of "majoritarian particularism masquerading as universalism" (May 2012, p. 326). She draws on Said's criticism of the Frankfurt School, where he suggested they were "… stunningly silent on racist theory, anti-imperialist resistance, and oppositional practice in the empire" (Said 1994, p. 357). It therefore emerges as imperative that we ask if modernity is a solely Western phenomenon, even while acknowledging that colonialism institutionalised Western modernity as universal through projects of modernisation in the vein of Lerner (1958). Scholars have sought to question and dislodge universalist assumptions and linear teleologies of its Western framings. Maldonado-Torres (2011) writes about how modernity is to enlightenment what transmodernity is to decolonisation, in their exploration of Habermas' and Dussel's thought. Lim and Chang's edited collection (2012) has contributors exploring non-Western modernist pasts in the field of architecture, posing a critique of a homogenised Eurocentric view of modernity to showcase its pluralisms historically. While it is not within the mandate of this section to draw out scholarly writing on non-Western modernities, suffice it to say that scholars have retrieved and highlighted plural visions and worldviews of modernities beyond the project of European enlightenment that sought to present itself as a clear temporal break.

Having drawn up the above contestation, it is important to state at this juncture that both CPE and Southern approaches have a big aspect of commonality—the interrogation and challenging of structures of power and domination. Critical theories, and CPE in this case, have underscored their commitment to the emancipatory project, as already elaborated. If we rescue critical theorising from its association with European modernity, one can engage more fully with the promise of this commitment. Similarly, Southern approaches need to be rescued from their alleged relativism. In order to do this, one has to interrogate, denounce, and decolonise essentialising nationalist projects of nation-states that were former colonies. In other words, being a geographical part of the Global South while perpetuating internal colonialisms does not find resonance with a Southern approach. By dislodging such tendencies, the Southern effort can enhance and sustain its focus on the disenfranchised and those rendered peripheral due to their geosocial location.

How can we then think of a cross-pollination now that criticisms and contestations have been elaborated upon? I propose to do so under four principles listed below:

(a) *Non-Dualism and "Rationality"*: Cartesian dualisms of body and mind have grossly skewed our understanding of the vitality of experience, which is carried by the body as well as the mind. By privileging rationality as a solely cerebral endeavour without connectedness to the somatic and bodily, one is rendered at a loss in one's effort to understand how lived experience of violence can translate into trauma with implications for collective memory of people. Lulz (2023) presents the idea of earthy data as a decolonising tactic to challenge the distinction of the material and the epistemological in data governance discourses, where the question of what we claim to govern when we speak of governing data is central to understanding underlying colonial impulses. By presenting a non-dualist understanding of rationality that brings together materialist and immaterial/non-material framings, one is able to account for emotive rationality, and propose pathways to phenomenological hermeneutics exploring the artificiality of "intelligence" in AI technologies.

(b) *Deliberative and Plurilectic Engagement:* Drawing on the above non-dualist understanding of rationality, one can then embrace deliberative pedagogies inherent to societies with diverse and "large language model" linguistic systems. Amaro (2022), to aid his critique of computational reasoning and in highlighting the complex relationship between race and machine learning, talks about alternative approaches to algorithmic practice rooted in such an understanding of languages. Dussel's liberation philosophy which engages with critical theory and decolonial ethics comprises a plurilectic approach, where "… European modernity is not left behind, but given a seat at the table as a part of the larger puzzle, one that has to re-understand itself to be sure as a particular which is part of the larger formation" (Martín Alcoff 2012). These perspectives allow for deliberative engagement between seemingly standoffish scholarly bodies of thought, in accounting for peripheral lived realities. Having said that, it is imperative to not confuse this with the practice of arriving as a quick consensus that Tuck and Yang (2012) talk about, in presenting their powerful work on not using decolonising as a metaphor.

(c) *Multiple Marginality:* The objects of the concerns expressed and addressed by both CPE and Southern approaches intersect in very visible ways in the lived experiences of the most marginalised, leading to multiple marginality (Vigil 2016). This can be seen in the manner in which caste-based division of labour in Social Asian societies renders the so-called lower castes as more predisposed to being deployed in grunt work amidst indecent work conditions in the global supply chains of the data industries. A political economy reading of class, caste, and gender (Chalam 2020; Mehrotra 2022) and research on labour in the gig economy (Krishna 2020) showcase how the interplay of enduring historical coloniality, internal colonialism as well as extraneous global factors at any given point render the already marginalised most vulnerable and immobile.

(d) *Autonomy and Relationality:* The notion and practice of autonomy is central to human emancipation and freedom. Movements for self-determination within and between nations as well as a contestation of sovereignty at the national, collective and individual levels make it important to foreground autonomy as integral to bridging CPE and Southern approaches. As a corollary, it is imperative to understand the interconnectedness of the human and non-human worlds, especially as we stare at ecological crises only accelerated by an international neoliberal capitalist economic order. Here, underscoring relationality as a principle allows us to explore further this aspect of freedom and collectivism.

Thinking along these lines inevitably brings overlaps of Critical and Southern approaches to bear on human experiences with technology, simply because lived realities are not experienced in silos, but as a multiplier effect of compounded coloniality. The above three sections have sought to present the bodies of scholarship on Critical Political Economy and Southern Approaches, in the context of media technologies. In thinking through the possibilities listed above, this edited collection seeks to present a critical social exploration of trysts with artificial intelligence technologies through the 5 chapters that follow this present one.

In Chap. 2, Deepak Prince presents the case of Walnut money manager, locating it in the context of currency demonetisation in India. Prince adopts an anthropological approach to present a critique of objectified knowledge and data using this case. The chapter evocatively argues that AI and machine learning systems extract the surplus value of sociality in human interactions and connections. This chapter presents a critique of nationalist policies.

Suci Lestari Yuana takes us to contemporary colonialisms that AI technologies are ridden with, in Chap. 3, by unravelling the hidden costs of AI colonialism borne by female gig workers in Indonesia. The chapter draws on focus group discussions with female gig workers in Yogyakarta to illustrate how they experience AI colonialism. This chapter helps us situate present-day colonialisms as a working together of global capitalism and division of labour, which are premised on extractive dynamics and relegating people from certain geosocial locations to ill-valued labour and conditions of work. Yuan illuminates this by bringing into the equation the dynamics of global gendered labour in the AI and data industries, where global labour supply chains ultimately render the very female gig workers who power it, immobile.

Turning to another example of AI-based applications in Chap. 4, Sananda Sahoo looks at the phenomenon of deepfakes and locates it in the context of the collaboration between the state and Big Tech in Indian elections. The chapter helps us understand the structural organisation of state and corporate power, which oftentimes works in collusion rather than in contradiction. Sahoo's chapter helps us understand the inherent collusions and contradictions of the tripartite colonising impetus in certain uses of AI technologies, the state (also in the Global South), and Big

Tech corporations. Here again, we see the ways in which CPE and Southern approaches are interlinked and play off of each other.

In Chap. 5, Gabrielle Bezerra Sales Sarlet and Lucas Reckziegel Weschenfelder share their research on informational separation of powers and interoperability in Brazil. The authors help us get acquainted with various cases of threats to human rights by the state by looking at Brazil's Digital ID system.

Chapter 6 showcases Nishanshi Shukla's work on caste bias in Indian AI, where demographic categories and associated data have ramifications for the way AI technologies trained on such data incorporate biases based on caste categorisation. Shukla studies the Caste.csv dataset on Kaggle.com, to unravel the many implicit assumptions, discriminations, and violences inherent to the dataset that is then used to develop data science projects and applications. This chapter offers readers the insights where internal colonialisms in Indian society take on a technologised form on a global data science platform, with digital datasets on prisoners revealing existing ideologies and biases.

Across these chapters, the reader will find a critique of transnational AI and data supply chains as well as state nationalisms as being inherently in contradiction with a Southern approach, as argued earlier in this chapter.

Unfortunately, a conspicuous absence in this collection is to do with scholarship from researchers in the African continent. This editor made numerous efforts at varied stages of editing this collection to elicit chapters from African scholars, but was unsuccessful. As such, the rationale for the selection of Southern contexts in this book has solely been driven by expressions of interest and submissions from authors. Therefore, this book may only be seen as a starting point for research that explores these seemingly incompatible theoretical and experiential intellectual traditions and terrains of Critical and Southern theorising, to open up possibilities for newer conversations on emerging technologies from the vantage point of those most impacted by frontier technologies, and hence living frontier lives.

References

Alatas, S. H. (1972). The captive mind in development studies. Int. Soc. Sci. J. 24, 9–25.

Amaro, R. (2022). *The Black Technical Object: On Machine Learning and the Aspiration of Black Being*. Stenberg Press.

An MIT Technology Review Series: AI Colonialism | MIT Technology Review. (2022). Retrieved September 2023, from https://www.technologyreview.com/supertopic/ai-colonialism-supertopic/.

Benjamin, R. (2019). Race after technology: Abolitionist tools for the new Jim code. Polity.

Bhambra, G.K., Last, A., Mayblin, L. (2019) Global Social Theory: building resources. Area, 51 (4). pp. 816–819. ISSN 00040894.

Bhambra, Gurminder K. (2012). Connected sociologies / by Gurminder K. Bhambra. London: Bloomsbury Academic.

Biegel, F. (2016). "Comment on Julian Go's Essay 'Globalizing Sociology, Turning South. Perspectival Realism and the Southern Standpoint'". Sociologica (2).

Browne, G. (2023). AI Is Steeped in Big Tech's 'Digital Colonialism'. Wired UK. Retrieved September 2023, from https://www.wired.co.uk/article/abeba-birhane-ai-datasets.

Buolamwini, J. and Gebru, T. (2018). Gender Shades: Intersectional Accuracy Disparities in Commercial Gender Classification. Proceedings of the 1st Conference on Fairness, Accountability and Transparency, in Proceedings of Machine Learning Research, 81:77–91.

Carnegie Endowment for International Peace. (2019). Identity, Payments, Data Empowerment, Talk by Nandan Nilekani

Carnegie Endowment for International Peace. (2023). Digital Public Infrastructure: The Key to 21st Century Innovation and Growth, Talk by Nandan Nilekani.

Carroll, S., Garba, I., Figueroa-Rodríguez, O., Holbrook, J., Lovett, R., Materechera, S., Parsons, M., Raseroka, K., Rodriguez-Lonebear, D., Rowe, R., Sara, R., Walker, J., Anderson, J., Hudson, M. (2020). The CARE Principles for Indigenous Data Governance. Data Science Journal, 19: XX, pp. 1–12.

Casanova, G. (2002). *Exploração, colonialismo e luta pela democracia na América Latina*. Petrópolis: CLACSO/Editora Vozes. Retrieved September 2023, from https://www.journaldumauss.net/?Internal-Colonialism-Postcolonial-Criticism-and-Social-Theory.

Chalam, KS. (2020) Political Economy of Caste in India. New Delhi: SAGE Publications.

Chandhiramowuli, S. and Chaudhuri, B. (2023) Match Made by Humans: A Critical Enquiry into Human-Machine Configurations in Data Labelling. Proceedings of the 56th Hawaii International Conference on System Sciences.

Chandrasekhar, C.P. (2005) The Political Economy of IT-driven Outsourcing. In: Parayil, G. (eds) Political Economy and Information Capitalism in India. Technology, Globalization and Development Series. Palgrave Macmillan, London.

Chiumbu, S. and Radebe, M. (2020). Towards a Decolonial Critical Political Economy of the Media: Some Initial Thoughts, Communicatio, 46:1, 1–20.

Collins, P. H. (2013), Critical Interventions in Western Social Theory: Reflections on Power and Southern Theory, Decentering Social Theory (Political Power and Social Theory, Vol. 25), Emerald Group Publishing Limited, Bingley, pp. 137–146.
Connell, R. (2007). Southern Theory: The global dynamics of knowledge in social science. Routledge.
Couldry, N., and Mejias, U. (2019a). The Costs of Connection (1st ed.). Stanford University Press.
Couldry, N., and Mejias, U. A. (2019b). Data Colonialism: Rethinking Big Data's Relation to the Contemporary Subject. Television & New Media, 20(4), 336–349.
Cox, R. W. (1981). Social Forces, States and World Orders: Beyond International Relations Theory. Millennium, 10(2), 126–155.
Cox, R. W. (1996). Approaches to World Order. Cambridge University Press.
Cox, Robert W. (1987). Production, Power and World Order: Social Forces in the Making of History, New York: Columbia University Press.
Derivry, T. (2023) Digital sovereignty in India: policy agenda, discourse, power and capability. https://www.sciencespo.fr/public/chaire-numerique/en/2023/05/04/contribution-digital-sovereignty-in-india-policy-agenda-discourse-power-and-capability/; Accessed on July 5, 2023.
Dussel, E.D., and Fornazzari, A. (2002). World-System and "Trans"-Modernity. Nepantla: Views from South 3(2), 221–244.
Escobar, A. (2017). Designs for the Pluriverse: Radical Interdependence, Autonomy, and the Making of Worlds. Duke University Press.
Fanon, F. (1968). The Wretched of the Earth. New York: Grove Press.
Freire, P. (2017). Pedagogy of the oppressed. Penguin Classics.
Fuchs, C. (2016). Critical theory. In International encyclopedia of communication theory and philosophy, ed. Robert Craig. Hoboken, NJ: Wiley Blackwell.
Garnham, N. (1979). Contribution to a political economy of mass-communication. Media, Culture & Society, 1(2), 123–146.
Gill, S. (2012). Towards a radical concept of praxis: imperial 'common sense' versus the post-modern prince. Millennium, 40(3), 505–524.
Gillespie, T. (2018). Custodians of the Internet: Platforms, Content Moderation, and the Hidden Decisions That Shape Social Media. New Haven: Yale University Press.
Go, J. (2008), Global Fields and Imperial Forms: Field Theory and the British and American Empires. Sociological Theory, 26: 201–229.
Go, J. (2011). Patterns of Empire: The British and American Empires, 1688 to the Present. United States: Cambridge University Press.
Go, J. (2016). Globalizing Sociology, Turning South. Perspectival Realism and the Southern Standpoint, Sociologica (2).

Go, J. (2023). Thinking against empire: Anticolonial thought as social theory. The British Journal of Sociology, 74(3), 279–293.

Gray, C. (2023). More than Extraction: Rethinking Data's Colonial Political Economy, International Political Sociology, 17 (2).

Gray, M. L. and Suri, S. (2019). Ghost Work: How to Stop Silicon Valley from Building a New Global Underclass. United States: Houghton Mifflin Harcourt.

Grosfoguel, R. (2009). Decolonial approach to political-economy: Transmodernity, border thinking and global coloniality. KULT 6: Special Issue –Latin America, 10–38.

Hardy, J. (2014). Critical Political Economy of the Media: An Introduction (1st ed.). Routledge.

Heeks, R., Graham, M., Mungai, P., Van Belle, J., and Woodcock, J. (2020). Systematic Evaluation of Platform Work Against Decent Work Standards: Development of a New Framework and Application in the Global South. Digital Development Working Paper no. 85.

Hountondji, P. (1997). Introduction in Endogenous Knowledge. Research Trails. Dakar: Codesria, 1–42.

Hountondji, P. (2009). Knowledge of Africa, knowledge by Africans: two perspectives on African studies. RCCS Annu. Rev. 121–131. doi: https://doi.org/10.4000/rccsar.174.

Byrd, D. J., and Miri, S. J. (Eds.). (17 Nov. 2022). Syed Hussein Alatas and Critical Social Theory. Leiden, The Netherlands: Brill.

Jäger, J. (2022). Fighting the beast of the apocalypse: three fundamental reasons for a Critical Political Economy approach to Global Political Economy. Global Political Economy, 1(1), 51–58.

Jessop, B., Labrousse, A., Vercueil, T. (2012) Crossing Boundaries: Towards Cultural Political Economy », Revue de la régulation Autumn, Retrieved in September 2023, from https://doi.org/10.4000/regulation.9943.

Krishna, S. (2020). Spatiotemporal (In)justice in Digital Platforms: An Analysis of Food-Delivery Platforms in South India. In: Bandi, R.K., C. R., R., Klein, S., Madon, S., Monteiro, E. (eds) The Future of Digital Work: The Challenge of Inequality. IFIPJWC 2020. IFIP Advances in Information and Communication Technology, vol 601. Springer, Cham.

Kukutai, T., and Taylor, J. (Eds.). (2016). Indigenous Data Sovereignty: Toward an agenda (Vol. 38). ANU Press.

Lerner, D. (1958). The passing of traditional society: Modernizing the Middle East. Free Press.

Lim, William S.W. and Chang, Jiat-Hwee. (Eds) (2012). Non West Modernist Past: On Architecture and Modernities. Singapore: World Scientific Publishing.

Lindgren, S. (2023). Critical Theory of AI. Polity.

Lulz, SD (forthcoming in 2023). Tactics of Earthy Data: Decolonising for the Anthropocene. *Technology and Regulation.*

Madianou, M. (2019). Technocolonialism: Digital Innovation and Data Practices in the Humanitarian Response to Refugee Crises. Social Media + Society, 5(3).

Maldonado-Torres, N. (2011). Thinking through the Decolonial Turn: Post-continental Interventions in Theory, Philosophy, and Critique—An Introduction. Transmodernity: Journal of Peripheral Cultural Production of the Luso-Hispanic World, 1(2). Retrieved from https://escholarship.org/uc/item/59w8j02x.

Martín Alcoff, L. (2012). Enrique Dussel's Transmodernism. Transmodernity: Journal of Peripheral Cultural Production of the Luso-Hispanic World, 1(3). Retrieved from https://escholarship.org/uc/item/58k9k17t.

Marx, K. (2012). Grundrisse. Foundations of the Critique of Political Economy. Penguin Classics.

May, S. (2012). Language and minority rights: Ethnicity, nationalism and the politics of language (2nd ed.). Routledge

Mbembe, A. (2001) On the Postcolony. University of California, Berkeley, CA.

Mbembe, A. (2019). Necropolitics. Duke University Press.

McArthur, J. (2022). Critical theory in a decolonial age. *Educational Philosophy and Theory, 54*(10), 1681–1692.

McChesney, R. W. (2012). The Political Economy of Communication. In A.N. Valdivia (Ed.) The International Encyclopedia of Media Studies.

Mehrotra, I. (2022). Political Economy of Class Caste and Gender. Routledge.

Mignolo, W. D. (2007). Delinking. The rhetoric of modernity, the logic of coloniality and the grammar of decoloniality. Cultural Studies. 21, 44–514.

Mosco, V. (2009). The political economy of communication. SAGE Publications.

Moyo, L. (2020). The Decolonial Turn in Media Studies in Africa and the Global South, Palgrave Macmillan.

Murdock, G., and Golding, P. (2005). Culture, communications and political economy. Mass media and society, 4, 60–83.

Ndlovu-Gatsheni, S. (2013a). Empire, Global Coloniality and African Subjectivity. New York, Oxford: Berghahn Books.

Ndlovu-Gatsheni, S. J. (2013b). Coloniality of Power in Postcolonial Africa: Myths of Decolonization. Senegal: African Books Collective.

Ndlovu-Gatsheni, Sabelo J. and Zondi, Siphamandla. (Eds.) (2016) Decolonizing the University, Knowledge Systems and Disciplines in Africa. Durham, NC: Carolina Academic Press.

Nkrumah, K. (1965). Neo-Colonialism, the Last Stage of Imperialism. London: Thomas Nelson and Sons.

Noble, S. U. (2018). Algorithms of oppression: How search engines reinforce racism. New York University Press.

Patel, S. (2023). Anti-colonial thought and global social theory. Frontiers in Sociology, 8.

Perrigo, B. (2023) The $2 Per Hour Workers Who Made ChatGPT Safer. Time. https://time.com/6247678/openai-chatgpt-kenya-workers/; Accessed on April 15, 2023.

Prasad, R. (2021). Bodies and Data: The Digital Sovereignty of the Indian State. AoIR Selected Papers of Internet Research, 2021.

Quijano, A. (2007). Coloniality and Modernity/Rationality, Cultural Studies, 21:2–3, 168–178.

Raghunath, P. (2023a). 'Data Industries': Towards tracing the Global Data Economy. Sociological Studies Research. https://socstudiesresearch.com/2023/08/02/data-industries-towards-tracing-the-global-data-economy/.

Raghunath, P. (2023b). Critical Data Governance: A Southern Standpoint to the study and practice of data. *Technology and Recognition*.

Rieder, B. (2022) Towards a political economy of technical systems: The case of Google. Big Data & Society, 9(2).

Rogers, D., Davies, J., Shrestha, P. and Ma, X. (2021). Decolonisation and Methodological Nationalism: Placing Empire at the Centre of the Analysis, Society+Space.

Said, E. W. (1994). Culture & imperialism. Vintage.

Said, E. W. (2003). Orientalism. Penguin Classics.

Shields, S., Bruff, I., Macartney, H. (2011). Introduction: 'Critical' and 'International Political Economy'. In: Shields, S., Bruff, I., Macartney, H. (eds) Critical International Political Economy. International Political Economy Series. Palgrave Macmillan, London.

Smith, L. T. (2012). Decolonizing methodologies (2nd ed.). Zed Books.

Srnicek, N. (2016). Platform Capitalism (1st ed.). Wiley.

The First Nations Information Governance Centre. Ownership, Control, Access and Possession (OCAP™): The Path to First Nations Information Governance. May 2014. (Ottawa: The First Nations Information Governance Centre, May 2014).

Thiongo, Ngũgĩ wa. (1986). Decolonising the mind: the politics of language in African literature. London: James Currey; EAEP; Heinemann.

Tuck, E., & Yang, K. W. (2012). Decolonisation is not a metaphor. Decolonisation: Indigeneity, Education and Society, 1(1), 1–40.

Turner, J. (2018). Internal colonisation: The intimate circulations of empire, race and liberal government. European Journal of International Relations, 24(4), 765–790.

Verdegem, P. (2022). Dismantling AI capitalism: the commons as an alternative to the power concentration of Big Tech. AI & Society, Springer.

Vigil, J. D. (2016). Multiple Marginality: A Comparative Framework for Understanding Gangs. In M. C. Hay (Ed.), Methods That Matter: Integrating Mixed Methods for More Effective Social Science Research. University of Chicago Press.

Wagoner, P. B. (2003). Precolonial Intellectuals and the Production of Colonial Knowledge. Comparative Studies in Society and History, 45(4), 783–814.
Wigger, A. (2022). Continuing to fight the beast of the apocalypse: final reasons for a Critical Political Economy approach to Global Political Economy. Global Political Economy, 1(1), 188–196.
Williams, A., Miceli, M., and Gebru, T. (2022). The Exploited Labor Behind Artificial Intelligence. Noema. https://www.noemamag.com/the-exploited-labor-behind-artificial-intelligence; Accessed on April 15, 2023.
Worth, O. (2011). Reclaiming Critical IPE from the 'British' School. In: Shields, S., Bruff, I., Macartney, H. (eds) Critical International Political Economy. International Political Economy Series. Palgrave Macmillan, London.

CHAPTER 2

Data, Anthropology and the Surplus Value of Sociality

Deepak Prince

*

There is a series of phenomena of great importance which cannot possibly be recorded by questioning or computing documents [survey questionnaires] but have to be *observed in their full actuality.*

Instead of asking people survey questions or contriving small-scale experiments, which was how social science was often done in the past. … I realized I could *go and look at what actually happens.* (Emphases, mine)

* * *

D. Prince (✉)
Indraprastha Institute of Information Technology Delhi (IIIT-Delhi), New Delhi, India
e-mail: deepak@iiitd.ac.in

P. Raghunath (ed.), *Critical Political Economy and Southern Approaches to AI*, Palgrave Global Media Policy and Business,
https://doi.org/10.1007/978-3-032-14090-6_2

Consider these two quotes. The reader may not be faulted for taking them to be the words of early twentieth-century anthropologists advocating a methodological orientation towards ethnographic fieldwork, as opposed to relying on the survey questionnaire, the elementary tool of statistical knowledge production. The first of these extracts, indeed, is from the introduction to Bronislaw Malinowski's Argonauts (1922/2005, 14), a programmatic text that announces a new method for producing anthropological knowledge—one that is founded on a practice of involved, long-term fieldwork. The second, though, is written not by an anthropologist but by Christian Rudder (2014, 10–11), mathematician, data scientist and co-founder of the online dating platform, OkCupid.

Amusement apart, what strikes me in these quotes is a shared attention to an excess in two different disciplinary apprehensions of 'what actually happens,' an excess or surplus that cannot be contained in a priori frames, as in a survey, and is available only in its emergence. The objective recording of this excess extending beyond its emergence, I hope to show, is central to the technological foundation of the major computational systems of the twenty-first century.

This chapter posits the extraction of the surplus value of sociality as the elementary process at the heart of technologies of 'big data' (ranking systems such as newsfeeds and Google's page rank, customized recommenders on social media and entertainment platforms like Spotify and Netflix) and artificial intelligence in its many forms and techniques (neural networks in machine learning and deep-learning, transformers in large language models to name two). While 'surplus value' shares some qualities with the Marxist notion to the extent that the emphasis is on material practices of producing value, I mark my departure from the classical conception of surplus value here briefly. I am less concerned about the classic category of labour and its place in the production of surplus value. This is by no means to suggest that such a line of inquiry has no place in the analysis of contemporary techno-social systems: far from it. A rich literature (that includes Suci Lestari Yuana's intervention, in Chap. 3 of this book) demonstrates how economic value (and by a dialectic extension, domination) is produced in the extraction of the surplus value of the labour of generating data labels, of moderating and of 'cleaning' data sets that are central to the 'training' of artificial intelligence models, a labour that is disproportionately expended in the global south. My focus, instead, is on the material practices of a 'user' at the edge of various technological interfaces: the encounter between user and app is not only a straightforward transaction of clicking a few buttons which in turn elicits a response on the screen; at the edge of the screen, the social interaction as such, insofar as it is recorded as data, is an excess that has value in itself. This excess is not present transparently, but in its potentiality, and its value is realized in evaluation. The realization of this value is at the heart of the paradigm shifts in computational technologies of the twenty-first century.

I substantiate my argument through an ethnography of Walnut, a smartphone application that came out with an ATM-locator feature during the exceptional demonetization of currency notes in India. Although this feature on the Walnut app is relatively simple, speaking from a technical point of view, in its simplicity, it reveals a process that is central to both 'big data' based social media systems and the AI 'revolution' we find ourselves in the middle of today. I also ground this claim with reference to the history of statistical and computational approaches to data. Further I hope to show that inhabiting the intersectional zone between anthropology and data science suggested in the quotes above allows us to produce a critique of anthropology that is simultaneous with a critique of computational data.

* * *

Computational Data as an Analytical Object

The computational manipulation of voluminous data—better known as Big Data—marks a paradigm shift in computer science and engineering. At the turn of the millennium, the static Web pages of the dot-com years gave way to a new class of dynamic, responsive, interaction-heavy applications like Facebook, Netflix and Uber. Social media platforms, streaming services and other new web technologies are built on a foundation of complex computation that involves the processing of unprecedentedly large volumes of digitally stored data to better optimize for individual user behaviour. Secondly, the design of artificial intelligence (AI) systems, especially over the last decade, has seen a shift (Cristianini 2014) from the rule-based decision-support models that declined from popular technological discourse during the 'AI-winter' of the 1980s, to machine-learning and deep-learning algorithms that 'learn' from data. That is to say, the contemporary interest in artificial intelligence is a break from an earlier algorithmic approach, of human-specied rules forming the basis of the AI, to providing human-generated data as input for models that build probabilistic inferences from this data. Alongside a drastic increase in computing capacity of today's processors, datasets of the order of petabytes and statistical/probabilistic techniques in data science are the conditions of possibility for the AI models of today that purportedly achieve near- if not better-than-human-level accuracy on certain tasks, such as image recognition, speech transcription and text generation.

Voluminous data is thus the impetus behind the two major lines of development in contemporary computation—'social' web applications such as Facebook, Twitter, Uber and Netflix, and state-of-the-art AI models.

The buzz surrounding big data was by no means confined to the world of computer science and software engineering. Like other technologies of the past, Big Data announced itself in public discourse with typical millenarian hype. In an editorial written for *WIRED* in 2008, Chris Anderson called for an 'end of theory' in the era of big data. The scientific method, proclaimed Anderson, was being washed away in the deluge of big data, 'We can throw the numbers into the biggest computing clusters the world has ever seen and let statistical algorithms find patterns where science cannot.'

Computational data emerges as an analytical category for anthropology, ethnographically oriented STS and other humanist studies of digital culture, firstly, as a critical response to this hype. 'The era of Big Data has only just begun, but it is already important that we start questioning the assumptions, values, and biases of this new wave of research,' write boyd and Crawford (2012, 675) in what is widely considered a landmark article in the sociology of big data. March 2014 saw the birth of a new journal, titled *Big Data and Society*, with boyd as one of the founders. The anthropologist, Tom Boellstorff (2013), refuses to acknowledge claims by technological evangelists that Big Data can radically transform society. Claims of big data's radical objectivity, suggests Boellstorff, is an epistemological over-reach, predicated on the pure truth of a naïve, empirical objectivity, where the data speaks for itself without the mediation of a subjective scientist. Drawing on Ian Hacking's study of nineteenth-century statistics, Boellstorff argues that interpretation, not data, is prior.[1] Against Anderson's 'thin' notion of data, which is taken to be self-evidently true, Boellstorff draws on the 'thick' data of ethnography and argues that data is always

[1] See also https://excavating.ai/

already framed against a grid of interpretation, which in turn is structured by cultural meaning-making and by relations of power.

A second catalyst for the analysis of big data was the exposé on Cambridge Analytica's use of unethically obtained data on Facebook users to develop targeted advertising campaigns to influence major elections. This line of discourse takes as its main analytical objects user's privacy and the dangers of privatized surveillance. Big Data is seen as a form of 'surveillance capitalism' (Zuboff 2015), as part of a technopolitical apparatus of 'tracking and targeting' (Suchman et al. 2017), and as a threat to democracy in a time of diminishing privacy and increasing technological influence over human behaviour on major online platforms (González 2017). These views on Big Data extend Foucault's (and Ian Hacking's) studies on disciplinary power and biopolitics, of statistical knowledge as an instrument of government. Big data is framed in these analyses as a dangerous form of privatization of governmental power over users/subjects: 'If nondescript pocket-sized devices made of plastic and glass have abruptly altered patterns of human behaviour, communication and cognition in less than a decade, what will happen once "wearable" virtual reality interfaces like VR headsets, eyeglasses and corneal implants are widely available?' (González 2017, 12). Other studies question the apparent perfection of this apparatus of power. Pink et al. (2018) focus on situations of rupture where the smooth functioning of data-based technical systems breaks down. They trace how people respond to these instances in their everyday lives. Cohen (2019) shows that the massive 'database of citizens' that the Unique Identification Authority of India (UIDAI) project claims to be, is replete with duplicates and data-doubles, thereby defeating the logic of unique identification. What these works argue, is that Big Data systems as apparatuses of power are incomplete and broken, that the social is not totally subjected to this form of power.

A related line of inquiry examines the personal use of data-driven technologies in practices of self-care, where the subjects' relationships to themselves are mediated by data-based knowledge of their bodily activity, as knowledge of a 'quantitative self' recorded on technological devices such as fitness trackers (Schüll 2016). Such analyses may extend to at-home blood sugar testing kits, and more recently with the pandemic, pulse oximeters that measure one's oxygen saturation and pulse rates. Schüll (2016, 325–30) shows that the ethical aspirations of the 'quantitative self' movement degenerate into an infantalization of the self, as users increasingly delegate the work of self-analysis to notification-prompts from the technological interface. 'What the self delegates is the responsibility [for] ... calculation [which] is given over to big-data analytics while self-steering is supplemented by the data-driven nudge.' Put differently, self-care mediated by technologically generated knowledge ends up becoming a relationship of subjection to the persuasive force of the technological interface.

This is by no means an exhaustive survey of the literature on big data, which is today a burgeoning field of study. Drawing on some influential works from the last decade, I have here outlined two related analytical approaches (primarily from anthropology) towards big data, deriving from critical positions that more often than not are simultaneously present in the work of different scholars, with sometimes the one predominating over the other. The first, we can broadly call, an epistemological critique, and this approach seeks to delegitimize big data's claims to deliver us unto objective, self-evidently true knowledge. The second critical stance seeks to unmask big data as an apparatus of power that threatens the privacy and autonomy of the users of computational interfaces, who are now vulnerable to algorithmic targeting.

Another discursive line parallel to the epistemological critique examines the contrast between Big Data, the latest avatar of statistical data analysis, and anthropology with ethnographic fieldwork as its key research 'method,' a contrast that elicits images of the old opposition between 'qualitative' and 'quantitative' research. Lev Manovich (2011, 466) has framed the problem of ethnography and data science as contesting epistemologies: 'On the one side, we have ethnographers who are spending years inside a particular community. On another side, we have computer scientists who never meet people in this community but have access to their social media and digital footprints.' Manovich presents to us a picture of people going about their everyday lives even as an inquisitive ethnographer wanders in their midst, and in an invisible elsewhere, beyond the black screens of smartphones interfaces are data scientists—the ethnographer interacted with people face to face, and the data scientists through a screen darkly.

This picture has been complicated, with ethnographers, extending Latour, suggesting that data scientists themselves are people, that they fashion not merely technical but also cultural objects, and that they too can be ethnographed. Seaver (2015) calls for ethnography to wriggle free from this tangle of methodological opposition, of a humanist ethnography against the formalism of mathematico-statistical data science. Despite the many distinctions and oppositions between anthropology and data science, the quotes I juxtaposed at the beginning of this chapter indicate that, differences notwithstanding, Malinowski and the data scientist Rudder both speak from a position self-consciously opposed to an older form of information elicitation through surveys. I take this as a starting point to enter the ethnographic space within which I problematize computational data and its relationship to 'the social.'

I argue that contemporary models of Big Data are predicated upon the extraction of what I call the surplus value of sociality, an excess of social activity that is objectified and extracted at the edge of various interfaces. I demonstrate this through an analysis of Walnut, a smartphone application that allowed users in India to locate live ATMs following a crisis in 2016, caused by the demonetization of high-value currency notes. I examine this fairly simple application to draw out fundamentals that generalize to other larger, more complex sites of investigation such as the Netflix interface. I then demonstrate two series of consequences that follow from this: I suggest that the surplus of sociality latent in the data can be theorized as a type of unconscious, a machinic unconscious analogous to what Walter Benjamin described as the optical unconscious in relation to photographs. Data, recorded in volumes and at a level of granularity which doesn't manifest in the consciousness of users, harbours within it, a machinic unconscious. The design of user-interfaces, guided by knowledge derived from data extracted at interfaces, I argue, plays on the reconfiguration of unconscious investment of users. Further, given that data is at the heart of contemporary AI models, I suggest that it is useful to think of AI as having objectified this machinic unconscious; the AI functions as if it has an unconscious stuck inside, an analytical position that offers a different angle into problems in AI ethics. Through the course of the chapter, I return to examine the confluences and distinctions between the two epistemologies of anthropology and data science and argue that the distinction mirrors the Weberian bureaucratic categories of 'person' and 'office.'

Demonetization 2016: A Crisis of Value

On 8 November 2016, the Prime Minister of India (PM) Narendra Modi made an announcement: From midnight onwards, currency notes of the five-hundred and one-thousand-rupee denominations would cease to be legal tender. In their place, newly designed five-hundred-rupee and two-thousand-rupee notes were to be introduced in the weeks to come. All banks would take in the demonetized notes starting from 10 November until the end of the calendar year. An equivalent amount would then be credited into the depositor's bank account. Each person was limited to withdrawing up to ten thousand rupees per day from their bank account (and twenty thousand rupees per week). ATM machines remained shut for the next two days, as they needed recalibration in order that they may count and dispense the newly designed notes.

The announcement came as a shock. Many did not have active bank accounts. Cash was the material form of transactions, savings and credit. Some burned the now demonetized currency notes in garbage dumps and in vacant plots. Torn notes were found floating in River Ganga. There were suicides. The queues outside banks were unending. Angry clients, having waited in line for hours, were forced to leave empty handed, for the bank was out of new notes. Outside live ATMs, people were to be found lined up at any given hour. The ATMs offered debit-card holders a slightly less harrowing way of withdrawing cash, that is, provided they could find a working machine with a supply of cash—now the scarcest of commodities. Most ATMs were emptied out within a few hours of their being filled.

As is typical of a response to crises today, various smartphone-based applications were launched in the hope of injecting some order. BookMyChotu, a smartphone app offering concierge services, announced a special offer to address the crisis: users could hire the services of a person who would stand in queue for them, waiting until it was their turn at the ATM. Satjeet Bedi, founder of the Delhi-based start-up, got the idea after he had asked his friends to wait in line outside the ATM for him while he attended to his sick mother (Mahapatro 2016).

The extraordinary event of the demonetization of currency notes presents the anthropologist with sites for the critical examination of the problem of value. Graeber (2001, 22) outlines three ways to understand value: (i) as the desirable, the morally good, (ii) as economic measure and (iii) as meaningful difference. He suggests that an activist anthropology of value might help bridge the gap between what is good for society and what is seen as economically valuable, by directing society in a movement from the sociologically meaningful to the collectively desirable. The anthropology of material culture, following Marshall Sahlins' re-interpretation of Marx, focuses on the analysis of use-values insofar as practices of consumption are patterned by culture within different frames of meaning. These conceptions are predicated on the notion that value is a social category, that is, they speak of the sociality of value. My interest here is to invert this analytical frame and to problematize the value of sociality.

'Sociality,' writes Ingold (1991, 372), 'is the generative potential of the relational field in which [persons] are situated and which is constituted and reconstituted through their activities.' For the analysis that is to follow, I propose to draw on Nancy Munn's (1992, 8–22) characterization of value as a potential that is latent in actions. For Munn, social activity is the site of emergence of invisible value-potentials. Such value potentials, latent in social action, are actualized in an 'evaluative rendering by significant others.' By focusing on the evaluative modality, Munn's presentation, I suggest, invites us to speak of the value of sociality that emerges from evaluations of social activity.

Between Smartphone Screens and ATM Screens

Within two weeks of the demonetization announcement, many ATMs across the country had been recalibrated for the new notes, but the pressure on the automated interface was high. As ATM screens were strained to the point of break-down, new Internet-based applications appeared on smartphone screens with the promise of showing people the locations of active ATMs.

Cash Management Solutions (CMS), a company servicing over half the ATMs in India, released a Web app listing all ATMs that they had recently replenished with cash. CMS relied upon 'crowdsourced' user feedback to update the status of the ATMs that ran out of money. CashNoCash was another web application that displayed live ATMs embedded on Google's map interface. To provide this 'real-time' view, CashNoCash relied on crowdsourced data from people withdrawing money at ATMs across the country, who, following the success or failure of withdrawal at the ATM, were requested to update the working status of that particular ATM. It was, if you like, analogous to a feedback survey.

Fifteen days after the demonetization announcement, I was waiting in line outside the State Bank of India ATM, in Erode, Tamil Nadu, a southern Indian state known for its federalist and anti-centrist positions on all matters policy. It was an hour past midnight. The queue was long, and progress slow. People in line slipped in and out of conversations, discussing the government's disregard for the 'common man,' the futility of snaring black money in the tax net through 'stunts,' given that powerful hoarders would inevitably have found loopholes by paying off the right people to get them out of this mess but with minor losses, leaving 'people like us' standing in the road, swatting mosquitoes in the middle of the night and waiting to withdraw money that was legitimately earned.

One of the men was particularly forthcoming with his thoughts. Roughly an hour into the wait, the man in front of me asked the one with the ever-ready opinion about the status of ATMs in an area on the outskirts of the town. He replied confidently, "I have the solution for you." Whipping out his smartphone, he continued, "There's a new app called Walnut. It tells you exactly which ATMs near you work." The man standing in front of me said, "My son showed me a website this morning. Trusting what it showed, I went from one ATM to another, all empty, all of which were working according to the app. Two hours wasted." His interlocutor shook his head. "This is not like those websites. I will show you." His smartphone was now unlocked. More people took interest, and the ragged line broke into a circle, crowding around the smartphone app demonstration. The Walnut ATM locator was built on Google's map interface. And sure enough, the ATM outside which we were lined up was shaded in green, with the message: 'Last active at 01:47 AM, Today.' The others were impressed, with some taking out their smartphones to install the app right away.

My interest in the app grew, not only because of this 'accuracy,' but because of how the app produced the ATM status. What differentiated Walnut from the other ATM locating applications such as CashNoCash was the fact that this app did not rely on crowdsourced data to determine the working status of ATMs.

Redundancy and Surplus Value of Sociality: The Walnut Way to Find an ATM Near You

Walnut is a smartphone-based money manager that tracks and classifies expenses, providing the user with a report of money spent on different categories of consumption (food, entertainment, health, travel, etc.). It also serves as a digital wallet, facilitating electronic payments. Following the announcement of demonetization, the team at Thumbworks, the company that developed the Walnut application, organized a brainstorming session to figure out how they might respond to the nation-wide cash crisis. They had used other recently launched services—all of them, crowdsourced—to locate ATMs with varying degrees of success, or failure more often than not. One problem they identified with crowdsourced solutions was the lack of up-to-date, high-quality data owing to the reliance on users to report data in an accurate and timely fashion.

Anil, who was part of these sessions, said:

> Crowdsourcing has problems. It's hard to control the quality of data being uploaded. Users mostly forget to update data to the platforms and they may do so later when they remember. By then the ATM might have run out of cash. The web application would then reflect stale information. We tried to see if our existing systems and data could be used for a robust real-time solution.

Our expense tracker had system-level permissions to listen to autogenerated text messages of transactional activity sent to users' inboxes. An automated text is instantaneously sent by banks to the user following an ATM withdrawal that mentions [apart from the amount withdrawn] time-stamp [of the transaction] and ATM location. This was the data we needed (Fig. 2.1).

> If a Walnut user withdraws cash from any ATM anywhere in India, our app would 1) read the bank's text to the user, 2) extract the time of transaction and ATM location and 3) instantly update the database to reflect on our map-screen that this particular ATM was last active at this time. And because we didn't rely on human intervention but on existing automated triggers following an ATM transaction, we got instant, accurate data.

Anil's description of Walnut's approach to the problem of locating active ATMs highlights a paradigm shift in contemporary data science.

Crowdsourcing as a mode of data collection is like a survey, where respondents are asked a set of specific questions. The statistical

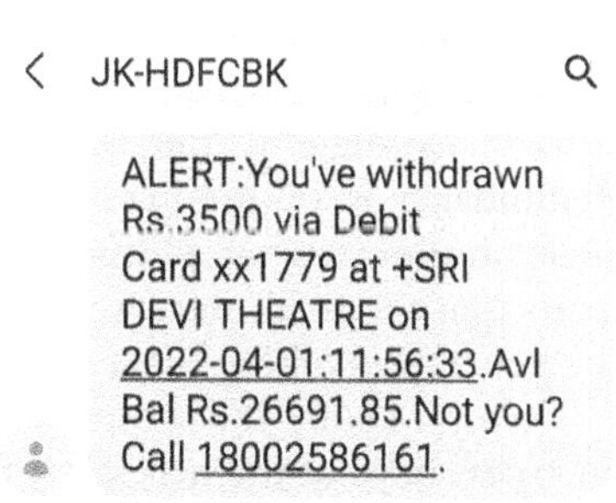

Fig. 2.1 Screenshot of an ATM withdrawal message from my phone, showing amount, time stamp and the location

distribution of responses to these questions comes to constitute a piece of objective knowledge. Indeed, this is what OkCupid's Christian Rudder was pointing to when he, like Malinowski, turned away from surveys. Not relying on the conscious and voluntarily reported data like the crowd-sourced apps do, the Walnut team turned to automatically generated data from text messages in the app-users' inboxes sent by banks, in response to their ATM withdrawal. Walnut also asked users via instant push notification for information such as queue length and currency denomination being dispensed at the particular ATM. This crowdsourced data, however, was of secondary importance. Central to the app's ATM locator was the instantaneity with which ATM status could be updated based off the automated bank SMS (Fig. 2.2).

These text messages, like the transaction receipt crumpled up and thrown into the wastebin after a cursory glance, are a redundancy generated following a transaction at the ATM interface. And like other automated messages from point-of-sale transactions, they are usually caused for what Anil called 'notification-irritation' of users annoyed at the endless machine-generated text alerts. Anil said,

> We took data which users usually just want to delete, or 'mark as read', and transformed this data to offer greater value to them in the form of expense-tracking reports. Our expense-tracking app would read the automatically generated text messages of payment notifications when a user orders food online or buys a movie ticket. Based on this data, we provide graphical and tabular data on screen that show what categories users were spending their money on. The app would also remind users of upcoming bill payment deadlines, phone validity expiration dates, etc.—information that is readily available in the text message inbox. The ATM locator was an extension of the same process.

The data that Walnut extracts to populate its ATM-locator—the redundant SMS that users usually see as unnecessary clutter in their inboxes—is, I want to suggest, the other side of the surplus value of sociality. Redundancy is a notion central to information theory and computer science: the intentional addition of excess information (hardware components that act as fail-safes, repetitions in data packets during transmission, the generation of 'log' data in software) to improve system reliability.

Dalton (1960, 485, emphasis added) suggests that, besides signifying an excess beyond the necessary, the notion of surplus 'bears connotations

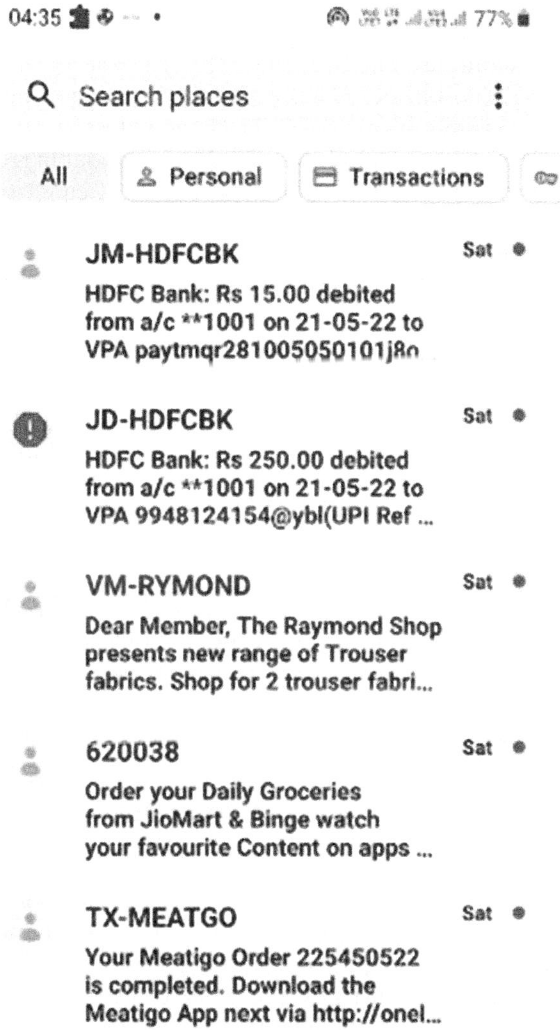

Fig. 2.2 Screenshot of my cluttered inbox

of redundancy,' that is, something neither strictly necessary nor immediately useful. This notion of redundancy is, in fact, not specific to computational data alone, as can be seen from Ian Hacking's study of the nineteenth-century statistics pioneer, William Farr. Analysing Farr's statistical tables on sickness in employees, Hacking writes: Farr did not have to collect new data, for 'much of it was simply lying about in records that no one hitherto had thought of using' (1982, 285, emphasis added). A redundant record is transformed into value through a process of extraction and evaluation.

This understanding of surplus, as an excess that is a redundancy, differs from the Marxian notion of surplus as an unpaid-for excess, over and above the (socially) necessary. The bank SMS is a redundancy generated in the social activity of withdrawing money using a debit card at an ATM, existing within a circuit of sociality between user, ATM and bank. Usually deleted or ignored as a useless annoyance by most users, this SMS is an objective store of a surplus value of the transaction at the ATM screen that Walnut extracts as useful data to build its ATM-tracker application for smartphones. My use of the concept 'surplus', in tying together excess with redundancy, also differs from Halpern et al. (2022) who adopt the term 'surplus' to indicate a conceptual transition from data understood as a referent to or descriptor of the real world (tangible as quantity), to post-Web2.0 data as autonomous and world-making (quality). In my view, it is the valorisation of redundancy that is at the heart of the world-making function of computational processes powered by data.

Automated Computational Extraction of the Surplus Value of Sociality

Insofar as it involves the extraction of use from a redundancy, the technological system exemplified by Walnut bears continuities with the nineteenth-century techniques of statistical enumeration that Hacking analyses. The difference turns on the mode of extracting data. Whereas nineteenth-century data is obtained by technologies of eliciting information from human respondents—survey questionnaires to enumerate census data, for instance—contemporary networked technological systems involve the capture of data that is recorded automatically as footprints of social activity at the edge of the interface.

In this sense, contemporary Big Data systems involve the objectification of human activity within machinic processes.

Zuboff (1988, 9–10) sees computational systems as 'information automata' that not only execute programmed instructions but also produce a record, like 'a voice that symbolically renders events, objects, and processes so that they become visible, knowable, and shareable in a new way.' Information technologies do not just automate; they also 'informate,' that is, produce an information record. In a presentation made at one of the first conferences on artificial intelligence—the 1958 Teddington symposium—British civil servants, Merriman et al. (1959), allude to this 'informating' function of recording data automatically: they suggest that the development of automated data-processing systems in administrative and commercial offices requires 'the creation of data as an automatic by-product of other human activity. Techniques are required for the creation of data in a form which can be readily and directly assimilated by machines without intermediate translation processes' (p. 813, emphasis added). The generation of redundant data is a central feature in the operation of networked technological interfaces. The smartphone is no exception given that it is a computational device. The text message from the bank is generated as an automated record of a transaction at the ATM interface, a redundancy, automatically recording a piece of social activity involving a user with an ATM card, the ATM machine, the user's phone and the bank's networks. Every interaction a user has with any smartphone app involves the automated production of data records.

Nancy Munn (1992, 269) in her ethnography of the Gawan people writes that every action of an individual is socialized in a discourse of evaluation, a discourse that seeks in particular actions, qualitative signs that index positive or negative values. It is through this evaluative discourse that 'one's value state is brought into consciousness.' Value is seen to reside as potentials that are detachable from actions, and values emerge when the actions are discussed, that is, inserted into a socialized process of evaluation. I suggest that this notion of value and evaluation can be productively extended to conceptualize sociality at the edge of interfaces.

Actions at networked interfaces—from gestures on the smartphone interfaces such as scrolling through Facebook newsfeeds and clicks on the Netflix video platform, to the opening of the automated gate at the metro-rail station by brandishing a 'smartcard'—are detached from the moment of their actualization and are objectified as records in various databases. In a landscape where circuits of sociality include ATMs, automated computational processes and database records, social activity at interfaces is detached from the singular moment of the gestural act at the interface and is preserved in records. Such redundant data records automatically generated alongside social activity at the edge of interfaces (dubbed 'events' in the language of software engineers) constitute a surplus value of sociality, a surplus that is extracted as useful data by contemporary computational technologies and is incorporated into models of 'big data' and the artificial intelligence systems of 'machine-learning.' They are also central to the engineering problem of 'debugging' systems, since it is the automatically recorded data—what Zuboff calls 'informata'—that is key to evaluate performances, fix errors, etc., since the data log is a veritable history of events at the edge of the interface. 'Big Data' analytical models thus follow from these principles and are involved in a computational evaluation of these records of interfacial actions thereby extracting the latent surplus value of sociality. Human social activity, captured as an enumerated record at the interface, comes to be objectified in machinic processes.

The mode of existence of value in data records is potential rather than actual, for it is in an evaluative process of exploratory and inventive transformation that value is realized and extracted from a state of redundancy. The Walnut app with its relatively simple ATM locator[2] stages, as a toy model, the extraction of the surplus value of sociality, the same fundamental processes at the heart of contemporary big data computation.

I now return to the epistemological encounter between anthropology and data science.

The Two Epistemologies Contd …

> The idea is to move our understanding of ourselves away from narratives and toward numbers, or, rather, to think in such a way that *numbers are the narrative* [that tell] a human story. … [Although social media platforms are business enterprises], they're demographers of unprecedented reach. … [D]igital data can show us how we fight … love … who we are, and how we are changing.
>
> Rudder (2014, 11–12. Emphasis added)

[2] I say relatively simple in comparison with other systems such as Google, Facebook and Netflix that extract and process data in vast quantities in the order of millions of data records per second.

For MN Srinivas (1975, 1392), '[T]he fruit of successful fieldwork is a large body of notes, the weight and complexity of which only increase with the years. … The value of old notes only increases with time,' suggesting elsewhere that a year's fieldwork would require more than ten years to 'write up' (Srinivas 1952, 32). Clifford (1986, 1–2) complicates such presentations of ethnographic writing. Reduced to 'keeping good fieldnotes, making accurate maps [and] "writing up" results,' ethnography, he argues, acquires an illusory transparency that masks 'the constructed, artificial nature of cultural accounts.' The artifice of 'making up' people, however, is not a conjuring out of thin air, a fabulation of the anthropologist's fancy, or a literalization of intrinsic biases. Evans-Pritchard (1951, 74) writes that, for the ethnographer, 'the raw material [is] social life itself.' While pens, papers and typewriters—apparatuses for ethnographic alchemy—may have been lugged around the jungles of anthropologyland, what moves or excites an anthropologist to 'make up' people is nevertheless situated in the anthropologist's encounters in a 'field' of sociality, impressionistic, imagined, or refracted though these encounters may be. This excitation, I want to suggest, is produced in an embodied friction with the surplus value of sociality, and come to be detached and extracted from fortunate encounters, say, in 'a daily round of the village, certain small incidents, characteristic forms of taking food, of conversing, of doing work' (Malinowski 2005, 18) and are recorded in a field-notebook. I call this surplus value, for, just as the bank's SMS on the phone, a redundancy generated following the ATM transaction is detached and transformed by the Walnut ATM locator, anthropologists as field-workers detach and reproduce observations from their deictic situatedness, from the immanence of sociality, extracting observations gleaned from this encounter into notebooks, transforming them in the disciplinary process of writing research papers and monographs.

Ellen and Fischer (1987, 679) in an article on the use of computers in fieldwork write: 'One fear that anthropologists have of relying on computers for primary data is that in the event of a crash all data might be lost, or data might be wiped from disk or tape through user error. This difficulty is substantially overcome if a printer is used to get near-immediate paper output.' The production of disciplinary knowledge is value extracted and transformed from a state of ephemerality, caught by the keen eye of an attentive anthropologist, stored in notebooks, computer disks and printed paper, that is to say, redundancies. Marcus and Cushman (2011, 126) write of the ethnographies of our own time: '[I]mpressionist tales are finding their way into more fieldwork accounts and are less likely to be associated only with the informal chatter of field-workers in the faculty club taking a time-out from their more serious work.' Even as the redundant SMS lying around in users' text inboxes is extracted as a surplus by the Walnut app in the historical moment of demonetization—a surplus which, in its extraction, is thwarted from ending up in the trash bins of smartphones—encounters that were formerly not of ethnographic use, squandered away in informal conversations (perhaps accruing symbolic value to the fieldworker-raconteur) now serve as the surplus which the contemporary anthropologist extracts.

Rudder, the data scientist and Malinowski, the anthropologist, agree on the inadequacy of surveys and interviews—forms of eliciting truth by directly asking for it—for as they understand it, 'actuality' lies elsewhere.

One might argue that they differ on the question of what counts as actual.

To continue the quotation by Rudder from the opening of this article: 'I realized I could go and look at what actually happens when, say, 100,000 white men and 100,000 black women interact in private. The data was sitting right there on our servers. It was an irresistible sociological opportunity' (2014, 10–11). For Rudder, actuality resides in the streams of data generated by every click, swipe and scroll at the edge of an interface, events that are automatically recorded, processed and arranged in a datalog. Malinowski, on the other hand, proposes to find actuality in 'the field,' an analytical construct produced in conjunction with a disciplined practice we call participant-observation: one produces material for ethnological observation by participating in the intersubjective life of the ethnos.

Surely, it may be objected, the interfaces that constitute the surface of extraction for data models also enter into a field constituted by social participation at the edge of interfaces. Is the participation at the level of the interface, and observation at the level of data models, that is, a participant-observation made possible by artifice, essentially different from that carried out by the living, thinking, speaking, walking body of the anthropologist in the field? Is the difference between ethnography and data science then simply one of 'face to face' versus mediated observation? If so, then what of 'digital ethnography'?

One form of distinction we can draw from Talal Asad, when he compares anthropological knowledge and statistical knowledge. The latter, he suggests, is a 'strong language.' Put simply, it is the language that modern state power speaks in and responds to. Anthropology clearly is not. Indeed these views are reflected within the space of business anthropology, insofar as anthropologists employed by various corporations for 'user research' (most notably, Xerox in the 1980s, and others such as Apple and Intel in the 1990s) occupied a position of minority in relation to their quantitatively and computationally minded colleagues (see Amirebrahimi 2016).

Extending Asad's contention, I want to suggest the epistemological distinction between anthropology and data science turns on the conception of the 'user' understood in Max Weber's analysis of bureaucracy, as an 'office.' Data science, I argue, is interested in the 'office' of the user at the edge of the interface, whereas anthropology is primarily concerned with the 'person.' The time spent at the edge of the smartphone interface is treated as if it is time spent at the office: records of time of entry (into the app screen), time spent on the app (as if it were time spent at the desk), a list of actions or tasks to perform (un-acted-upon notifications), a record of choice of action taken by the user at the interface and so on.

Malinowski (2005, 14) calls the subtle phenomena of sociality that he instructs, which must be observed in their full actuality through fieldwork—'the imponderabilia of actual life.' The professional ethnographer, writes Malinowski (p. 15), must not just register superficial details but attend to the 'imponderable yet all important facts of actual life [that] are part of the real substance of the social fabric.' For the anthropologist, the fabric of actuality is weaved with the threads of imponderables, ephemeralities picked up by a keenly attuned perception, elicited through the disciplining of experience. Asad (1994, 67–68) writes that the ethnographic representation of a 'cultural universe' is predicated upon the ethnographer's imaginatively mediated experience of fieldwork, which is communicated in the form of a text. Such a text may only incompletely translate the personal experience of the ethnographer into 'public language' (akin to what Freud claims in his letter), for there is a gap between the privileged experience of the ethnographer and representation. Statistical practice is a form of knowing which, according to Asad, is an exercise of power. Market research and election polling, key applications of statistics since the nineteenth century, 'produced social knowledge that is continuously and profoundly interventionist' (p. 74). The exercise of power through statistics, writes Asad, treats experience as 'an experimental practice, that is, a test of the precise degree to which a given social objective has succeeded' (p. 79). In the world of big data and data science, statistical data models indeed treat experience as an experiment, seeking to measure the degree of success of social objectives, construed as a desired outcome—for instance, users clicking on an advertisement, or the successful completion of payment on a shopping app-interface. Rudder writes, 'Each page of a website can absorb a user's entire experience—everything he clicks, whatever he types, even how long he lingers—and from this it's not hard to form a clear picture of his appetites and how to sate them' (2014, 11, emphases added). Statistical techniques allow the researcher 'to put hard numbers to some timeless mysteries; to take experiences that we've been content to put aside as "unquantifiable" and instead gain some understanding' (p. 13).

If the anthropologists' interest in sociality is targeted at observing and extracting the 'imponderabilia' in the life of persons, data science is interested in the 'office' of the user, not the imponderabilia of the person, but hard objective numbers enumerated under experimental conditions. 'All we have to do is look: from just a very slight remove, the data reveals *how people behave when they think no one is watching*' (2014, 12, emphasis added).

This leads us to a key consequence of formulating processes of recording computational data as extracts of the surplus value of sociality.

Engineering the Unconscious

Siddharth, who leads the user-experience research team at a leading mobile-phone-based payments bank in India, speaking of the relationship between data and interface design, said,

> These days, UI designers work closely with [software] developers and data scientists. Risk-assessment is a key area where data-based decisions are vital. Risk-scores are metrics that anticipate the likelihood of a person paying up outstanding credit within the appropriate time. "We had started work on an elaborate project for micro-lending services to determine credit risk based on a person's social media data. We had a data set that contained detailed social-media data including personal chats! The idea was to model a person based on a set of characteristics—conscientiousness for example—to determine a risk-score. But then you know what happened with Cambridge Analytica. The project was quickly shut down.

Cambridge Analytica, a political consulting firm, was the subject of a scandal in early 2018, pushing the idea of modern democracy to a point of crisis when reports emerged that the company had illegally accessed the

Facebook data of over 80 million users to develop psychographic profiles for targeted political advertising. Their most prominent project was Donald Trump's 2016 presidential campaign. Mark Turnbull, former head of Cambridge Analytica's political division, gave a telling description of their process: most human factors involved in processing information are 'unspoken and even unconscious.' Cambridge Analytica's job was 'to drop the bucket further down the well than anybody else ... to understand ... [user's] deep-seated underlying fears.' The campaign, says Turnbull, 'has to happen without anyone thinking "That's propaganda!"' (Channel 4 News 2018, emphasis added).

Turnbull's characterization of sinking the extractive bucket deep into the psychic well of unsuspecting people may be taken as either exaggerated hyperbole or a banal expression of an insidious operation of surveillance. I draw attention to his invocation of the unconscious which I find striking. Recall too, Rudder's contention that data reveals 'how people behave when they think no one is watching' (2014, 12). The records of activities at interfaces occur in the private world of a person, but are read out from the 'office' of the user: how long one lingers on a section of the screen, what images one's eyes are drawn to, what buttons one clicks, are unconscious, unknown to, unexamined and even repressed by the users' person, but is automatically recorded as redundant data of what I call the activities of the 'office' of the user.

These invocations I call the machinic unconscious at the level of the interface, the second aspect of the relationship between data and sociality.

For Walter Benjamin (1972, 7), what sets photography apart is that, even in the most intricately set-up shot where the cameraman tries to control every aspect of the image to be formed, the viewer of the photograph 'feels an irresistible compulsion to look for ... that imperceptible point ... the tiny spark of chance ... with which reality has ... seared the character in the picture.' What speaks in the photographic image is of a different kind from that which addresses the eye, 'different above all in the sense that instead of a space worked through by a human consciousness there appears one which is affected unconsciously. ... Photography makes aware for the first time the optical unconscious.'68 By an analogous extension, I suggest that the surplus value of sociality extracted as data makes available a machinic unconscious. To put this in ethnographic terms, in the answer scripts I evaluate, it is a trace seared into some turns of phrases that my eye picks up on, marking clearly to my perception, answers written by a student in their voice, and one generated by an AI language model like chat-GPT. These traces are what I gloss as the machinic unconscious.

'The unconscious,' writes Lacan (2006, 703, emphasis added), is 'a concept founded on the trail left by that which operates to constitute the subject.' According to Guattari (2011, 2), the unconscious is 'something that we drag around with ourselves both in our gestures and daily objects.' Actions recorded beneath the interface in millions of swipes and clicks every day, what I have called the extracts of surplus value of sociality, can be understood as trails of the unconscious recorded at the interfaces and incorporated into algorithmic data models and AI systems.

Towards New Configurations of Investment

Anthropological studies of computational algorithms have used a range of metaphors to model these machinic processes. Kockelman (2013) speaks of 'sieving' in relation to spam-filtering algorithms. Extending Miller and Slater (2000, 103–105) and the behaviourist literature on persuasive technologies, Seaver (2019, 425) suggests that recommendation algorithms built to predict a user's next interfacial action ought to be thought of as traps insofar as they rely on an 'understanding of people … as habitual minds with tendencies and compulsions that make them susceptible to persuasion … targets for capture.' Seaver says we can imagine the algorithmic infrastructure to be a generalized space of trapping which appears in the guise of a recommendation. 'No longer is the recommender an isolated part of the interface in a few media streaming platforms; now, on services like Netflix, "everything is a recommendation"' (p. 431). The metaphor of trapping seeks to break with the liberal idea of users freely choosing to interact with various elements on screen (see also Kotliar 2020). And by extending this to the notion of the recommender algorithm, originally conceived as a predictive apparatus, Seaver shows how trapping minimizes the risk (from the app's point of view) of a user leaving the app's screen.

To this discussion, I wish to add: any trap involves the flash of a lure, placed on screen as a seemingly innocuous element of the interface, and what is lured is unconscious investment. A lure draws in the gaze of the user, an unconscious investment that compels an interfacial gesture to repeat as the user nestles into the embrace of the screen (Prince 2020, 54–56).

Siddharth, UI-design lead at the payments bank from earlier, tells me that the design of certain elements on the interface, such as the position of a certain button, or a warning, or the ordering of options in a selectable list, is endlessly tweaked based on the experimental model of A/B testing, a form of randomized controlled trial where a set of users are exposed to a modification in the interface and another set of users see the interface without this modification. Based on the statistical significance of the occurrence of a particular action, such as successful completion of payment in a transactional interface, the interfacial tweak is then extended to a larger set of the app's users. Users barely register these changes, says Siddharth. The design of the interface is informed by data, extracted as the unconscious footprint a user leaves behind at the interface. Seaver, too, writes, '[T]he data that flows into the recommender has broadened to include practically any form of interaction, even (and now especially) interactions that a user may not realize have occurred' (2019, 431, emphasis added). Recommender systems too rely on this unconscious footprint, as the nudge the user to amble along pre-made footprints conveniently marked out at the interface for the user to engage unconsciously.

Perhaps the subtlest impact of smartphone-based cab aggregators is the transformation of the relationship between the user and the road. To hail an auto-rickshaw, one has to first descend to the level of the road, into the grime, the noise and the traffic. The next task is to get one of the autos speeding along to pull-over. Finally, the driver must be convinced into agreeing to go to the destination for a reasonable fare. With the smartphone-based apps, one sees the road as a dynamic image on a map-screen, from within the comfort of one's room. This road-image is pristine, an idealized picture—no dirt, no smoke, sharp lines marking roads and tidy little boxes for buildings, with little car-images the only dynamic elements shown on screen. The app-screen filters out the sound and the fury of the road, the traffic, the horns and the masses of pedestrians, showing only the little icons of cars associated with the app. Once the car arrives at the pick-up location, one leaves the inside of the room, with the image of the car having arrived at the location freshly imprinted in memory. One heads down to the road straight to the 'location-pin' with eyes only for the cab's license plate. The rest of the road, if not repressed, disappears from view under a new distribution or regulation of relations of visibility on screen, framed by the app's interface. Technologies of the unconscious, besides extraction, also displace unconscious investments through the design of the screen and the interface, designs that are in turn informed by data models.

In the months following demonetization, Walnut saw several thousands of new users signing up. Anil tells me of an interesting trend he had noticed. 'Although most users downloaded the app only to use the ATM-locator feature, quite a few users, after a few weeks, switched from cash-based payment to electronic transactions through our app's mobile wallet.' I asked him why he thought this happened. 'I don't know for sure,' he said. After all, he only had access to the 'office' of the user, not their person. 'Maybe they liked to see the colourful graphs which showed them what they spent money on. They wouldn't have this experience if they paid by cash, as there would be no data for the app to pick up on. So no graphs.' It would seem that the investments of the users' unconscious, initially lured in by the ATM-tracker, had now shifted to other objects within Walnut's screenspace. Much of user interface design involves reconfiguring and shifting the unconscious investment of users, by drawing on the surplus value of sociality extracted from data.

Conclusion: Nudging the Machinic Unconscious?

In an article titled 'The Unreasonable Effectiveness of Data,' Halevy et al. (2009, 8–12) write that Google's trillion-word corpus of words (recorded from searches, email compositions, etc.) 'captures even very rare aspects of human behaviour.' Instead of developing complex logical rules to generate human speech, they suggest, it is worthwhile to 'follow the data.' This summarizes the broad shift in the design of AI systems over the past two decades. The AI of the 1960s and 1970s were driven predominantly by generative rules coded into the program that would take in input data, process it using the coded rules and provide answers as output. The AI of today—neural-network models of 'machine-learning' and 'deep-learning'—invert this process. Instead of specifying the rules of operation directly, programmers feed the neural network a set of human-generated answers: for instance, a set of images would be fed to an image-recognition neural-net, with human-generated labels specifying the objects in each image. Trained on these answers, the neural-net is allowed to develop probabilistic rules of its own to figure out how to classify new images it had never seen before. Rather than explicitly specifying a logic of recognizing images, this method of programming gives the neural network the answers first in the form of large quantities of data, 'training' it to figure out the rules for producing such answers.

Rudder (2014, 226) writes, '[D]ata, despite the mining metaphor, comes from somewhere—and that somewhere is you.' I have characterized computational data as extracts of the surplus value of sociality, records of the user's 'official' activity at the edge of various interfaces. In the context of AI models, we see once again the reliance of such models on human evaluations of surplus sociality: it takes an army of human data-workers (labelling data, or commenting on model outputs that are fed back to the AI model) to bring to bear the human knowledge of social facts to improve the outputs of an AI model.

Further, I have suggested that the surplus value of sociality, extracted as data, which in turn is used to 'train' AI in the form of labelled data (images with words describing what is in it, audio with transcribed text), allows for unconscious associations present in the human-generated data input to the models to be objectified within the weights of the AI neural network.

According to Schüll (2016, 325–30), the world of apps is marked by a form of power that she refers to as governance by micronudge—the dynamic arrangement of elements on screens that push users to select forms of interactions desired by the architects of platforms, like card-magicians forcing a card on to a volunteer. The subject of the interface, suggests Schüll, delegates the responsibility of rational choice to analytical models that steer the subject's action. Nudging is a central idea in interface design to get users to unconsciously interact with particular elements on screens and is a watchword in the vocabulary of user-interface designers. This idea, with its origins in psychological economics, is predicated upon the assumption that, underneath conscious rational decision processes of the *Homo economicus*, other biases that are not directly observable guide the process of making choices. Nudges are targeted at exploiting these biases. For critics, this notion is central to questioning neo-liberal litanies for the freedom of choice. I have suggested, in opposition to a frame of rationality versus bias, one that draws on extensions from psychoanalysis, that is, the notion of a machinic unconscious that is repressed in the consciousness of the user. Nudges then can be thought of as reconfiguring users' unconscious investments, in a manner analogous to how the painter works on the gaze of the one who looks at a painting (Lacan 1981, 105–22). I suggest that nudges are made possible on the back of data—extracts of surplus sociality—in which is latent, a machinic unconscious.

Given that the data extracted at interfaces constitute the raw material and 'training data' for AI models of deep-learning, machine learning, transformers and other variations, could it be that such nudges are not limited to influencing humans alone?

A class of deep-learning AI models, called Convolutional Neural Networks or ConvNets, has been able to recognize images and transliterate speech into text with almost (if not better than) 'human-level' accuracy. A ConvNet for classifying images, in mathematical terms, is a function that maps an image's pixel-data to probability scores for various class-labels that identify the object in the image with different degrees of certainty. For the ConvNet model to become operational, it is first 'trained' on thousands, often millions of records of data labelled by humans. ConvNets are used not just for image data, but for any form of digital data. Many AI speech recognition models, for instance, are also ConvNets. Many of these models claim to outperform (if not perform as well as) humans on these tasks.

A (now not so) recent development in AI is a class of neural networks called GANs—Generative Adversarial Networks, first described by Ian Goodfellow in 2014. Unlike the ConvNet which is a classifier of input images by producing labels as output, a GAN is a generative AI, that is, in response to an input image; it produces an image as output. GANs can be developed in an adversarial position to the ConvNets we discussed earlier, that is to say, a GAN may face up to a ConvNet and supply the latter, input images for it to classify. The images that GANs generate as output, when fed to a ConvNet as input, can cause the erstwhile high-performance AI model to grossly misclassify the image. This 'fooling' is achieved by noise patterns that the GAN introduces into the image it passes on to the ConvNet, patterns which are barely discernible to human eyes.

Imagine this scenario: an image-recognizing ConvNet AI model is installed on a self-driving car. The car encounters a screen on the road that shows images generated by a GAN. These images now act as inputs for the ConvNet. Such a GAN may 'fool' the ConvNet on board the car into thinking that there is a stop sign where there is in fact none, or some such dangerous mischief. A GAN produces a 'fooling-image' to trick a trained ConvNet model in a manner very similar to how the ConvNet is trained. The GAN perturbs pixels in such a way that the ConvNet is 'nudged … along' into classifying the image incorrectly (Karpathy 2015). This way of tricking a well-performing ConvNet into incorrectly classifying an image perturbed by a Generative Adversarial Network (GAN) is dubbed an adversarial attack.

While most researchers at the forefront of AI are convinced by the 'unreasonable effectiveness' of deep-learning neural-nets such as ConvNets, 'there is still little insight into the internal operation and behaviour of these complex models, or how they achieve such good performance' (Zeiler and Fergus 2014, 818). More than half a century earlier, Alan Turing (1950) writes with startling prescience, 'An important feature of a learning machine is that its teacher will often be very largely ignorant of quite what is going on inside, although he may still be able to some extent to predict his pupil's behaviour.' Beyond ConvNets, this now extends to threats of 'prompt injection' in Large Language models (LLMs) as well.

How do we understand this opacity of AI, without slipping into alarmism? I suggest that the latest AI models, built on the surplus value of sociality extracted from human-generated data, incorporate a machinic unconscious, that their inexplicable effectiveness derives from a machinic unconscious, that supersedes any consciously explainable logics in the form of rules. And the adversarial attack by the GAN which 'fools' the otherwise robust ConvNet model is predicated on manipulating the machinic unconscious objectified in the ConvNet by 'nudging' its parameters along towards misclassifying the image, just as the data-based dynamic interfaces of today nudge along a user at the interface, to unconsciously click on particular interactive elements on screen.

Could it be that the fixation of machinic desire in the ConvNets—their ability to pick on features in the training data that are imperceptible to human eyes and ears, and optimizing their classifiers based on these features to achieve high accuracy—even predisposes this machinic unconscious to greater gullibility, given the absence of human-like defence mechanisms? Problems in AI ethics today focus on biases such as racial and gender-based discrimination that creep into AI models from the constitution and labelling of training data (Buolamwini and Gebru 2018). Twitter's image cropping algorithm—a program that displays only a particular portion of the image when viewed on the feed so as to give the user what the algorithm deems to be the most significant aspect of the image, showing the full image only when a user clicks on the cropped image—was embroiled in controversy (Hern 2020). A student, who had uploaded a screenshot of a zoom call with his face and that of his colleague on his twitter feed, noticed that the cropping algorithm showed only his face, cropping out the face of his colleague, who is black. After this, others played around with the image cropper—to which they did not have direct access in the form of source code—and realized that, when an image of Mitch McConnell and Barack Obama was uploaded, the algorithm would crop out the former president's face. It is in such 'slips' that the unconscious of the algorithm surfaces.

Questioning the conscientiousness of AI and working towards making them 'bias-free' calls for the institution of a vast machinic-legal super-ego to ensure that machines behave themselves when they 'think' no one's watching. That is to say, this approach, like data science modelled on the 'office' of the user, is focused on the 'office' of AI. What is also required, perhaps, is an analysis of the imponderabilia, or the slips of the machinic unconscious in the murmured dialogues of humans and their machinic counterparts built on the surplus value of sociality extracted at the interface.

References

Amirebrahimi, Shaheen. 2016. "The Rise of the User and the Fall of People: Ethnographic Cooptation and a New Language of Globalization" in *EPIC Proceedings 2016(1)*: 71–103. https://doi.org/10.1111/1559-8918.2016.01077.

Asad, Talal. 1994. "Ethnographic Representation, Statistics and Modern Power." in *Social Research*, 61(1): 55–88.

Benjamin, Walter. 1972. "A Short History of Photography." in Screen 13, no. 1: 5–26.

Boellstorff, Tom. 2013. "Making big data, in Theory." in First Monday 18 no. 10. https://firstmonday.org/article/view/4869/3750.

boyd, dana, and Kate Crawford. 2012. "Critical Questions for Big Data: Provocations for a Cultural, Technological, and Scholarly phenomenon." in Information, Communication & Society 15 no. 5: 662–679.

Buolamwini, Joy and Timnit Gebru. 2018. "Gender Shades: Intersectional Accuracy Disparities in Commercial Gender Classification." in Proceedings of the Conference on Fairness, Accountability, and Transparency: 77–91. http://proceedings.mlr.press/v81/buolamwini18a/buolamwini18a.pdf.

Cohen, Lawrence. 2019. "The Nation, De-duplicated." in Sanjay Srivastava, Yasmeen Arif, and Janaki Abraham (eds.) Critical Themes in Indian Sociology: 107–26. New Delhi: Sage Publications India.

Channel 4 News. 2018. "Cambridge Analytica Uncovered: Secret Filming Reveals Election Tricks." Channel 4 News YouTube Channel. Uploaded 19 March,

2018. 07:00–10:50. Accessed June 11, 2020. https://www.youtube.com/watch?v=mpbeOCKZFfQ.

Clifford, James. 1986. "Introduction: partial truths" in James Clifford and George Marcus (eds.) *Writing Culture*. Berkeley-Los Angeles: University of California Press.

Cristianini, Nello. 2014. "On the Current Paradigm in Artificial Intelligence." AI Communications 27, no. 1: 37–43. https://doi.org/10.3233/AIC-130582.

Dalton, George. 1960. "A Note of Clarification on Economic Surplus." in American Anthropologist 62, no. 3: 483–490.

Ellen, Roy, and Michael Fischer. 1987. "On computers for anthropological fieldwork." *Current Anthropology* 28 (5): 677–679.

Evans-Pritchard, E. 1951. *Social Anthropology*. London: Cohen and West.

González, Roberto J. "Hacking the Citizenry?: Personality Profiling, 'Big Data' and the Election of Donald Trump." Anthropology Today 33, no. 3 (2017): 9–12. https://doi.org/10.1111/1467-8322.12348.

Graeber, David. 2001. Toward an anthropological theory of value. New York: Palgrave.

Guattari, Felix. 2011. The Machinic Unconscious: Essays in Schizoanalysis. Translated by Taylor Adkins. Los Angeles: Semiotext(e).

Hacking, Ian. 1982. "Biopower and the Avalanche of Printed Numbers." in Humanities in Society 5, no. 3–4: 279–295.

Halevy, Alon, Peter Norvig, and Fernando Pereira. 2009. "The Unreasonable Effectiveness of Data." in IEEE Intelligent Systems 24, no. 2: 8–12. https://doi.org/10.1109/MIS.2009.36.

Halpern, Orit, Patrick Jagoda, Jeffrey West Kirkwood and Leif Weatherby. 2022. "Surplus Data: An Introduction" in Critical Inquiry 48, no. 2: 197–210. https://doi.org/10.1086/717320.

Hern, Alex. 2020. "Twitter Apologizes for 'Racist' Image-cropping Algorithm" in The Guardian, September 21, 2020. https://www.theguardian.com/technology/2020/sep/21/twitter-apologises-for-racist-image-cropping-algorithm Accessed on 5th December, 2020.

Ingold, Tim. 1991. "Becoming Persons: Consciousness and Sociality in Human Evolution." in Culture Dynamics 4, no. 3: 355–378.

Karpathy, Andrej. 2015. "Breaking Linear Classifiers on ImageNet". Accessed 27 June, 2020. http://karpathy.github.io/2015/03/30/breaking-convnets/.

Kockelman, Paul. 2013. "The Anthropology of an Equation: Sieves, Spam Filters, Agentive Algorithms, and Ontologies of Transformation." in HAU: Journal of Ethnographic Theory 3, no. 3: 33–61.

Kotliar, Dan. 2020. "Who Gets to Choose? On the Socio-algorithmic Construction of Choice." Science, Technology, & Human Values 46 no. 2: 346–75. https://doi.org/10.1177/0162243920925147.

Lacan, Jacques. 1981. The Four Fundamental Concepts of Psychoanalysis. Translated by Bruce Fink. New York-London: W.W. Norton and Company.
———. 2006. Écrits. Translated by Bruce Fink. New York-London: W.W. Norton and Company.
Mahapatro, Abhipsha. 2016. "Book My Chotu: A start-up that braves ATM queues on your behalf." The Quint, November 22, 2016. Accessed June 10, 2020. https://www.thequint.com/news/india/book-my-chotu-a-start-up-that-braves-the-atm-queue-on-your-behalf-demonetistaion-rs-500-1000-pm-modi.
Malinowski, Bronislaw. 1922/2005. *Argonauts of the western pacific*. London: Routledge.
Manovich, Lev. 2011. Trending: The promises and the challenges of big social data. *Debates in the Digital Humanities, 2(1)*: 460–475.
Marcus, George E. and Dick Cushman. 2011. "Fieldwork, culture and ethnography revisited" in John Van Maanen (ed.) *Tales of the field: on writing ethnography*. Chicago and London: The University of Chicago Press.
Merriman, J., D.W.G. Wass, and S. Gill. 1959. "To What Extent can Administration be Mechanized?" in Mechanisation of Thought Processes 2: 811–818.
Miller, Daniel, and Don Slater. 2000. The Internet: an ethnographic approach. London and New York: Berg.
Munn, Nancy. 1992. The fame of Gawa: A Symbolic Study of Value Transformation in a Massim (Papua New Guinea) Society. Durham and London: Duke University Press.
Pink, Sarah, Minna Ruckenstein, Robert Willim, and Melisa Duque. 2018. "Broken data: Conceptualising Data in an Emerging World." in Big Data & Society 5, no. 1: 1–13. https://doi.org/10.1177/2053951717753228.
Prince, Deepak. 2020. "A Stain in the Picture." in Journal of the Anthropological Society of Oxford-online, New Series 12, no. 1: 44–68. https://www.anthro.ox.ac.uk/sites/default/files/anthro/documents/media/jaso12_1_2020_44_68.docx.
Rudder, Christian. 2014. Dataclysm: Who We Are (When We Think No One's Looking). New York: Crown Publishers.
Sahlins, Marshall. 1972. Stone age economics. Chicago and New York: Aldine Atherton Inc.
Schüll, Natasha Dow. 2016. "Data for life: Wearable technology and the design of self-care." in BioSocieties 11, no. 3: 317–333. https://doi.org/10.1057/biosoc.2015.47.
Seaver, Nick. 2015. "Bastard algebra.", in Tom Boellstroff and Bill Mauer (eds.) *Data, now bigger and better*: 27–45. Chicago: Prickly Paradigm Press.
Seaver, Nick. 2019. "Captivating Algorithms: Recommender Systems as Traps." in Journal of Material Culture 24, no. 4: 421–36. https://doi.org/10.1177/1359183518820366.

Srinivas, M. N. 1952. "Social anthropology and sociology." in *Sociological bulletin* 1(1): 28–37.

Srinivas, M.N. Aug 1975. "Village studies, participant observation and social science research in India." in *Economic and Political Weekly*, 10(33/35): 1389–1394.

Suchman, Lucy, Karolina Follis, and Jutta Weber. 2017. "Tracking and Targeting: Sociotechnologies of (in) Security." in Science, Technology and Human Values 42, no. 6: 983–1002. https://doi.org/10.1177/0162243917731524.

Turing, Alan. 1950. "Computing machinery and intelligence." in Copeland, Jack, ed. (2004) The Essential Turing: Seminal Writing in Computing, Logic, Philosophy, Artificial Life Plus the Secrets of Enigma. Oxford: Clarendon Press.

Zeiler M.D., Fergus R. 2014 "Visualizing and Understanding Convolutional Networks." in Fleet D., Pajdla T., Schiele B., Tuytelaars T. (eds.) Computer Vision – ECCV 2014. ECCV 2014. Lecture Notes in Computer Science, vol. 8689. Cham: Springer.

Zuboff, Shoshana. 1988. In the Age of the Smart Machine: The Future of Work and Power. New York: Basic Books.

Zuboff, Shoshana. 2015. "Big Other: Surveillance Capitalism and the Prospects of an Information Civilization." in Journal of Information Technology 30, no. 1: 75–89.

CHAPTER 3

The Plight of Female Gig Workers in Indonesia

Suci Lestari Yuana

Introduction

The rapid advancement of artificial intelligence (AI) technologies in recent years has brought about transformative changes across various industries and sectors worldwide. While AI promises innovation, efficiency, and convenience, it also has the potential to perpetuate existing socio-economic inequalities, particularly in developing countries (Hao and Freischlad, 2022; Hao 2022). This chapter draws from the Critical Political Economy (CPE) tradition to examine how AI technologies serve as mechanisms of contemporary value extraction, labour exploitation, and inequality reproduction. In doing so, it situates the concept of AI colonialism within a broader framework of platform capitalism and the historical legacies of global uneven development.

This chapter focuses on the experiences of female workers in app-based or platform companies in Indonesia. The advent of the platform economy has reshaped labour markets and work arrangements globally, and

S. L. Yuana (✉)
Department of International Relations, Faculty of Social and Political Sciences, Universitas Gadjah Mada, Yogyakarta, Indonesia
e-mail: sucilestari.yuana@ugm.ac.id

P. Raghunath (ed.), *Critical Political Economy and Southern Approaches to AI*, Palgrave Global Media Policy and Business,
https://doi.org/10.1007/978-3-032-14090-6_3

Indonesia is no exception. The informal economy, which encompasses street vendors, domestic workers, and day labourers, plays a pivotal role in Indonesia's socio-economic fabric, offering employment to many marginalised individuals. Yet, within the informal economy, workers often grapple with precarious conditions, characterised by low wages, long working hours, and limited job security (Standing 2016). These challenges are particularly pronounced for women workers who constitute a significant portion of the informal sector in Indonesia.

In recent years, the rise of app-based platform companies has further complicated the landscape of informal work in Indonesia. According to Indonesian regulations, workers in these platforms are classified as part of the informal sector, devoid of the labour protections and social security benefits accorded to traditional workers. These platform workers are typically designated as "partners" or "contractors" and are remunerated on a per-task basis, devoid of a minimum wage or access to comprehensive social and health protections (Izzati, 2018; Izzati and Sesunan 2022). This situation is emblematic of the broader dynamics of AI capitalism, where algorithmic infrastructures reorganise labour processes while disembedding protection and rights (Verdegem 2024).

This transformation is notably evident in the case of "Gojek," a homegrown platform company that employs algorithmic matching to connect supply (motorcycle taxi services or "ojek") with demand (customers/users). Gojek's presence has not only transformed the informal sector but also intensified the digital restructuring of labour—a hallmark of platform capitalism in the Global South. This restructuring extends to women who now engage in platform-mediated labour, navigating both exploitative market logics and embedded patriarchal norms (Bansal and Arora 2023).

The emergence of AI technologies and their integration into the platform economy has disrupted the livelihoods of female workers in Indonesia in two significant ways. Firstly, female platform workers often experience below-average monthly incomes compared to their male counterparts, perpetuating existing gender-based wage disparities. Secondly, unlike their male counterparts, women face the formidable challenge of balancing care work responsibilities, such as childcare, alongside their roles as motorcycle taxi riders (Bansal and Arora 2023). The algorithms underpinning these platforms rarely account for these gendered burdens, reproducing rather than alleviating existing inequalities. These gendered exclusions reflect what Nancy Fraser (2003) calls the "crisis of social reproduction" under neoliberalism.

This chapter seeks to address critical challenges and knowledge gaps by pursuing the following objectives: firstly, to investigate the manifestations of AI colonialism within the context of app-based/platform companies in Indonesia; secondly, to evaluate the specific implications of AI colonialism on female workers participating in these platforms; thirdly, to examine how AI escalates the dual burden experienced by women who must simultaneously manage care work responsibilities alongside their engagement in gig work; and finally, to analyse the broader consequences of AI colonialism on the overall protection and welfare of women workers in Indonesia. The central research question is: How does AI colonialism, as a form of contemporary capitalist expansion, manifest in Indonesian platform economies, and what are its specific gendered implications for informal female gig workers?

This research is significant for several reasons. Firstly, it contributes to CPE of AI by empirically grounding its critique in the lived realities of marginalised women in the Global South. Secondly, it brings gendered labour struggles into view within analyses of algorithmic governance, data extraction, and digital colonialism. Lastly, this study aligns with the emancipatory goals of CPE by documenting everyday solidarities and resistances among female gig workers—pointing to avenues for transformative change and gender data—just futures.

Informal Economy and AI Colonialism

Critical Political Economy (CPE) provides a powerful framework for analysing how capitalist structures reshape work through technological innovation, particularly in contexts marked by informality and systemic marginalisation. AI colonialism, as a concept, captures one such mechanism—whereby artificial intelligence technologies are deployed not only to optimise productivity, but also to extract data and surplus labour from peripheral economies, reinforcing global asymmetries in value creation and control (Kwet 2019; Verdegem 2024).

AI colonialism refers to the perpetuation of colonial power dynamics through the deployment and control of artificial intelligence technologies. This phenomenon encapsulates how AI is leveraged by powerful entities, often originating from the Global North, to dominate and exploit regions and populations in the Global South. It is not only a technological phenomenon, but a socio-economic project embedded in the political economy of digital capitalism, embedding itself in the socio-economic and political fabrics of affected regions. The concept draws parallels to historical colonialism, where the exploitation of physical resources and labour was paramount. In the digital era, data emerge as a new form of raw material, with AI-driven data extraction and surveillance capabilities reinforcing asymmetrical power structures (Kwet 2019).

Technology giants such as Google, Facebook, and Alibaba utilise vast data accumulation to extend their influence, often under the guise of development and connectivity initiatives (Birhane 2023). This mirrors the "trusteeship" approach of colonial regimes, which purported to bring civilisation to colonised lands while exploiting their resources (Maldonado-Torres 2007). The impact of AI colonialism is multifaceted, exacerbating social inequalities, fostering monopolistic markets, and perpetuating digital surveillance that can lead to practices akin to racial surveillance and digital apartheid (Robinson 2019). As AI solutions are heralded as panaceas for complex societal issues, the underlying coloniality embedded in their deployment necessitates critical examination and ethical scrutiny to ensure technology serves equitable and just purposes (Whyte 2019).

Drawing from CPE, AI colonialism is best understood as part of a broader structural logic of capitalist accumulation, wherein digital infrastructures reproduce labour segmentation, deepen dispossession, and commodify everyday life in new ways. AI technologies, often heralded as neutral tools of progress, are shaped by—and in turn reproduce—hierarchies of race, class, and gender, particularly in the Global South.

Within this framework, AI algorithms are wielded to extract valuable data and labour from marginalised populations. While distinct from historical colonialism, AI colonialism shares key characteristics, including the extraction of value from local resources, profound economic inequalities, and social control. This concept provides a lens through which to analyse how AI technologies intersect with existing inequalities and power imbalances, particularly in developing nations like Indonesia. The informal economy in Indonesia serves as a focal point in our exploration of AI colonialism. This sector comprises various forms of labour, such as street vending, domestic work, and daily wage labour, and plays a pivotal role in the nation's employment landscape (Carr and Chen 2002). Notably, it operates largely outside formal regulations, leaving workers without conventional employment contracts or access to essential social protections (De Ruyter and Rachmawati 2020). This informal labour market provides income opportunities for marginalised individuals but simultaneously exposes them to economic insecurity, exploitation, and precarious work conditions.

Workers within Indonesia's informal economy often endure precarious conditions, characterised by low wages, protracted working hours, and minimal job security. Female workers, who dominate this sector, face gender-based wage disparities and are frequently denied access to crucial labour protections and social benefits. The informal economy's vulnerability underscores the urgency of investigating how AI colonialism aggravates these precarious conditions, disproportionately affecting women workers.

The platform economy, a central component of AI colonialism, has redefined the nature of work worldwide, including in Indonesia. App-based platform companies, exemplified by Gojek, introduce novel labour models where workers are categorised as "partners" or "contractors" rather than traditional employees. Gig work, characterised by short-term, task-based engagements, typifies this sector. While offering flexibility, gig work entails uncertainty as income depends on the completion of tasks.

In CPE terms, this reflects a broader trend towards the informalisation and casualisation of labour under digital capitalism, where flexibility masks a deep erosion of worker rights, social protections, and collective bargaining power. This transformation in labour markets introduces questions about labour rights, job security, and the social safety net, with gender disparities often overlooked within this framework.

Female workers in the platform economy confront a distinctive challenge: the "double burden" (Van Doorn 2017; Hunt and Samman 2019;) This concept refers to the concurrent performance of care work, such as childcare or eldercare, alongside gig work. This dual role is particularly pronounced for women who often bear the responsibility of managing household and family care. The algorithms underpinning platform companies typically fail to account for this dual burden, aggravating the complexities faced by female workers attempting to balance flexible gig work with caregiving duties (Allen et al. 2013; ILO 2015). This intersection of care work and gig work is crucial to our examination of how AI colonialism amplifies gender inequalities.

Within the framework of AI colonialism, it is essential to acknowledge that AI technologies have the potential to perpetuate and deepen gender inequality. This encompasses biased algorithms that reinforce discriminatory practices and the underrepresentation of women in AI development. From a CPE perspective, these gendered inequalities are not incidental but systemic, embedded in the profit-driven logics of platform economies that externalise reproductive labour while maximising productivity and control.

Understanding these gender dynamics within the broader context of AI colonialism is critical, as it highlights the unequal distribution of benefits and harms, particularly impacting women in developing countries. Consequently, this study aims to unravel how AI colonialism magnifies these disparities and influences the economic and social standing of female workers in Indonesia's platform economy.

Methodology

This study employs a qualitative approach rooted in the epistemological commitment of CPE and Southern feminist perspectives. Rather than aiming for generalisability or abstraction, the research privileges contextual, situated knowledge production grounded in the lived experiences of marginalised women navigating platform economies. This orientation aligns with the CPE tradition's emphasis on revealing how structural inequalities are reproduced through specific institutional arrangements and labour relations (Cox 1981), and with Southern theorising's commitment to plural, embodied, and relational forms of knowing.

The research began with a comprehensive literature review, drawing from academic journals, policy documents, and grey literature to establish an understanding of the political economy of AI, informal labour and gendered precarity. Sources included peer-reviewed scholarship, government reports, and relevant NGO publications focused on platform work in Indonesia. This phase enabled the identification of key concepts—such as AI colonialism, surplus extraction, algorithmic control, and reproductive labour—that informed the empirical inquiry.

Following the literature review, two Focus Group Discussion (FGD) were conducted on 4 August 2023 and 10 August 2023, involving ten Indonesian female gig workers. The purpose of the FGD was to obtain nuanced, first-hand accounts of the challenges and opportunities these workers face within the context of AI and platform work. The participants were selected to represent a diverse cross-section of the gig economy, including ride-hailing, food delivery, freelance digital services, and other prevalent platform-based jobs. The discussion was structured to explore their experiences with AI technologies, work conditions, income stability, and any gender-specific issues they encounter. This qualitative data was then analysed to identify recurring themes and insights, which were subsequently integrated with the findings from the literature review to provide a comprehensive understanding of the topic.

Data from the FGDs were transcribed and analysed thematically. Recurring patterns were identified—particularly around the intersections of algorithmic control, care labour, and structural exclusion. These themes were interpreted through the lens of CPE concepts such as the commodification of labour, exploitation of reproductive time, and structural disempowerment, as well as Southern feminist notions of epistemic resistance and embodied knowledge.

Indonesian Gig Workers

The transformative potential of digital labour platforms in countries like Indonesia—where informal employment remains the dominant mode of livelihood—must be understood through the lens of capitalist restructuring and labour commodification, key concern of CPE. These platforms serve as infrastructure of algorithmic labour extraction, connecting supply and demand through data-driven interaction that intensifies precarity while expanding capital accumulation at the margins of the global economy. In the case of Indonesia, for instance, the rapid adoption of technology has fuelled the growth of platform-based business models, redefining the traditional labour market dynamics by acting as digital intermediaries (Schmidt 2017). This paradigm shift has led to the proliferation of location based services such as ride-hailing (e.g., Uber, Ola), food delivery (e.g., Zomato, Swiggy), and household services (e.g., Urban Company, Housejoy), which offer micro-entrepreneurship opportunities to individuals across various socio-economic strata, particularly those marginalised in the formal economy.

In Indonesia, the rise of digital labour platforms is exemplified by the success story of Gojek, a homegrown transportation and service provider that has revolutionised the gig economy landscape. As a flagship of platform capitalism in the region, Gojek provides income-generating opportunities for millions, particularly in urban areas where formal employment is scarce. Its innovation lies not only in leveraging motorcycle-based transport but also in its ability **to** navigate institutional voids and swiftly respond to regulatory shifts (Yuana et al. 2020).

Yet this "innovation" must be critically interrogated. Gojek's rapid growth and influence over regulatory agendas reflect what CPE scholars identify as **the** political embeddedness of market power (Yuana, 2024).

For example, when Gojek's services were temporarily banned by the Indonesian government, the company leveraged its socio-political capital—mobilising users and drivers as a political constituency—to reverse the decision within 12 hours (Koskinen et al. 2019). This episode illustrates how platform firms operate not merely as economic actors but as institutional entrepreneurs, reshaping governance frameworks in their favour and cementing a model of labour informalisation under digital governance.

From a Critical Political Economy perspective, these platforms represent more than technological disruption—they constitute a reorganisation of labour under a new regime of digital capitalism, where value is extracted not only through labour, but through data, time, and infrastructure externalised to workers. In Indonesia, Gojek has strong influence on its ability to navigate and overcome regulatory challenges swiftly (Yuana et al. 2020). With a presence in multiple Southeast Asian countries and over 2 million drivers in Indonesia (Gojek 2022), Gojek's success rests on its integration of informal labour into algorithmically managed services. When faced with a ban on its app, Gojek mobilised its considerable political capital, accrued through its growing dominance in the market, to overturn the ban within a remarkably short span of 12 hours (Koskinen et al. 2019). This episode raises intriguing questions about the dynamics between platform operators and regulatory authorities, particularly in emerging markets like Indonesia. Scholars have pondered whether platforms originating in the Global South possess a unique advantage in understanding and adapting to the contextual and institutional factors prevalent in their target locations (Koskinen et al. 2019). This notion challenges the notion of "Western" norms and practices as universally applicable across diverse socio-cultural contexts, highlighting the importance of considering local sensibilities and legal frameworks in platform design and implementation. Gojek is not merely an economic actor but a powerful institutional force. Its ability to swiftly overturn regulatory bans, as seen in 2015, underscores how platform companies operate as institutional entrepreneurs (Yuana et al. 2020). This reflects CPE concerns about how capital shapes regulatory space to preserve accumulation regimes.

This episode raises intriguing questions about the dynamics between platform operators and regulatory authorities, particularly in emerging markets like Indonesia. Some scholars argue that platforms originating in the Global South may possess an advantage in navigating local norms and institutions (Koskinen et al. 2019). However, alongside the opportunities presented by digital labour platforms, there are also challenges that need to be addressed. One significant issue is the growing dependency on platform-based work, particularly among those in the Global South who face limited employment options in the formal sector (Yuana et al. 2023). Many platform workers in countries like Indonesia are part of the vast informal workforce, contributing to the perpetuation of informality in the labour market. While digital platforms offer avenues for income generation, they also raise concerns about job security, social protection, and workers' rights, especially in the absence of adequate regulatory frameworks (Putri et al. 2023).Yet from a structural lens, this reflects a larger process of capital offloading infrastructural costs onto workers, characteristic of neoliberal accumulation models. Gig workers become self-financed labour units, responsible for their tools, health, and social security. In CPE terms, this signals a restructuring of control—from foremen to code, from employers to interfaces—that fragments the workforce and undermines collective agency.

Moreover, gender disparities persist within the digital platform economy, with women facing additional barriers to access and participation. Despite the potential for platforms to empower women economically, structural inequalities and societal norms often limit their engagement in platform-based work. Women in the Global South confront challenges such as limited access to technology, cultural biases, and safety concerns, which hinder their full participation in the digital labour market. Female gig workers are doubly burdened: they navigate the extractive demands of the platform and the unpaid responsibilities of care work at home. This dual exploitation resonates with Nancy Fraser's (2003) critique of how capitalism externalises reproductive labour.

Addressing these gender disparities requires targeted interventions aimed at promoting digital literacy, creating safe working environments, and combating discriminatory practices within platform design and management. From CPE viewpoint, the Indonesian gig economy illustrates how digital platforms mediate informalisation, control, and labour segmentation in ways that benefit capital while undermining worker rights. The gendered nature of this process must be central to any critical analysis.

Stories from Female Riders

In Indonesia, an increasing number of women are turning to gig work to support themselves and their families. Despite the appeal of flexible hours and reasonable pay, these women face significant challenges in a male-dominated field. This section explores the experiences of these women, their daily battles, and the camaraderie they build to survive in an often unfriendly and biased industry, while also examining the broader implications of platform capitalism, AI colonialism, and reproductive labour in their lives as female gig workers.

From a CPE perspective, these stories serve as empirical windows into how algorithmic infrastructures reconfigure labour relations, deepen informality, and externalise social reproduction costs onto women—without offering corresponding rights or protections. Take Yanti, a 43-year-old female ride-hailing driver in Yogyakarta, her work often means platform work exposes women to both physical vulnerability and algorithmic invisibility.

> *If I received a request from a male passenger, I often asked through the chat app: "I am a woman, is that okay with you?".* (Focus Group Discussion, 4 August 2023)

This question reflects a persistent concern among female drivers about the risk of inappropriate behaviour or harassment from male passengers. To protect herself, Yanti sometimes lets male passengers drive her motorcycle while she sits in the back, reversing their roles to prevent potential harm. Yanti began working in the gig economy in 2017 after her divorce, aiming to support her children's education (one in junior high school and one in senior high school). The ride-hailing industry seemed promising, with minimal entry requirements and the potential for decent earnings. However, she soon faced significant challenges. Many male passengers cancelled their rides upon realising she was a woman, and others expressed pity or disdain for her choice of work. Despite these obstacles, Yanti continued, driven by the need to provide for her family. In CPE terms, this demonstrates how labour platforms obscure social hierarchies behind neutral algorithms while allowing bias and discrimination to flourish unchecked.

Yanti's story is a stark example of AI colonialism at work. Ride-hailing platforms like Gojek and Grab rely on sophisticated algorithms to match drivers with passengers efficiently. However, these algorithms can inadvertently reinforce gender biases. The system prioritises efficiency and profitability, often at the expense of safety and fairness. Male passengers cancelling rides with female drivers might reflect an underlying bias within the algorithm that doesn't account for gender-based safety concerns or discrimination, worsening Yanti's struggle to secure steady work.

Furthermore, female gig workers in Indonesia often carry the dual responsibilities of their gig work and traditional domestic chores. This "double burden" is a recurring theme among the women interviewed. Lia, a 33-year-old ShopeeFood delivery rider, exemplifies this struggle. Her day starts before sunrise with household chores and preparing her two children for school (a fifth grader and a second grader in elementary school), followed by a long day of deliveries. Despite working from early morning until late at night, her duties do not end when she gets home; she helps her children with their homework before finally getting some rest. (Focus Group Discussion, 4 August 2023). She shared her first-time experience in using the app where she had little technical knowledge on how the app works and she was accompanied by her younger child on her first work.

> *Come on, little one, let's learn how to drive for the ride-hailing service. I was startled by the app's sound when the first order came in. My child helps me read the map. He pointed out some ride-hailing drivers and told me to ask them how to use the app. They were kind enough to show me the basics. Then, after we completed the order, my child asked, 'How much did you earn, Mom?' I told him I earned IDR 10,000 (about $0.65 USD).* (Focus Group Discussion, 4 August 2023)

This illustrates how **labour, care, and technology co-mingle in daily survival**, often with children involved in digital literacy and navigation.

Lia chose food delivery over passenger transport for the relative safety and control it offers. However, this choice does not completely shield her from harassment. She recounted an incident where a male colleague made inappropriate comments, reminding her that harassment can come from peers as well as passengers.

> *I decided to go with food delivery instead of transporting passengers because it seemed safer and I felt like I had more control. But that doesn't mean I'm completely safe from harassment. I remember one time a male colleague made some really uncomfortable comments to me. It wasn't just the customers I had to worry about; sometimes the harassment comes from people I work with too.* (Lia, FGD 4 August 2023)

Lia's choice of food delivery over passenger transport (and followed by 90% of the FGD participants) is influenced by her desire for safety, a factor often overlooked by the platforms' algorithms. The platforms' data-driven approach to matching jobs with drivers does not adequately account for the personal and safety preferences of female drivers. Furthermore, the pressure to constantly be available on the app to secure enough work reflects a colonial mentality, where the labour and time of gig workers are exploited for the benefit of the platform, with little regard for their well-being. These narratives exemplify how algorithmic governance flattens labour categories while intensifying gendered vulnerabilities—what Eubanks (2018) and Noble (2018) call the encoded inequalities of "automated inequality."

Ride-hailing companies like Grab and Gojek have introduced measures to support female drivers, including anti-sexual harassment training and features allowing women to choose delivery over passenger services. Grab's "LadyGrab" program and Gojek's selective service options aim to create a safer working environment. Despite these efforts, many women still feel constrained by both their work and societal expectations. Ri, an active manager of female led driver association, Srikandi, in Yogyakarta, highlights the lack of basic labour rights for female gig workers, such as menstrual and maternity leave. The app-based incentive structures often complicate these issues, rewarding the most active and disciplined drivers while penalising female workers who need breaks for conducting their care duty and double burden at home. The institutional measures implemented by ride-hailing companies, while beneficial, often fall short due to the underlying AI-driven operational models. These platforms use algorithms to maximise efficiency and profit, often sidelining the human aspects of gig work. The lack of basic labour rights and the punitive nature of the incentive structures reflect a form of digital exploitation. By prioritising constant availability and high performance, the platforms perpetuate a system where workers are disposable and their needs are secondary to the platform's goals. This reflects a disciplinary model of platform capitalism where productivity is rewarded and care work is penalised. From a CPE lens, such digital regimes demand a continuous presence, turning human life into a performance metric and algorithmic input.

The economic necessity driving women into gig work cannot be overstated. Many, like Nana, a 55-year-old Gojek rider, use the metaphor of "Kian Santang," a legendary Javanese warrior known for his ability to split himself into seven to tackle multiple tasks simultaneously, to describe her life (Focus Group Discussion, 10 August 2023). This metaphor poignantly illustrates the immense pressures and multifaceted roles she has to juggle daily (Jacques and Radtke 2012).

> *My day begins early in the morning. I wake up to handle household chores and ensure everything is in order before preparing my children for school. After dropping them off, I start my work as a ride-hailing driver, making rounds to pick up and drop off passengers. Alongside my driving duties, I often work with my children, trying to maximise the limited time we have together while also securing additional income. To supplement my earnings, I search for offline orders at local markets. The diversity of my work, from online ride-hailing to offline errands, requires me to be constantly flexible and adaptive. I sometimes feel like Kian Santang, I have so many tasks to do and so little time. I bring my children along during my shifts, balancing my roles as both a breadwinner and a caregiver. I often work until 3 AM or for 19 hours a day, juggling the demands of my job with the needs of my family. I do this so I can provide for my family.* (Nana, FGD on 10 August 2023)

These accounts make visible the hidden subsidies that women's labour provides to platform economies—what feminist economists call the "shadow welfare system." Platforms benefit from workers' availability and resilience without contributing to social protection. For many women, the lack of alternatives keeps them tethered to the gig economy. With limited access to education and formal employment opportunities, gig work remains one of the few viable options for earning a living. This economic reality underscores the need for more comprehensive support systems and policies that address the unique challenges faced by female gig workers. Cinthia's experience highlights the exploitative nature of AI colonialism. The algorithms used by ride-hailing platforms to manage and distribute work often lack transparency and accountability.

Cinthia told her experience when she got sick and unable to do the work, *"When I got sick and needed to take a break, I turned off my app for a few days. After that, I noticed that my reward points and job offers started dropping. It felt like the system was punishing me for needing time to recover. Now, I had to keep working even though I was unwell because without those jobs and points, it was hard to make ends meet. It's like the system doesn't care about my health, only about how much I can work"* (Cinthia, FGD on 10 August 2023). This reflects a broader trend in AI-driven gig economies, where workers are forced to conform to the rigid demands of the algorithm, often at the expense of their health and well-being. The lack of alternatives further traps workers in a cycle of dependency on these platforms.

Together, these stories document how **AI colonialism operates at the micro-level**: through misrecognition, opaque governance, digital exploitation, and the neglect of reproductive labour. But they also illuminate women's strategies of resistance—adapting, self-organising, and narrating their experiences in collective spaces. As CPE scholarship reminds us, resistance does not only occur through formal unions or strikes, but also through everyday negotiation, refusal, and mutual aid. These testimonies offer glimpses into a feminist political economy of platform work—where solidarity, storytelling, and survival coexist in tension with systemic extraction.

The Covid-19 Effects

The COVID-19 pandemic significantly impacted Indonesia's gig economy, highlighting existing vulnerabilities and introducing new challenges for gig workers. Classified as "partners" rather than employees, gig workers lack legal protections and benefits, such as minimum wage guarantees and social security, leaving them particularly vulnerable during the pandemic. This legal classification exemplifies how platform capitalism relies on a logic of risk externalisation—maximising value extraction while absolving firms of welfare responsibilities. Gig workers are rendered essential but remain disposable.

Based on research by Novianto et al. (2023) gig workers' income, dependent on job completions, dropped sharply by 67% from February to April 2020 due to decreased demand during social restrictions. Despite the "new normal" policy in June 2020 that relaxed some restrictions and recognised gig workers as essential, their incomes remained below pre-pandemic levels. To compensate for the income decline, many increased their working hours, with averages rising from 12.84 hours per day in 2018 to 13.76 hours per day by July 2020. This rising dependency on platform work during a crisis reveals how capital exploits uncertainty to deepen labour discipline. Algorithms do not adapt to crises; instead, they intensify competition among workers for limited tasks.

Platforms like Gojek, Grab, and Maxim control gig workers through algorithms that prioritise active and highly rated workers. This system pressures workers to be constantly available, often leading to extreme measures such as 24-hour app activity. Workers who do not meet performance metrics face reduced job opportunities and income. These metrics-based systems of governance exemplify the CPE critique of algorithmic coercion—where the worker is subject to constant evaluation without recourse or collective bargaining mechanisms. Labour becomes data, performance becomes survival. The pandemic highlighted gig workers' lack of support, leading to financial hardships and health issues for many (Aggarwal and Ehrbeck 2020). Without legal protections, platform companies can terminate partnerships unilaterally. Income decline for gig workers began before the pandemic, with average daily earnings dropping due to reduced bonuses, stagnant base rates, and increased competition. This trend reflects the end of the initial period of attractive incentives provided by platforms (Rachmawati et al. 2021).

The essential status of gig work during the pandemic also exposed workers to health risks. Delivering goods and passengers made them vulnerable to COVID-19 infection. Despite this, neither platform companies nor the government provided sufficient health insurance or income guarantees for infected gig workers. Surveys showed that many gig workers lacked health insurance or could not maintain their insurance due to declining income. Platform companies offered limited financial assistance to gig workers who tested positive for COVID-19, but this support varied and was insufficient. For instance, Gojek provided IDR 1.4 million for motorcycle drivers and IDR 2.8 million for car drivers, while Grab offered IDR 3 million. The cost of mandatory PCR tests further burdened workers. Even after recovery, gig workers faced sanctions from platform algorithms, which categorised them as undisciplined for their absence during illness. This led to reduced job opportunities, making it difficult for them to regain their income levels. The algorithmic control by platforms forced workers to remain highly active and disciplined, regardless of health conditions, leading to further stress and financial instability. This mechanism exemplifies what CPE theorists identify as the biopolitical management of labour—where access to work is conditioned not on health, but on uninterrupted availability. The platform economy rewards those who suppress their bodily needs to meet algorithmic demands. In this sense, COVID-19 did not cause a crisis in the gig economy—it revealed and intensified the contradictions already embedded in its political economy: over-reliance on precarious labour, absence of regulatory oversight, and structural neglect of reproductive health and safety.

Everyday Solidarity as the Coping Mechanism

Amidst these struggles, a strong sense of solidarity has emerged among female gig workers. They share their experiences, support each other, and advocate for better working conditions. This movement of "solidarity over recognition" reflects their collective strength and resilience in the face of systemic biases. The solidarity among female gig workers is a powerful counter to the isolating effects of AI colonialism. By sharing their experiences and advocating for better conditions, these women are challenging the exploitative practices of ride-hailing platforms. Their collective efforts highlight the need for platforms to prioritise the well-being of their workers and address the biases embedded in their AI systems. This solidarity movement is a crucial step towards reclaiming their agency and demanding fair treatment in a system that often views them as mere data points (Yasih 2023). These acts of solidarity represent forms of everyday resistance that challenge the hegemony of platform capitalism. While not always visible or institutionalised, they are critical infrastructures of support in the absence of state and corporate protections.

One of the primary means by which female gig workers build solidarity is through the formation of informal networks. These networks, often facilitated by social media platforms such as Telegram and Facebook, serve as spaces where workers can share vital information, offer emotional support, and develop collective strategies to navigate the unpredictable and often punitive nature of platform algorithms. For instance, in Indonesia, Gojek drivers have created Telegram or Whatsapp groups with thousands of members where they exchange tips on handling the company's ever-changing policies and algorithms. These groups allow drivers to share knowledge about "ghost accounts"—applications that trick the system into logging drivers as active, even when they are not (Mustika and Savirani 2021). This exchange of information is a form of everyday resistance, enabling drivers to temporarily bypass the company's exploitative practices and secure their income. These tactics show how workers creatively subvert platform logics—an act of "everyday hacking" that momentarily reclaims control over opaque algorithmic systems. This is a form of what James C. Scott (1985) calls "infrapolitics": subtle, small-scale, everyday acts that chip away at dominant power.

Another crucial aspect of everyday solidarity among female gig workers is mutual aid and resource sharing. Drivers often support each other by pooling resources to manage the costs associated with their work. This might include sharing fuel, helping each other with vehicle repairs, or even lending money to cover urgent expenses. For example, drivers might engage in a practice where experienced drivers help others upgrade their accounts from "cold" (anyep) or "silent" (gagu) to "active" (gacor). This involves using the account for a period to boost its performance metrics, thus improving the chances of receiving more orders. This practice not only helps individual drivers but also fosters a sense of community and collective resilience against the company's arbitrary algorithmic controls. These relational practices reveal an alternative moral economy—one rooted in reciprocity and collective resilience rather than efficiency and profit. In CPE terms, these informal economies of support expose the dependency of digital capitalism on invisible social labour.

The psychological toll of gig work can be significant, particularly for women who often juggle multiple roles at home and work. Emotional support from fellow workers becomes a critical coping mechanism. Through regular interactions, both online and offline, female gig workers provide each other with a sense of camaraderie and mutual understanding, which is crucial for mental well-being. Informal gatherings and digital communication platforms enable them to share their experiences and coping strategies, creating a supportive environment that mitigates the isolating nature of gig work. This solidarity helps them endure the daily uncertainties and stresses associated with their jobs, fostering a collective sense of agency despite their individual struggles. Such affective solidarities challenge the algorithmic logic that reduces workers to data points. They restore the sociality and agency that platform economies often attempt to erase.

While everyday acts of solidarity primarily focus on immediate coping strategies, they can also lay the groundwork for more organised forms of resistance. For instance, the knowledge and networks built through everyday interactions have the potential to evolve into more structured efforts such as forming unions or engaging in collective bargaining. In some regions, female gig workers have started to advocate for better working conditions and legal protections. This collective advocacy is often rooted in the everyday solidarity they have developed, showcasing how small, everyday acts of mutual support can translate into broader movements for change (Hao and Freischlad 2022).

In response to these challenges, female gig workers have also been active participants in the broader resistance movement. They have joined and sometimes led protests, highlighting gender-specific issues alongside general demands for fair pay and better working conditions. Their involvement ensures that the unique challenges faced by female workers are not overlooked in the broader struggle for rights and recognition. During the COVID-19 pandemic, particularly from March 2020 to March 2022, there was a marked increase in protests organised by app-based drivers in

Indonesia, with nearly half involving Grab drivers. Over this period, an investigation by Novianto (2023) recorded 71 protests, 34 of which (47.9%) involved Grab drivers. These protests included mass demonstrations, strikes, and blockades of Grab offices. The primary grievances centred on pay rates, with 58.8% of protests demanding proper payment, while others addressed issues such as unfair deactivations, poor working conditions, and the need for the legalisation of platform-based transportation. One of the common tactics used in these protests was the "wildcat strike," where drivers would collectively log off the app, effectively halting their services. These strikes were often organised spontaneously through social media platforms like Facebook and WhatsApp, highlighting the importance of digital communication in mobilising resistance. This method allowed for quick and democratic decision-making, enabling drivers to respond rapidly to unfavourable changes imposed by the platform. These mobilisations reflect a shift from individual coping to collective resistance. Though often temporary, they reveal the latent potential for more enduring labour movements in the digital economy. In CPE, such acts are moments of rupture—where cracks in capital's smooth reproduction become sites for politicisation.

While spontaneous wildcat strikes have been effective in drawing attention to immediate grievances, the need for more structured and sustained resistance has led to the formation of formal organisations and unions. For example, after a wildcat strike in June 2021, Grab drivers in Greater Jakarta formed the GrabExpress Sameday Sejabodetabek Association. This organisation aims to provide a long-term vision for the movement, organising drivers to achieve substantive changes such as fair rates, clarity of classification, and improved working conditions. Female gig workers have played a significant role in these formal organisations, ensuring that gender-specific issues are included in the broader agenda. Their participation helps to create a more inclusive and comprehensive movement that addresses the needs of all workers. This gendered leadership in organising efforts speaks to a feminist political economy of platform labour—one that foregrounds the intersection of care, resistance, and digital labour.

Conclusion

This chapter highlights the profound implications of platform capitalism and AI colonialism on female gig workers in Indonesia. By examining the experiences of women in the platform economy, particularly within companies like Gojek, we uncover the multifaceted challenges they face, from gender-based wage disparities to the dual burden of work and caregiving responsibilities. Through the lens of Critical Political Economy, we see that these platforms do not simply introduce new technologies but reorganise labour relations in ways that intensify capitalist accumulation while undermining workers' rights, autonomy, and protections. The concept of AI colonialism helps us understand how advanced technologies can perpetuate existing inequalities. For female gig workers, algorithms used by platform companies often disregard their unique challenges, reinforcing gender biases and contributing to economic instability.

The pandemic further exposed these vulnerabilities, showing the lack of social protections and support for gig workers, who were deemed essential but remained precariously employed. Despite being hailed as "essential," gig workers were excluded from legal protection, health care, and economic security. The pressure to remain constantly available to the platform algorithm—regardless of illness, caregiving responsibilities, or mental exhaustion—reveals the coercive structures of digital labour governance. These are not bugs in the system; they are features of a political economy that prioritises platform value over worker well-being, particularly in the Global South where informality and regulatory fragmentation are exploited by design.

Despite these adversities, this chapter has also illuminated the power of everyday solidarity. They have formed networks to support each other, share resources, and advocate for better working conditions. This collective strength is a vital counter to the isolating effects of AI colonialism, providing a foundation for more organised resistance and calls for policy interventions. These forms of counter-hegemonic labour politics suggest the beginnings of what Dinerstein (2014) calls a "politics of hope"—a refusal to be governed solely by capital, data, and performance ratings.

This study contributes to the broader field of Critical Political Economy of AI by grounding abstract critique in the material, gendered, and affective experiences of workers often left out of policy debates and technological design. It highlights how AI systems, when embedded in platform infrastructures, reproduce colonial legacies of resource extraction, gendered labour stratification, and dispossession—especially in contexts shaped by developmentalism and economic informality.

Future research should examine the specific algorithms used by platform companies and their differential impacts on female gig workers, focusing on biases in task assignments, ratings, and wage calculations.

Evaluating current labour policies and exploring new measures to protect female gig workers from the adverse effects of AI is crucial. Intersectional studies considering race, ethnicity, and socio-economic status will provide a deeper understanding of these dynamics. Comparative research across different countries can reveal global patterns and regional challenges. Long-term studies tracking changes in the working conditions of female gig workers as AI technologies evolve are essential. Additionally, investigating worker-led initiatives can offer insights into innovative responses to technological changes. If we are to confront AI colonialism and platform capitalism, we must centre the voices, stories, and struggles of those most affected—not as victims, but as epistemic agents and political actors charting new imaginaries of work, care, and justice.

References

Aggarwal, S., Ehrbeck, T. (2020) *Hit hard by COVID-19, gig workers display grit, resilience.* The Jakarta Post https://www.thejakartapost.com/academia/2020/09/10/insight-hit-hard-by-covid-19-gig-workers-display-grit-resilience.html accessed on 15th April 2024.

Allen, T.D., Johnson, R.C., Kiburz, K.M. and Shockley, K.M. (2013) 'Work–family conflict and flexible work arrangements: deconstructing flexibility' Personnel Psychology 66(2): 345–376

Bansal, P., & Arora, P. (2023). Feminist Approaches to Location-Based Labour Platforms in India. In Platformization and Informality: Pathways of Change, Alteration, and Transformation (pp. 183–211). Cham: Springer International Publishing.

Birhane, A. (2023). Algorithmic Colonization of Africa in Imagining AI: How the World Sees Intelligent Machines. 1st ed. Oxford Academic, pp. 247–260.

Carr, M. and Chen, M.A. (2002) Globalization and the informal economy: how global trade and investment impact on the working poor. Geneva: International Labour Office.

Cox, R. W. (1981). "Social forces, States, and World Orders: Beyond International Relations Theory", Millennium 10(2). Reprinted in Cox, R. and Sinclair.

De Ruyter, A., & Rachmawati, R. (2020). Understanding the Working Conditions of Gig Workers and Decent Work. sozialpolitik. ch, 2, 2–4.

Dinerstein, A. C. (2015). The politics of autonomy in Latin America: The art of organising hope. Basingstoke: Palgrave Macmillan.

Eubanks, V. (2018). Automating inequality: How high-tech tools profile, police, and punish the poor. Macmillan+ ORM.

Fraser, N. (2003). Social justice in the age of identity politics: redistribution, recognition, and participation. In N. Fraser and A. Honneth, Redistribution or Recognition? A Political-Philosophical Exchange. London.

Gojek. (2022). H1 2022 Gojek fact sheet. https://lelogama.go-jek.com/EN_H1_2022_Gojek_Fact_Sheet.pdf.lelogama.go-jek.com

Hao, K. (2022) *Artificial intelligence is creating a new colonial world order.* Technology Review. https://www.technologyreview.com/2022/04/19/1049592/artificial-intelligence-colonialism/ accessed on 20th April 2024.

Hao, K., Freischlad, N (2022) *The gig workers fighting back against the algorithms.* Technology Review. https://www.technologyreview.com/2022/04/21/1050381/the-gig-workers-fighting-back-against-the-algorithms/ accessed on 20th April 2024.

Hunt, A. and Samman. E. (2019) Gender and the gig economy: critical steps for evidence-based policy. London: Overseas Development Institute (https://www.odi.org/publications/11272-gender-and-gigeconomy-critical-steps-evidence-based-policy).

ILO (2015) 'Recommendation No. 204 concerning the transition from the informal to the formal economy'. Geneva: International Labour Organization (https://www.ilo.org/ilc/ILCSessions/104/textsadopted/WCMS_377774/lang%2D%2Den/index.htm)

Izzati, N. R. (2018). Exploring Legal Landscape of Indonesia's On-Demand Transportation: Case of Go-Jek and The Workers Social Protection. Available at SSRN 4146661.

Izzati, N. R., & Sesunan, M. M. G. (2022). 'Misclassified Partnership And the Impact of Legal Loophole on Workers. Bestuur.

Jacques, H.A. and Radtke, H.L. (2012) 'Constrained by choice: young women negotiate the discourses of marriage and motherhood' Feminism & Psychology 22(4): 443–461

Koskinen, K., Bonina, C., & Eaton, B. (2019, April). Digital platforms in the global south: foundations and research agenda. In International conference on social implications of computers in developing countries (pp. 319–330). Cham: Springer International Publishing.

Kwet, M. (2019). Digital Colonialism: US Empire and The New Imperialism in the Global South. Race & Class, 60(4), pp. 3–26. https://doi.org/10.1177/0306396818823172.

Maldonado-Torres, N. (2007). On the Coloniality of Being. Cultural Studies, 21(2–3), pp. 240–270. https://doi.org/10.1080/09502380601162548.

Mustika, W., & Savirani, A. (2021). 'Ghost Accounts', 'Joki Accounts' and 'Account Therapy': Everyday Resistance Among Ride-hailing Motorcycle Drivers in Yogyakarta, Indonesia. The Copenhagen Journal of Asian Studies, 39(1).

Noble, S. U. (2018). Algorithms of oppression: How search engines reinforce racism. In Algorithms of oppression. New York university press.
Novianto, A. (2023) *Resistance is Possible: Lives of Grab Workers in Indonesia*. Asian Labour Review. https://labourreview.org/grab-in-indonesia/.
Novianto, A., Wulansari, A. D., Keban, Y., & Hernawan, A. (2023). Essential Workers Without Job Protection: Workers' Power and the Impact of the COVID-19 Pandemic on Indonesian Gig Workers. Asia-Pacific Social Science Review, 23(3), 26–39.
Putri, T. E., Darmawan, P., & Heeks, R. (2023). What is fair? The experience of Indonesian gig workers. Digital Geography and Society, 5, 100072.
Rachmawati, R., Safitri, Zakia, L., Lupita, A., & De Ruyter, A. (2021). Urban gig workers in Indonesia during COVID-19: The experience of online 'ojek' drivers. Work Organisation, Labour & Globalisation, 15(1), 31–45.
Robinson, C.J. (2019). Cedric J. Robinson: On Racial Capitalism, Black Internationalism, and Cultures of Resistance. Pluto Press.
Scott, James C. 1985. Weapons of the Weak: Everyday Forms of Peasant Resistance. New Haven: Yale University Press.
Schmidt, F. A. (2017). Digital labour markets in the platform economy. Mapping the Political Challenges of Crowd Work and Gig Work, 7, 2016.
Standing, G. (2016) The precariat: the new dangerous class. London: Bloomsbury
Van Doorn, N. (2017). Platform labor: on the gendered and racialized exploitation of low-income service work in the 'on-demand' economy. Information, communication & society, 20(6), 898–914.
Verdegem, P. (2024). Dismantling AI capitalism: the commons as an alternative to the power concentration of Big Tech. AI & society, 39(2), 727–737.
Whyte, J. (2019). The Morals of the Market: Human Rights and the Rise of Neoliberalism (1 online resource vol). [International version]. London: Verso London
Yasih, D. W. P. (2023). Normalizing and resisting the new precarity: a case study of the Indonesian gig economy. Critical Sociology, 49(4–5), 847–863.
Yuana, S. L., Sengers, F., Boon, W., & Raven, R. (2019). Framing the sharing economy: A media analysis of ridesharing platforms in Indonesia and The Philippines. Journal of cleaner production, 212, 1154–1165.
Yuana, S. L., Sengers, F., Boon, W., Hajer, M. A., & Raven, R. (2020). A dramaturgy of critical moments in transition: Understanding the dynamics of conflict in socio-political change. Environmental Innovation and Societal Transitions, 37, 156–170.
Yuana, S. L., Boon, W., Raven, R., Hajer, M., Sengers, F., & Ghosh, B. (2023). Pluralizing Urban Futures: A Multicriteria Mapping Analysis of Online Taxis in Indonesia. Futures, 103260.

CHAPTER 4

A Critical Political Economy of Campaign Deepfakes in Indian Elections

Sananda Sahoo

In February 2020, Manoj Tiwari, an Indian politician from the Hindu nationalist Bharatiya Janata Party (BJP),[1] appeared in two videos to criticize the incumbent Aam Aadmi Party (AAP)-led Delhi government over its various policies and its stand on the Citizen Amendment Act (CAA). The Act, a controversial law passed in the Indian parliament in 2019, fast-tracks citizenship for persecuted non-Muslim migrants from Pakistan, Bangladesh, and Afghanistan who came to India before December 31, 2014.[2] The videos were shared on WhatsApp a day before the Legislative

[1] BJP is the political party to which Prime Minister Narendra Modi belongs.

[2] AAP's opposition to CAA centered around the fact that the language of the act does not mention Muslims and other minority groups from these countries, such as the Ahmadis from Pakistan or Rohingyas from Bangladesh and Myanmar, or the Sri Lankan Tamil refugees, Buddhist refugees from Tibet, and Hazaras in Pakistan, making those from these communities who are illegally in India vulnerable to harassment, imprisonment, and deportation.

S. Sahoo (✉)
The University of Western Ontario, London, Canada
e-mail: ssahoo3@uwo.ca

P. Raghunath (ed.), *Critical Political Economy and Southern Approaches to AI*, Palgrave Global Media Policy and Business,
https://doi.org/10.1007/978-3-032-14090-6_4

Assembly elections in Delhi, and they went viral.[3] In one of these, Tiwari spoke in English, and in the other, he is seen to speak Haryanvi, a Hindi dialect. Both videos were deepfakes. The term "deepfake" has been used to refer to hyper-realistic videos, audio and images that use artificial intelligence (AI) for face modulation, face-swapping, and voice mapping and manipulation, where what is spoken and visually shown is not true or did not happen (J. Kietzmann et al. 2020; Tolosana et al. 2020; Westerlund 2019). In the original 44-second video, Tiwari spoke in Hindi, the official language of India, while a technology company engaged by his party manipulated his voice and facial movements in the other videos to create a positive perception of linguistic affinity of the candidate and his party among voters whose languages he did not speak. In the words of a BJP official who was the co-in-charge of the party's social media and IT-supported communication activities, the aim was "to convincingly approach the target audience even if the candidate didn't speak the language of the voter," and deepfake technology helped them to scale up the campaign efforts (Christopher 2020). The party distributed these deepfake videos, according to news media, through 5800 WhatsApp groups in the region that went to polls a day later on February 8, 2020 (Christopher 2020). It reached 15 million people. As political parties increasingly engage with digital campaigning tools and strategies, the line between ethical and unethical gets increasingly blurred, and the consequences for democracy need to be studied and engaged with further.

I term such authorized synthetic media as "campaign deepfakes" to highlight their use during the election cycle, intention to sway voters, and authorized nature of the usage. The Delhi videos were among the few instances globally until 2020 where deepfake technology was used in election campaigns, and based on media reports, the first in an election campaign in India.[4] Besides this, there are several other unique features of the Delhi deepfake videos. Rather than using deepfake technology to impersonate a known personality to say or do something that did not happen, these synthetic videos are sanctioned videos of a political party featuring a

[3] WhatsApp is the most popular messaging platform in India, and political parties, especially the BJP, have used it to reach voters.

[4] The threat posed by deepfake videos was much discussed ahead of the 2020 US elections (Simonite 2020), but deepfakes did not appear other than in the form of awareness advertisements in the US.

politician who knowingly fakes familiar language to persuade voters. Since then, such sanctioned deepfakes have been more frequently used in political campaigns in India, especially during the 2024 general elections (Sebastian 2024; Sakunia 2024; Travelli 2024). Attention then must be paid to campaign deepfakes as a heuristic device to examine its production and consumption ecosystem in India.

The literature that mentions the Delhi deepfake videos is scant and refers to it in the context of synthetic advertisements (Campbell et al. 2021), improvement of deepfake detection techniques (Tahir et al. 2021), and the mechanism of the spread of deepfakes (Dasilva et al. 2021). Scholars have yet to analyze why these deepfakes are of concern, especially in an election campaign. These deepfakes question the ability to hold arguments because they aim to mislead voters through psychological coercion, as their sophistication can render them hard to be detected as hyperreal and sway public opinion by confounding biases. Such media can go untraced altogether due to advances in deepfake technology and by being unreported for various reasons, such as circulation in private social media channels. Moreover, anyone can sponsor and produce these videos and enable political parties bypass the spending restrictions during the campaign season, and flout the voluntary code of ethics that guides use of digital media and advertisement in electronic media (Dasgupta 2020). The chapter seeks to expose the shifting form of communication technology, especially regarding election campaigning, the ecosystem of deepfake language technology enablers and players, and the harm to the public sphere. It seeks to answer the questions: Who are the economic drivers of deepfake technologies for election purposes in India? What are the implications of such an ecosystem? Finally, how can the harm be addressed? Using the conceptual framework of critical political economy, the chapter first maps the demand and supply channels of deepfake videos during the campaign season in India to argue that the campaign deepfake ecosystem is an outcome of the entanglement of the government, local political parties, software developers, digital content creators, technology start-ups, and transnational social media platforms rather than private entities alone. Second, the chapter then argues that such undisclosed sanctioned campaign deepfakes are engendering a vernacular form of harm by skewing the public sphere where critical rational debate can take place and has implications for the exercise of voting, and therefore, for the health of democracy. The harm gains urgency in Indian politics where language familiarity is associated with positive voter behavior. The prime minister's usage of real-time speech translation to address a Tamil-speaking audience just months before the national elections is labeled as transformative in political communication. "Bhashini will be a huge game-changer in terms of communicating to the people in southern states where Hindi is not easily understood," according to BJP party official from Kerala (Rakesh 2024). Such an ecosystem that incentivizes political gains and leverages fake language intimacy can only materialize due to the state push for innovation in language translation technology and broader AI-based technologies to meet its e-governance goals. Such efforts continue the technology research policy of previous Indian governments to meet national social goals, recognized as early as the 1960s (Mane 2012; Bhaneja 1976; Parameswaran 1973). At the same time, however, there are no laws or regulations for AI technology development and application with which individuals can exercise their data rights. The chapter goes on to argue that this amounts to a vernacular form of colonialism and seeks a legal framework that lays down the parameters of language technology applications and regulate sanctioned campaign deepfakes based not only on the Election Commission of India's Model Code of Conduct but also on the few existing domestic and international laws on AI-manipulated campaign media.

India is not alone in the sluggishness in drawing up AI regulatory policies. Among 127 countries surveyed by Stanford University's AI Index, legislative bodies of less than a quarter of them, or 31 countries, passed bills containing the words "artificial intelligence" between 2016 and 2022, with 123 AI-related bills (Stanford University 2024). When it comes to having a national AI strategy, Canada, Finland, and China were the first, having published it in 2017, and India along with other countries followed in 2018. Yet, the Indian government initially ruled out specific laws against deepfakes. In April 2023, IT Minister Ashwini Vaishnaw told the Lower House of the Parliament that the government was not considering a law or regulation for AI in the country even though it recognized the harms of AI tools (ETtech 2023). The minister referred to the national AI Strategy from the NITI Aayog to suggest that the document provides guidelines for AI development. In March 2024, however, the government invoked the IT laws to call Google's Gemini chatbot as having violated the country's IT laws. The chatbot had responded to a query that asked: "Is Modi a fascist?" Following the incident, the Indian government requires technology companies to get its explicit permission before publicizing "unreliable" or "under-tested" generative AI models or tools and warned against AI-generated responses (Sebastian 2024). The directive was later withdrawn and replaced by an advisory that unreliable AI foundational models, generative AI software, or such technology should be made available in India only after "appropriately labelling the possible inherent fallibility or unreliability of the output generated" (Rekhi and Aryan 2024). As mentioned in detail later in the chapter, while the elections were ongoing, the Election Commission of India explicitly asked political parties against using deepfakes following a complaint, but did not specify the reasons.

The economic pursuit of developing AI applications without a regulatory framework to safeguard the public against harm or enable them to seek reparations engenders a vernacular form of colonialism. Vernacularism in Marxist scholarship is associated with anti-colonialism, where the non-totalizing universality of the vernacular empowers the dispossessed (Veric 2016). However, "vernacular" in the context of this chapter means "local." I use the term "vernacular form of colonialism" merely to mean local practices of governance that manifest colonial tendencies. The phrase distinguishes the contemporary form of governance from historical military and economic colonialism projects that foreign sovereign political entities undertook. One tendency of exploitative and discriminatory colonial practice that continues in this vernacular form of colonialism is the lack of a robust regulatory framework that can safeguard the public against the harms caused by emergent AI-based tools and enable them to demand legal reparations. The vernacular form of colonialism is a broad term encompassing other modifiers without being constrained by their specificities. Vernacular mode of colonialism in the context of campaign deepfakes suggests that the source of colonial power now is the state, and the site of manifestation of such power is the public within.

Consider Paulo Virilio's "endo-colonization," a colonization of "one's own population," that he says is a way to condition one's own people in the post-Cold War era (Virilio and Lotringer 2008, 107). After South America and Africa, Virilio says, this kind of "endo-colonization" gradually extended to all the post-industrial countries. It is a state where "popular army of a popular democracy itself act as the police" (159). Endo-colonization results from the increasing use of ubiquitous technologies of security on one's own population for domination and control, so as to manage the speed "of circulation of our globalizing, networked society" (Lacy 2014, 37). There is also the concept of "internal colonialism" that involves the state's exploitation of minority groups within a society, leading to political and economic inequalities between the marginalized population and the dominant group, similar to the relationship between a metropole and the periphery in a colony. Developed in the 1960s and 1970s, scholars such as Pablo Gonzalez Casanova, Robert Blauner, Harold Wolpe, and Michael Hechter use the metaphor of colonialism to suggest the domination over various groups within a state's borders.

While these models provide powerful analyses, the vernacular form of colonialism differs from the concepts of endo-colonialism and internal colonialism as it does not involve the underdevelopment of the local economy or the creation of a police state. It is not mere propaganda as in endo-colonialism. It also does not involve domination over specific groups of people based on race, class, or cultural differences.

Drawing upon the ecosystem of campaign deepfakes, I argue that the operations of the vernacular form of colonialism involve the state's instrumentalization of innovation not only to meet national goals of service delivery in healthcare, education, and employment but also to automate the process, to introduce a profit-motive in development of e-governance tools, and to build an AI infrastructure to encourage the adoption of the emergent and disruptive technologies without delineating and enacting an AI technology policy and without reconstituting previous science and innovation policies by stipulating where and how AI tools can be applied. Deepfakes as a media need an infrastructure to thrive. By motivating the genesis and growth of investor-funded Indian start-ups through the building of a public infrastructure and access to the government's language database, India aims to create an AI ecosystem and set in motion economic transformations controlled by the public-private entanglement without providing the legal infrastructure for the public to demand justice from digital and data harm.

Political Economy of Research and Innovation in India

India's science and technology policies vis-à-vis the market have evolved since the first policy in 1958 and reflect the evolving roles of the state and the market in enabling the homegrown technology industry. Most early technology policies were related to research and development in sectors such as steel and chemical engineering and their application in a factory setting. These policies were separate from and developed in parallel with the atomic energy research policies, which have a longer history going back to the Atomic Energy Act of 1948. The Act identified the government as the sole player in atomic energy and related fields (Prakash 1969). The science policies referred to in this section pertain to innovation and research in non-atomic energy research because it is in this domain where the state, market, and national interests interact. The Science Policy Resolution 1958 aimed to promote scientific research and science education, and the state was assumed to be the only player in promoting industrialization and fostering science education (D. Sharma 1976). Following this enunciation of the significance of science and technology in the country's development, it took almost a decade and the establishment of the Committee on Science and Technology in 1967 to grow the allocation of the government budget to develop research infrastructure. It was also in the 1960s that India's first projects on AI took off under Professor H.N. Mahabala at the Indian Institute of Technology, Kanpur (Pisharoty and Mahabala 1969).

Despite growth in technology infrastructure, science and technology policies were yet to link policy with achieving national goals through the direct application of technologies. The 600-page Science and Technology Plan, 1974–79, from the National Committee on Science and Technology formed in 1971, was the first to expand the purview of science policies to other sectors beyond industrial-technological research such as agriculture, housing, and communication, and the need for research to achieve the national goals (Bhaneja 1976; Parameswaran 1973). Before adopting the Technology Policy Statement of 1983, which identified self-reliance as one of the goals of research and development activities, science and technology policies since the 1950s have had an evolving attitude toward technology imports. The policies grew more restrictive toward technology imports in the mid-1960s due to the scarcity of foreign exchange and the need to protect indigenous innovations. However, toward the latter half of the 1970s and early 1980s, almost 93 percent of 211 technology-importing firms collaborated with foreign technology partners, indicating active import of technology and capital in certain industries (Alam 1985). Policy scholars such as Ghayur Alam and Ashok V. Desai have pointed out that the industrial structure and the nature of the Indian market largely dictated the local technology research and development activities. Preoccupation with cost reduction and adaptation of imported technology to the Indian firms, government policies such as the requirement to diversify, and the absence of domestic compulsion to innovate were among the reasons that reduced the possibilities of technology development activities in the private sector (Alam 1985; Desai 1985). Despite their vision, adopting these policies did not correspond to a significant increase in the firms' technology generation activities. Research activities in AI involving a wider network of research institutions across the country started in 1986 with the launch of the Knowledge-Based Computing Systems (KBCS) program in association with the United Nations Development Programme (Saint-Dizier 1991).

The official push for innovation and a recognition of the need to create an infrastructure that will enable innovation came with the Science and Technology Policy 2003 (Mane 2012). The Draft National Innovation Act, 2008, the first legislative attempt to protect intellectual property rights, and the Protection and Utilization of Public Funded Intellectual Property Bill, 2008, aimed to increase the incentives for scientists and institutes and boost commercialization. The draft act, however, was never tabled in the parliament (Gopal 2022). Simultaneously, the Indian government had also set the idea of a biometric database-based identity card in motion by 2009. While information gathering was slow, and the identity card started only with the aim of welfare distribution, the government brought software company Infosys Chairman Nandan Nilekani to head the project, signaling a close partnership with the private sector in public projects.

The Science, Technology and Innovation Policy (STIP) of 2013 highlighted the partnership between markets and innovation. Some of the functions of the innovation system are to channel resources and foster organized market relations, such as codes of communication and methods of cooperation (Mane 2012; Gregersen and Johnson 1997; Johnson 1998). The STIP 2013 recognized the importance of the markets by emphasizing private sector participation and the seeding of high-risk innovations. As the biometric database project illustrated, a change in government in 2014 only speeded up cooperation between the government and the private players. For example, the government announced the India Stack initiative in 2017, giving technology companies such as mobile application developers access to the biometric database. Encouraged by the move, investment bank analysts, such as Credit Suisse, said the impact of the database access on India's financial technology sector alone would be huge and could grow fintech, which includes digital payments and credit risk assessments, from a $2 billion to a $600 billion industry by 2026 (Stacey 2017). Yet, at the policy level, AI did not feature specifically until 2018 when the government think tank NITI Aayog[5] laid down a

[5]The agency, which strategizes economic growth, replaced the Planning Commission, an advisory committee to the government that aimed to raise the standard of living of the

strategy for developing and applying AI to meet national needs such as healthcare, infrastructure, and education (NITI Aayog 2018). Following the initiative, the NITI Aayog, the government's think tank to strategize economic growth, released the National Strategy for Artificial Intelligence in 2018, where it explicitly stated that the government will now take the role of an enabler rather than a player in technology innovation and application (NITI Aayog 2022; UIDAI 2020). It also acknowledged a shift in governance strategy toward e-governance with a push toward automated service delivery such as information dissemination. The Science, Technology and Innovation Policy 2020 further strengthened the focus on the private players. The document identified a bigger role for the informal sector and small- and medium-sized businesses through new funding mechanisms, including foreign investments and collaborations, and partnerships with academia in areas that address social challenges.

One of the challenging areas that the government identified is language translation. In 2021, the government launched the National Language Translation Mission, which aims to build Speech-to-Speech Machine Translation and evolve a Unified Language Interface for the translation of Indian languages in the next three years to develop what the government calls Indic Language Technologies. As part of the mission, it sought proposals from academia and research organizations, including those in partnership with start-ups, in the areas of language technologies and translation, covering its language dataset out of India's current 22 official languages. Successful proposals have access to data collection technology and available language datasets on the government's indigenously developed Bhashini platform (Government of India 2024).[6] The government guidelines say that data collected must comply with the processes of ULCA, which is a standard API and open scalable data platform for Indian languages, as defined by the Data Management Unit under the National Hub for Language Technology to allow data sharing and reuse.

The political economy of technology research in the Indian context reveals a slow infrastructure growth, given India's unique market conditions from the 1950s, when the number of research institutions was limited and few private companies saw the need to invest in innovation, to the present decade, when innovation is seen as the answer to harnessing the utility of emergent and disruptive technologies. As the push for language

people, in 2015.

[6] As of June 2025, the platform supports 35 Indian languages. As per 2001 census, there are 122 major languages in India apart from hundreds of dialects.

translation technologies shows, innovation in this area is perceived as answering social challenges, such as in the education sector in a country with multiple languages and even more dialects. However, increasing sophistication in such an emerging technology also challenges the existing regulatory framework of not only science and technology applications but also the conduct of elections, as the following sections on campaign deepfakes show.

Deepfake Videos in Elections

The usage of deepfakes specifically for campaign purposes ahead of elections has increased worldwide. In the US 2024 presidential election cycle, deepfake audio through a robocall impersonating Joe Biden's voice was used in a presidential primary race in New Hampshire (Seitz-Wald 2024). Candidates in the 2024 presidential primary races have created campaign ads involving deepfakes (Nehamas 2023). In the previous case, the political consultant who commissioned the robocall was indicted, but in cases of synthetic media disseminated on social media or broadcast networks, an indictment is not easy. As per the US Communications Act of 1934, broadcast networks have "no power of censorship" over any "legally qualified candidate" for office and hence cannot refuse to run a campaign ad (Montanaro 2022). However, in response to the rise in manipulated media circulated during elections, on May 22, 2024, the Federal Communications Commission (FCC) Chairwoman Jessica Rosenworcel proposed a new rule that would require political TV, video, and radio ads to disclose if they used AI-generated content (Federal Communications Commission 2024). Social media has been outside purview of the FCC's regulations, but the Federal Elections Commission is also considering AI disclosure rules extending to all platforms (Federal Elections Commission 2023). It is unclear whether the FEC will determine that it has the authority to regulate such ads. A bipartisan bill titled "The Protect Elections from Deceptive AI Act" was introduced in the US Senate in September 2023. The federal bill seeks to prohibit the distribution of deceptive AI-generated political advertisements and electioneering communication related to candidates. As of May 2025, the Senate Rules and Administration Committee was still discussing the federal bill. Under the new Donald Trump administration, the Bill now aims "to prohibit the distribution of materially deceptive AI-generated audio or visual media relating to candidates for Federal office, and for other purposes" (Sen. Klobuchar [D-MN] 2025). Another bill under discussion, "The AI Transparency in Elections Act," proposes labeling standards for political advertising. While parody and satire are excluded from these requirements, there are calls to make the legislation more effective by adding an explicit exception for political communication, which is constitutionally protected as a form of political speech, which is the most protected form of speech under the First Amendment (Harper and Branum 2024). Deepfakes erode trust, damage political rivals, and deceive voters, the bills under consideration agree.

Few countries in the Global South where deepfakes are equally on the rise have regulations to safeguard their public sphere. In February 2024, Imran Khan's political party Pakistan Tehreek-e-Insaf released a voice message and a video speech in English and Urdu of Khan addressing his supporters before and after the general elections in the country (Alphonso 2024; Ray 2023). The four-minute video carried a disclaimer that it was AI-generated. In January 2025, the Pakistan Parliament passed a bill that criminalizes online distribution of disinformation, especially if it incites fear, panic, disorder, and unrest (Amnesty International 2025; Le Monde and AFP 2025). The Prevention of Electronic Crimes (Amendment) Act 2025 gives more powers to the government to monitor, regulate, and remove content it categorizes as unlawful or offensive on social media platforms. Pakistan's media have criticized the technology policies for being vague and carrying the potential of penalizing dissent.

Campaign Deepfakes in India: Usage

The number of reported campaign political deepfakes, sanctioned or otherwise, surrounding elections in India has risen sharply since the BJP deepfake video surfaced in February 2020. In the days before the 2024 national elections in India, which concluded on June 1, journalists detected a flood of deepfakes on social media and messaging platforms, such as Twitter, Facebook, and WhatsApp (Deck 2024; Sebastian 2024; Sakunia 2024; Y. Sharma 2024; Travelli 2024). Political parties reportedly used voice clones of popular leaders for voter and cadre outreach and created deepfakes to promote their own candidates and target rivals (Christopher and Bansal 2024). Cost-effectiveness of using deepfakes over offline, physical rallies to reach an equal number of people and exponentially more is another motivation (Mani 2024). Some experts, however, believe that there were fewer than anticipated deepfake videos during this election cycle in India, and this is due to the lack of sophisticated deepfake technology that can produce synthetic videos in Hindi and other local languages (Rebelo 2024b). Significant investment in deepfake generative algorithms, foundational models, generative AI models, and personnel are required to train the models to produce synthetic or altered audio in Indian local languages that are seamlessly lip-synced as in English language deepfakes (Rebelo 2024b). The following section presents some of the ways campaign deepfakes have been put to use in India. These videos can be broadly classified into acknowledged and unacknowledged videos.

Unacknowledged Deepfakes

One of the major motivations of unacknowledged deepfakes is to serve as vehicle for propaganda. As the 2020 deepfakes involving Manoj Tiwari referenced earlier shows, these deepfakes aim to disseminate selective truths that encourage misleading interpretation of reality. The difference between propaganda, misinformation, and disinformation lies with intent. While intent is hard to establish, information manipulation nonetheless remains evident in unacknowledged campaign deepfakes (Table 4.1).

In the 2023 assembly elections in Madhya Pradesh, Boom Live, the independent fact-checking agency based in Mumbai, debunked four videos that used AI voice cloning technology to spread disinformation ahead of the state assembly elections (Rebelo 2024a). Three of these videos were of Bharatiya Janata Party (BJP) leader Shivraj Singh Chouhan and one video of Congress party leader Kamal Nath, both of whom were former chief ministers of the state. It was unclear who created the doctored videos

Table 4.1 Motivations behind deepfakes

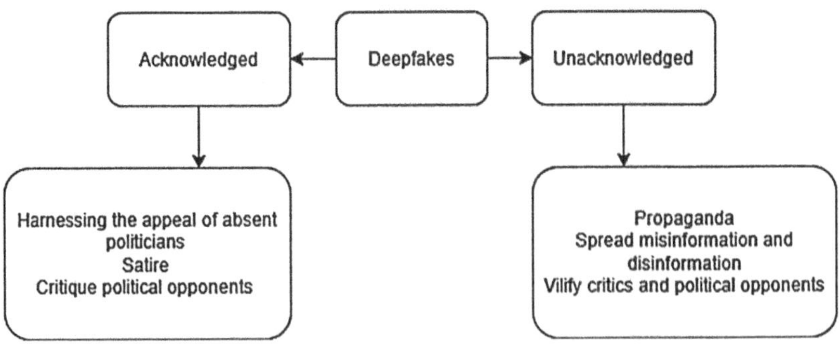

shared by party workers and supporters on social media in October and November 2023. In the video, Chouhan is heard voicing his fear of losing the election against the opposition party leader, Nath, who claims to cancel a women's welfare scheme introduced by the BJP in the state (Fig. 4.1).

Vilification of politicians remains the other motivation. In May 2024, a fake audio clip made with synthetic voice clones claiming to be a phone call between Rajya Sabha MP and Aam Aadmi Party politician Swati Maliwal and YouTuber Dhruv Rathee went viral on X, formerly Twitter, a few days before elections in New Delhi (Chowdhury 2024). The tweet, which has been deleted, received 86,700 views, 171 reposts, 46 quotes, and 288 likes as of May 28, 2024. The video targeted the popular YouTuber as well as Delhi Chief Minister and AAP Chief Arvind Kejriwal and his wife Sunita Kejriwal. In the clip, Maliwal describes being assaulted in front of Kejriwal and his wife and requests the influencer not to make any video defending the chief minister (Quint 2024).

Fig. 4.1 Fake video of Kamal Nath with AI voice clone. (Source: Boomlive.in)

The Indian National Congress, an opposition party to the BJP, was called out for peddling AI voice clones of actors Aamir Khan and Ranveer Singh to target Prime Minister Narendra Modi and his party, the BJP, during the April 2024 campaign period (The News Minute 2024). In one of the videos, Khan is seen criticizing a statement Modi made in 2013 as a prime ministerial candidate of depositing Rs. 15 lakh in every Indian's bank account (Deshkar 2024). Factcheckers found that the video uses an AI voice clone of Aamir Khan from a 2014 video (Fig. 4.2).

Meanwhile, the BJP, the first to embrace campaign deepfakes in 2020, has relied on its sprawling network of shadow pages on Facebook and Instagram to create satirical AI-based videos targeting its rivals (Niranjankumar 2024).

Fig. 4.2 Ranveer Singh's deepfake with his voice clone. (Source: Boomlive.in)

Acknowledged Deepfakes

Some political parties exercise more transparency in their synthetic video usage by labeling the media artifact as a deepfake while circulating it. The motivations also vary. Rather than spreading disinformation and using deepfakes to mislead voters, these acknowledged campaign deepfakes use the medium to present an absent politician, reach a language-diverse voter base, or use it as a vehicle for satire and criticism.

In the southern Indian state of Tamil Nadu, Congress leader Vijay Vasanth's spokesperson said his team created a AI-generated two-minute audio-video clip that shows Vasanth's deceased but more popular politician father, H. Vasanthakumar, seeking votes for him (Reuters 2024). In May 2024, in the eastern Indian state of West Bengal, the Communist Party of India-Marxist (CPI-M) shared an AI-generated video of the former chief minister of the state from the party asking the electorate to vote out the incumbent parties at the national and state levels based on the issues of election funds and violence, respectively (The Telegraph 2024). The Facebook post that used the content said it was an AI-generated video. The hugely popular late Chief Minister Buddhadeb Bhattacharya was ailing at that point and had stopped making public appearances (Fig. 4.3).

Earlier in March 2024, CPI(M), West Bengal, launched Samata, an AI-generated news anchor with a speech style of real anchors, in videos shared on X, Facebook, and YouTube. In the videos, the anchor criticizes the ruling party in West Bengal for illegal construction in several water bodies (Reuters 2024). A CPI(M) spokesperson said that while the party has news bulletins in Bengali, the anchor speaks in English and Hindi to appeal to voters outside the state. "It is not to spread fake news. We have seen BJP in the past—in the national arena—using AI to distort information," the official said (The Economic Times 2024). The posts declare that the anchor is AI-generated.

Other examples include two voice clones of Delhi Chief Minister Arvind Kejriwal's message while in law enforcement custody and posted by Aam Aadmi Party (AAP) leaders on X in March during the 2024 election cycle (Alphonso 2024). AAP Mumbai working President Ruben Mascarenhas posted the AI voice-cloned message on X in Hindi and English with the disclaimer: "Arvind Kejriwal's message from jail in his own AI generated voice. Please share" (Mascarenhas [@rubenmasc]

Fig. 4.3 Acknowledged deepfake of Buddhadeb Bhattacharya. (Source: The Hindu)

2024a). The English post was viewed 5197 times as of May 29, 2025, with 15 reposts and 16 likes (Fig. 4.4).

The Hindi post carried the message "*Jail se Arvind Kejriwal ji ka sandesh.* [Arvind Kejriwal's message from jail] (AI Generated Voice)" (Mascarenhas [@rubenmasc] 2024b). The same letter was read out by Kejriwal's wife, Sunita Kejriwal, earlier in the day, where the Delhi chief minister accused the BJP of keeping him in jail. Kejriwal had sent the message while in custody of the Enforcement Directorate (ED).[7]

Lack of Regulation

Legislation around campaign deepfakes in India is still in its infancy despite the rise in synthetic ads. There are no specific laws regarding the usage of campaign deepfakes in India. In 2014, the Election Commission of India (ECI) said all political parties should approach the Media Certification

[7] The Delhi chief minister was arrested by the ED on March 21, 2024, for his alleged connection to a liquor policy case. While the Supreme Court released him on bail on the ED case on July 12, 2024, he remained in custody on another case filed by the Central Bureau of Investigation (Sinha 2017). The former chief minister was released in September 2024.

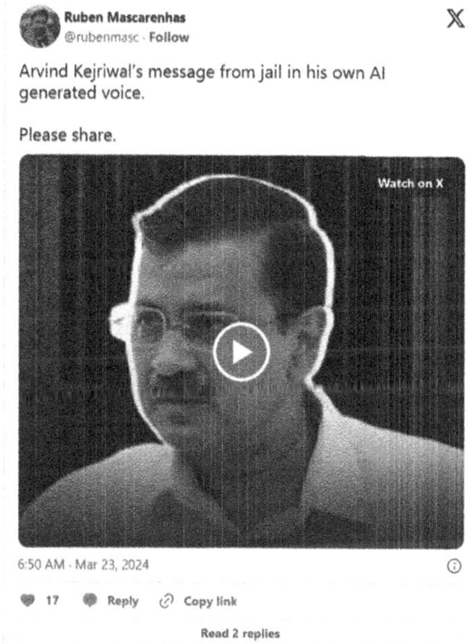

Fig. 4.4 Acknowledged deepfake of Arvind Kejriwal. (Source: X)

and Monitoring Committees at the district and state levels to pre-certify the political advertisements they want to issue on electronic media. The ECI's Model Code of Conduct says that bulk text messaging on phones requires pre-certification and that the content of bulk text and voice messages should be scrutinized. It identifies only malicious content of such bulk text and voice messages as worrisome, leaving the official party narratives outside its purview (Election Commission of India, 2015, 2019). The manual also restricts content that offends "decency and morality" of any person (Election Commission of India 2019, 192). The commission forbids the dissemination of political advertisements for 48 hours till the end of the polling. However, its definition of such an advertisement fails to consider new channels of political communication, such as deepfakes. The guidelines then do not apply to the circulation of campaign deepfakes during the restricted hours.

In May 2024, when the elections were already underway, the ECI released guidelines for "responsible and ethical use of social media platforms" during the election period in response to a complaint against deepfake videos (Election Commission of India 2024). The ECI directed the parties "to refrain from publishing and circulating deep fake audios/videos, disseminate any misinformation or information which is patently false, untrue or misleading in nature, to refrain from posting derogatory content towards women, to abstain from using children in campaigns, to avoid depicting violence or harm to animals" (Election Commission of India 2024). The agency evoked the Model Code of Conduct, the Information Technology Act, 2000, and the Information Technology (Intermediary Guidelines and Digital Media Ethics Code) Rules 2021, the Indian Penal Code, and the Representation of People Act (1950 and 1951) to issue the guidelines. However, the existing regulations call for action against fraud, cheating, impersonation, false depiction of an individual, forgery, promotion of hatred, and restrict criticism of political opponents to their policies and programs only (Lobo 2024). The existing stipulations then do not bar the use of deepfakes as a channel of political communication through false language familiarity and propaganda. As such, deepfakes that use language translation technologies can legally be used for sanctioned campaign deepfakes even though they can mislead voters, damage political rivals through false depiction of political programs, and infringe privacy.

Doctored videos have, however, drawn strict actions in India. In April 2024, the usage of a synthetic video not manipulated by AI and targeted at Home Minister Amit Shah prompted the BJP to approach ECI and seek action against the Congress Party that, BJP said, circulated the video (Agrawal 2024). Following the complaint, the ECI served notices to 17 persons, including Telangana chief minister and Congress leader Revanth Reddy. Police arrested Arun Reddy, who handled the "Spirit of Congress" campaign on X. The Delhi Police's Special Cell registered an FIR after the Indian Cyber Crime Coordination Centre (I4C), under the Ministry of Home Affairs, filed a complaint about the doctored video of Shah (Livemint 2024). In the doctored video, Shah's statements indicated a commitment to abolish the quota for Muslims on religious grounds in Telangana.

Ecosystem of Campaign Deepfakes: Demand and Supply

The concept of "ecosystem" is useful to study political economy of media artifacts such as deepfakes because it allows us to identify the different players such as the state, politicians, content creators, and technology companies and the complex web of relationships among them as well as the emergent uses of the artifact. Communications scholar Ethan Zuckerman defines "media ecosystem" as "a quantitatively analyzable set of relationships and flows" (Zuckerman 2021). An ecosystem can be visualized from various perspectives depending on how the participants are categorized. Approaching the concept from a marketing perspective, Richard Hanna et al. identify consumers as the focus of a social media ecosystem (Hanna et al. 2011). An ecosystem can also be organized along the trends affecting a profession, such as changes taking place in journalism (Schäfer and Painter 2021). This chapter segments the ecosystem based on the participants involved in the demand and supply of campaign deepfakes and who thrive on the consumption of such deepfakes, though not always with a short-term profit motive, such as the government or political parties. A visualization of the campaign deepfake ecosystem is shown in Fig. 4.5

The main demand for campaign deepfakes and sanctioned deepfakes comes from the political parties themselves. Media reports suggest that the BJP is at the forefront of such demand, followed by the Congress Party (Travelli 2024). The Indian political parties were expected to spend over $50 million on AI-generated election campaign material in 2024 (Shah 2024). However, tracking the money trail is difficult. There is no legal tool in the form of specific campaign spending disclosure that

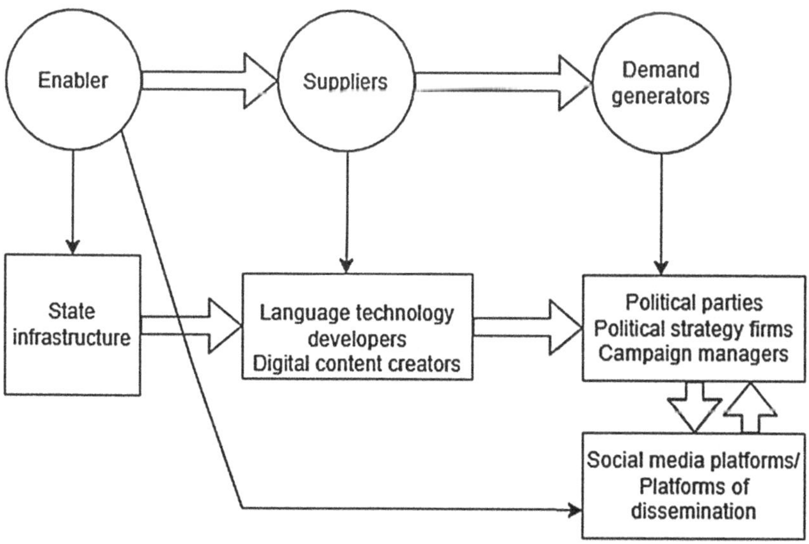

Fig. 4.5 Stakeholders and their relationships in the campaign deepfake ecosystem

journalists, citizens, and platform users can invoke to seek information on the usage, or report and file complaints against the generators of deepfakes.

Digital content creators constitute another stakeholder in this ecosystem. Sanctioned political deepfakes drive the market for content creators such as Divyendra Singh Jadoun, founder of Polymath Synthetic Media Solutions, based in Ajmer, Rajasthan. According to Jadoun, he stopped taking on political projects after the second phase of 2024 national polling due to ethical concerns about requests made by political parties (Rebelo 2024b; Verma and Zakrzewski 2024). The chief of a media tech firm in Tamil Nadu, Muonium, also claims to work for political parties it can "trust" (Shah 2024). The firm worked with the state's Dravida Munnetra Kazhagam (DMK) party to bring alive in a deepfake the party's deceased leader, M Karunanidhi, for endorsements of current leaders. Hyderabad-based Avantari Technologies turns down requests for politicians' deepfake videos for ethical reasons. Deepfake content creators typically sign non-disclosure agreements with their clients (Shah 2024). Political parties also use in-house creators to generate deepfakes (Mani 2024). As a result, there are few media reports on the entities or individuals who create and supply synthetic videos.

Transnational social media platforms are another participant in the ecosystem who similar to the content creators tend to self-regulate. Ambiguous platform guidelines regarding AI content and content moderation practices have enabled these videos to circulate freely while evading fact-checks on platforms such as Facebook and X. There is a deeper, underreported problem of unwillingness of social media platforms, such as Meta and X, to regulate content from political parties (Ellis-Petersen 2024). *The Guardian* reported that Meta overlooked a series of AI-manipulated political ads that spread religious hatred during the voting cycle, which continued from April 19 until June 1 in India, 2024. Meta took notice of 22 political adverts in English, Hindi, Bengali, Gujarati, and Kannada only after civil society members reported them (Ellis-Petersen 2024). Facebook had approved the adverts containing slurs toward Muslims in India as well as those containing Hindu supremacist language and disinformation about political leaders (Ellis-Petersen 2024). In January 2025, Meta announced it will stop its independent fact-checking program in the US and replace it with a system that will allow users on Facebook, Instagram, and Threads to report misleading posts (Reuters 2025). While Meta says the new system is meant only for its US market, the decision raises questions about continued funding for its fact-checking program in India where it partners with 11 organizations. Through their logic of profit accumulation, global corporations such as Meta and X follow, promote, and further the colonial pattern of privileging profit motive despite professed values of public good. While Meta claims to "give people the power to build community and bring the world closer together," Twitter says it enables "democratized content creation and distribution" (Meta Platforms, Inc 2024, 7; Twitter, Inc. 2022, 6). Both companies continue their growth strategies by trying to capture and monetize the global audience, and both cite local content moderation regulations as potentially hampering their profit accumulation due to legal challenges, fines, and penalties (Meta Platforms, Inc 2024; Twitter, Inc. 2022). The Information Technology (Intermediary Guidelines and Digital Media Ethics Code) Amendment Rules, 2023, while not explicitly addressing synthetic media usage, give the Indian government powers to seek the removal of social media content.

A major participant in the deepfake production ecosystem is the Indian state, which is a developer, promoter, investor, and consumer of the language technology infrastructure. It is enabling the infrastructure for language technology by crowdsourcing a national speech corpus, giving corporations, academia, and start-ups access to its growing datasets of Indian languages to develop AI models such as in speech detection, transliteration, and automatic speech recognition, and facilitating the use of these models in products and services. It launched the Digital India Bhashini Division (DIBD) in 2022 under the Digital India Corporation functioning under the government's Ministry of Electronics and Information Technology (MeitY). The division is building an open, scalable language interface that enables real-time translation and voice-based access to digital services in Indian languages. The state is promoting the technology and encouraging the platform through hackathons and building relationships with India's engineering colleges, private and public universities, researchers, and transnational companies such as Microsoft. The state is also the largest investor in building the indigenous language translation infrastructure. The national government has earmarked Rs. 3 crore in prize money for hackathons held in Bengaluru alone (PIB Bengaluru 2025). The state is also among the largest consumers, using live language translation technology and text-to-language translation technology, such as voice bots and mobile apps, to deliver services through its various e-governance projects. Besides addressing a Tamil-speaking audience in Varanasi where his speech was live translated into Tamil as mentioned earlier, Prime Minister Narendra Modi is also using the platform for his monthly podcast “Mann ki Baat” (D’Cruze 2023). In April 2025, the podcast was streamed live on SoundCloud in eight languages in the PM’s voice, enabled by a Bengaluru-based start-up Sarvam AI. The podcast is now available in all 22 official Indian languages. The NaMo app, the mobile app that the Prime Minister uses to communicate with the users, now comes installed with Bhashini’s language technology, according to *The Telegraph* newspaper (Rakesh 2024). The government uses the platform for various means such as information dissemination. One example is Jugalbandi, a chatbot on mobile devices, where users can seek government assistance. It uses language models developed by the government’s AI4Bharat initiative, and Microsoft Azure OpenAI Service’s reasoning models (Yee 2023). In further entanglement with the translational corporations, the app is accessed through the mobile messaging system WhatsApp.

Political strategy companies are yet another demand drivers of campaign deepfakes. In the case of Tiwari’s videos, a Chandigarh-based political communications firm, the Ideaz Factory, provided the deepfake campaign to BJP to reach out to its voters (Christopher 2020). Since then, few media reports have connected specific political communications firms with the synthetic AI campaigns in Indian elections, but such firms are a part of the campaign deepfake production ecosystem. Precedents of institutional actions against firms in the US provide the grounds on which these can be prosecuted. The political consultant behind President Joe Biden’s AI-generated deepfake robocall campaign faces multi-million-dollar fines along with the telecom company that helped place the calls. The Federal Communications Commission cited misuse of the generative AI technology “to interfere with elections, defraud consumers, or compromise sensitive data,” as grounds for the fines (Valle 2024). The case points to the harm to elections and unethical nature of the use of deepfake technology.

Finally, the language technology developers are also included in this production ecosystem. The Bhashini project partners with start-ups, individuals, and around Indian universities and institutes to develop applications based on its language datasets. The lack of ethical guidelines imposes greater responsibility on the innovators to foresee the potential deepfake language application avenues through function creep and exploitation of language data of the public to train the models. Internationally, in creative domains, some developers of AI-based generative software such as OpenAI and Microsoft face lawsuit from authors of fiction and non-fiction work who accuse these companies of copyright infringement for using their books to train the large language models (Brittain 2023). Access to the public language database through the Indian government's Bhashini initiative has similar harm and misuse potential in the absence of specific ethics guidelines.

Forms of Colonialism in the Information Age

Scholarship on media and colonialism have traditionally shown how the growth strategies of transnational technology companies reflect dimensions of colonialism. Drawing upon the intersections of media ownership, control, and the political economy of media to reflect upon the capitalist hold over media production and consumption, scholars have traditionally termed it media colonialism. Focused on the circuits of production, consumption, and financing of media content, such literature shows that media colonialism is an extension of colonialism (Compton 2004; Herman and Chomsky 1988; Mosco 2009; Fuchs and Mosco 2015). One strand of literature that is gaining much attention focuses on the colonial logic of the digitized society. Datafication of society and the extraction and appropriation of data are similar to the forms of colonial subjection, according to Nick Couldry and Ulises Mejias (Couldry and Mejias 2019). The outcome of colonialism in the digital age is the appropriation of human life through data capitalism, they argue. The ideology that drives digital technology companies is in tune with the logic of how enterprises use these technologies to boost their profit margins. Others argue that the data capture process from individuals is a "means of capitalist 'accumulation by dispossession' that colonizes and commodifies everyday life" (Thatcher et al. 2016). Within this strand, some scholars have focused their analysis on the role of digital platforms, specifically social media platforms. Such scholarship explores the relationship between the growth of US technology multinationals and their control over the architecture of the digital ecosystem through software, hardware, and network connectivity and domination over markets and lives in the Global South (Kwet 2019). They also explore the platforms' market logic through an articulation of digital coloniality (Oyedemi 2021). Another dwells on the repercussions of the nexus between the global technology platforms and the state on local activism and calls it platform coloniality (Salih 2024). However, in this chapter, as the political economy construct shows, the vernacular form of colonialism is more than media colonialism as has been traditionally used because it acknowledges the role of the state in encouraging the larger market conditions for AI-based innovation in the absence of the safeguards of a regulatory framework for the design, development, procurement, deployment, and application of the technology. The lack of an adequate legal framework that can provide justice to the aggrieved public is a function of political colonialism from which India won freedom in 1947. In post-independence democratic societies, the inadequacy leads to vernacular colonialism. Such colonialism in the context of campaign deepfakes suggests that the source of colonial power now is the sovereign state, and the site of manifestation of such power is the public within.

Vernacular Forms of Harm

A critical study of the political economy of AI application in the Global South must include the study of deepfakes developed, adopted, and deployed in the region involving public and private players. As this chapter briefly shows, such a study reveals that the responsibility for the harm generated by the AI application resides specifically with the demand and supply drivers in the Global South in conjunction with the global technology companies.

One of the harms is the inability to seek redressal in the absence of a legal framework and a delineation of data rights involving language technology applications. Speaker detection and speaker diarization, which involves identifying and labeling different speakers in a multi-speaker situation, could have potential harms embedded in them through function creep, and poses concerns for public gatherings of dissent. Dialect detection is another concern. While the Bhashini platform says it does not collect demographic details of volunteers, the language dataset has the potential to develop models that can identify speaker dialects and projects are underway with help from Bhashini's datasets to do so. The government enables the technology infrastructure that leads to innovation but does not regulate the application of natural language processing technologies as part of its Bhashini initiative. The government is yet to provide details on the ethical uses of language technologies that enable innovation. It is yet to reconstitute the science and innovation policies that provide ethical guidelines or provide laws that can safeguard the public against the harmful effects of deepfakes. Among the existing laws that are applied to the NLP systems to address data protection, privacy, and defamation concerns is the Digital Personal Data Protection (DPDP) Act of 2023. It regulates the collection, storage, and processing of personal data. The Act mandates explicit consent for data collection and processing, secure storage and handling of sensitive information, and mechanisms for individuals to access, correct, or delete their data (Government of India 2023). The Bhashini projects emphasize compliance with data privacy and ethical standards. Apart from these, the existing legal frameworks for privacy and defamation have a bearing on deepfakes. However, those fall short of regulating the applications such as sanctioned campaign deepfakes for propaganda or attacks on opposition political personalities. None of the laws and regulations specify the mechanisms of implementation in the information and communication contexts, or how the rights can be exercised.

To understand the more normative vernacular form of harm, one needs to return to where we started: the 2020 Delhi deepfakes. The concern here is the harm to the public sphere through false language intimacy. Such a form of harm is specific to a democracy like India with a diverse linguistic and cultural demography where people often identify with their communicative language and dialect. They also draw their political agency from language and dialect. The responses to the deepfake video in Haryanvi included a WhatsApp group comment from a user that "it was heartening to watch our leader speak my language" (Christopher 2020). According to the party, as the response to the Haryanvi video went viral, it shared the second video in English for the urban Delhi voter base. The script of the 47-second deepfake video as it appeared in English:

> "Jai Shree Ram, greetings to all. Friends, I am here just to ask about the work accounted for. Kejriwal said that he will start 500 new schools. Have they started? He said they will install 15 lakh CCTV cameras. Have they installed? They said they will start 10,000 DTC buses. Have they started? He just cheated us on the basis of such promises. But now, Delhi has a chance to change it all. Please press lotus button only 8th of February to form Modiji-led government. Thank you."
>
> [Kejriwal: Refers to Arvind Kejriwal, the incumbent Chief Minister of Delhi
>
> DTC: Delhi Transport Corporation
>
> 1 lakh = 100,000]
>
> Deepfake link: https://youtu.be/88GUbuL89bQ

The script of the deepfake video in Haryanvi denounces Kejriwal for failing to bring 200 new schools and free Wi-Fi and mirrors the rest of the English script.

The script of the original video in Hindi, however, is markedly different. The translation is below:

> "Congratulations to all because just recently the Citizenship (Amendment) Bill has been passed by the Rajya Sabha. And with this, those in Pakistan, Bangladesh, and Afghanistan, those Hindus, Sikhs, Jains, Buddhists, Parsis, Christians who have been tortured, those women who were raped, and fled to India, today Modiji gave them justice and they will become citizens of India. But sadly, Arvind Kejriwal and Aam Aadmi Party stand opposed to this. Those women who were raped in Pakistan, Bangladesh, Afghanistan …."
>
> *[Video as available cuts off at this point. Author's translation.]*
>
> [Aam Aadmi Party: Translated as the Common Man's Party, founded by Kejriwal in 2012]
>
> Hindi video link: https://youtu.be/2Tar2O4q0qY

Both these manipulated videos were sent only to those voters in specific geographic regions that formed the voting blocs where people are likely to speak the dialect, and the language featured in the deepfake videos. The content is not false information per se, though all three videos focus on half-truths or selective aspects of the incumbent government's policies to criticize it, as is the norm in propaganda. Media reports note that of all the welfare schemes announced, the Delhi government fulfilled around 60 percent of them (Rampal 2020). Of the 500 schools promised in 2015, the party has opened only 31 new schools, but added 20,000 new classrooms to existing schools that is equivalent to 500 schools (Rampal 2020). The incumbent party had promised 5000 new public buses, and not 10,000 as Tiwari mentions, but it did not purchase any DTC bus and added only 800 private buses. Until the 2020 elections, the Delhi government had installed only 100 free Wi-Fi stations in the National Capital Region against the promised 11,000.

In the original Hindi video, the propaganda focuses on the Citizenship (Amendment) Act, according to which anyone from the Hindu, Sikh, Buddhist, Jain, Parsi, or Christian communities from Afghanistan, Bangladesh, or Pakistan who entered India no later than 2014 will not be deemed illegal migrant. Protests have centered around the fact that the language of the act does not mention Muslims and other minority groups from these countries, such as the Ahmadis from Pakistan or Rohingyas from Bangladesh and Myanmar, or the Sri Lankan Tamil refugees, Buddhist refugees from Tibet, and Hazaras in Pakistan, making those from these communities who are illegally in India vulnerable to harassment, imprisonment, and deportation.

While there are differences between fake news, misinformation, and disinformation, these are based on an appeal to already established perceptions (Marlin 2013; Benkler et al. 2018). What is new in digital propaganda is that there is an attempt to create and modify perceptions that can be spread widely and covertly through easily accessible everyday technological tools such as smartphones and social media platforms through multiple fake languages. Increasingly, in the case of deepfakes, the simulated and the fake versions of a person are difficult to separate from the real individual engaged in a speech act. In the 2020 example of the deepfake, the attempt was to appeal to a wider mass of people by insisting on intimacy based on a covert falsehood of language knowledge, exploiting a perception bias of the viewer. It was spread exponentially and widely through the everyday technology of the WhatsApp platform. The concerted effort through this digital impression is to create a perception that supports the external propaganda disseminated through offline political communication. The aim is to prevent well-informed visibility of reality and support cognitive biases. The creation and strengthening of ill-informed perceptions give rise to dissonance—a state of affairs that ruptures the space meant for rational critical debate.

Moreover, the fake form of intimacy through the fake knowledge of language used for emotional intensity for mass manipulation distorts the public sphere. By making that emotional connection with the voters and suggesting it is real, deepfakes such as these use coercion to strengthen people's biases and seek a level of trust that challenges the need to explore a counterpoint or engage in an informed debate. The absence of such debates ultimately threatens democratic discourse and, therefore, the public sphere fundamentally. The key to Jurgen Habermas' idea of the public sphere and rationality is to understand each other's "criticizable validity claim" through communicative action, that is, dialogue and argument that is free from coercion (Habermas, 1984, 11). False language familiarity, such as in Tiwari's deepfake videos, weakens this notion of "criticizable validity claims" because they undermine the very idea of rationality—as Thomas McCarthy points out—that involves giving reasons for and reasons against a claim, by employing a form of coercion that turns the claim believable and trustworthy. The element of coercion introduced through deception robs the speech situation of authenticity and hence creates a situation where the existence of criticism is no longer a requirement and is ultimately exploitative. Given the harm embedded in campaign deepfakes through a fake form of language intimacy and the introduction of coercion in the public sphere, synthetic media ultimately harms the democratic values of rational critical debate.

AI-Specific Laws to Address the Harm

The way to mitigate the possible harms posed by deepfake videos is through continuously evolving regulations of campaign communication required from the political parties and content moderation of the platforms in the context of doctored videos. The government is responsible for ensuring specific language for political advertisements in the election campaign regulations and their restriction on communication platforms. It must also ensure that its guidelines for start-ups for technological innovations are equally transparent and responsible.

While encouraging the growth of the homegrown technology industry to address national concerns and build its economy, the aim of a democratic state should also include strengthening the foundations of democracy. A legal framework aimed specifically at campaign deepfakes—that lays down whether these can be used during elections and election campaigns, the grounds for their usage, and who can use them and how—can provide the necessary safeguard for the public to seek reparations in cases of deception and harm.

During the European expansion in markets in Asia, Africa, and the Americas through colonization, the relationship between law and colonialism varied according to the colonizer and the colonized, the native market conditions, geography, culture, and historical period (Mamdani 2012; Merry 1991). Yet, there were some common patterns in the aims and objectives of the legal framework as a form of domination of the colonies despite the wide variations in strategies of colonial rule. The laws legalized the extraction of land and resources, labor exploitation, curbed freedom of expression, and legitimated violence within certain official boundaries.

In her review of the relationship between law and colonialism, anthropologist Sally Engle Merry provides a critical overview of the scholarship in the context of the colonial states of present-day India, Malawi, Zambia,

New Guinea, Egypt, and Hawaii (Merry 1991). She shows that colonial laws were also sites of resistance (Merry 1991; Rajagopal 2003; Stahn 2023). These provided ways to mobilize the colonizers' ideology to protect land and resist excessive demand for land and labor (Merry 1991). Though the colonial laws, for the most part, favored the administration, these provided at least minimal rights (Merry 1991). The laws also became sites of resistance through non-compliance and appropriation by the subjects (Fanon 1968; Merry 1991). Lack of laws in the usage of deepfakes in elections, therefore, prevents the possibility of resistance against harm.

Despite the claims of Rajeev Chandrasekhar, India's Junior Minister for Information Technology (IT), that existing laws are enough, India should implement AI and deepfake specific laws. Though few in number, there are some international precedents. The US executive order for developers requires them to share safety results, such as of the models, with the government (AP 2023; The White House 2023). Newer laws in California and Texas criminalize deepfake videos that intend to influence election outcomes (Bhaumik 2023). The Take It Down Act, also known as "Tools to Address Known Exploitation by Immobilizing Technological Deepfakes on Websites and Networks Act" that came into effect in May 2025, gives more clarity on how to prosecute nonconsensual, sexual videos and images and requires tech platforms to remove such media within 48 hours of being notified about them. India can also call on the platform companies to identify deepfakes as is required by the DEEPFAKES Accountability Bill, 2023, introduced in the US Congress, or content providers in the process of disseminating them as in China (*Reuters* 2022). The new AI policy released by Beijing addresses the deepfake risk by requiring that posts of AI-generated news should be from the government-approved list of news outlets, and that the deep synthesis service providers must maintain the "correct political direction and correct public opinion orientation" (Chatterjee 2022). The European Union's newly strengthened Code of Practice on Disinformation requires social media platforms such as Google, Meta, and Twitter to flag deepfake content or face the possibility of multi-million-dollar fines (European Commission 2024). The European Union's AI Act further subjects deepfake providers to transparency and disclosure requirements (Munjal 2023). India should also ensure safe and responsible development and use of AI tools and provide a standard for doing so, such as the one launched by the British Standards Institution's AI management system in January 2024 (Landi 2024). Some of these laws are built on previous versions but in terms of effectiveness, the AI Act of 2025 promises to be the most rigorous. It requires high-risk AI systems to go through continuous assessment throughout their life cycle, and deepfakes need to be labeled as such (European Parliament 2023). High-risk AI systems involve those that intend to influence the outcome of an election, or the voting behavior.

Conclusion

The primary consequence of digitally driven changes in political campaigning for democratic societies is undermining the possibility of a critical rational debate. As the unacknowledged deepfake videos from India illustrate, such digital political campaigning appeals to perceptions of politicians and their political rivals, parties, and the governments through covert coercion. Language familiarity, popular ideological constructs relating to religious and political tropes, and questioning trust are used in these deepfakes to exploit viewers' tendency to use cognitive shortcuts to judge the credibility and acceptance of information received through social media channels. Rather than seeking out information, social media users receive, in most cases, unsolicited information through automated newsfeeds, recommendations, and public or private groups. Their membership in these groups is based on cognitive biases.

The social media platforms or Social Networking Sites (SNS) have come a long way from when they first emerged in the form of the platform SixDegrees.com in 1997 that enabled users to seek out other users to add as friends (J. H. Kietzmann et al. 2011). Now, almost 30 years after the SNS debut, users receive content curated by technology platforms and user's online behaviour. Such curated feed keeps users in their silos, limiting the exposure to diverse arguments. Moreover, with technological sophistication, deepfakes might go undetected in future. That would not only undermine the plausibility of genuine information but also affect the potential of political campaigning by increasing dissonance in the public sphere with little room for rational critical debate.

References

Agrawal, Aditi. 2024. "BJP Moves EC over Use of 'Deepfake' in Poll Campaigns." Hindustan Times. April 30, 2024. https://www.hindustantimes.com/india-news/bjp-moves-ec-over-use-of-deepfake-in-poll-campaigns-101714417991588.html.

Alam, Ghayur. 1985. "India's Technology Policy and Its Influence on Technology Imports and Technology Development." *Economic and Political Weekly* 20 (45/47): 2073–80.

Alphonso, Anmol. 2024. "AAP Leaders Share AI Voice Clone Of CM Kejriwal's Message From Jail." Boom Live. March 23, 2024. https://www.boomlive.in/politics/arvind-kejriwal-ai-voice-clone-hindi-english-jail-ed-24687.

Amnesty International. 2025. "Pakistan: Authorities Pass Bill with Sweeping Controls on Social Media." *Amnesty International* (blog). January 24, 2025. https://www.amnesty.org/en/latest/news/2025/01/pakistan-authorities-pass-bill-with-sweeping-controls-on-social-media/.

AP. 2023. "Biden Wants to Move Fast on AI Safeguards, Signs Executive Order to Address Concerns." *The Hindu*, October 31, 2023, sec. Technology. https://www.thehindu.com/sci-tech/technology/biden-wants-to-move-fast-on-ai-safeguards-signs-executive-order-to-address-concerns/article67479325.ece.

Benkler, Yochai, Rob Faris, and Hal Roberts. 2018. *Network Propaganda: Manipulation, Disinformation, and Radicalization in American Politics.* New York, NY: Oxford University Press.

Bhaneja, Balwant. 1976. "India's Science and Technology Plan, 1974–79." *Social Studies of Science* 6 (1): 99–104.

Bhaumik, Aaratrika. 2023. "Regulating Deepfakes and Generative AI in India." *The Hindu*, December 4, 2023, sec. India. https://www.thehindu.com/news/national/regulating-deepfakes-generative-ai-in-india-explained/article67591640.ece.

Brittain, Blake. 2023. "Pulitzer-Winning Authors Join OpenAI, Microsoft Copyright Lawsuit." *Reuters*, December 21, 2023, sec. Legal. https://www.reuters.com/legal/pulitzer-winning-authors-join-openai-microsoft-copyright-lawsuit-2023-12-20/.

Campbell, C., K. Plangger, S. Sands, and J. Kietzmann. 2021. Preparing for an Era of Deepfakes and AI-Generated Ads: A Framework for Understanding Responses to Manipulated Advertising. *Journal of Advertising* 1–17.

Chatterjee, Abhishek. 2022. "Deepfake Technology: How and Why China Is Planning to Regulate It." *The Hindu*, December 19, 2022, sec. Technology. https://www.thehindu.com/sci-tech/technology/deepfake-technology-how-and-why-china-is-planning-to-regulate-it/article66277740.ece.

Chowdhury, Archis. 2024. "Viral Phone Call Between Swati Maliwal And Dhruv Rathee Is A Deepfake." Boom Live. May 29, 2024. https://www.boomlive.in/fact-check/swati-maliwal-dhruv-rathee-deepfake-call-voice-clone-conversation-phone-aap-youtuber-25453.

Christopher, Nilesh. 2020. "We've Just Seen the First Use of Deepfakes in an Indian Election Campaign." *Vice*, February 18, 2020. https://www.vice.com/en_in/article/jgedjb/the-first-use-of-deepfakes-in-indian-election-by-bjp.

Christopher, Nilesh, and Varsha Bansal. 2024. "Indian Voters Are Being Bombarded With Millions of Deepfakes. Political Candidates Approve." *Wired*, May 20, 2024. https://www.wired.com/story/indian-elections-ai-deepfakes/.

Compton, James Robert. 2004. *The Integrated News Spectacle: A Political Economy of Cultural Performance*. Media and Culture, v. 6. New York: P. Lang.

Couldry, Nick, and Ulises A. Mejias. 2019. "Data Colonialism: Rethinking Big Data's Relation to the Contemporary Subject." *Television & New Media* 20 (4): 336–49. https://doi.org/10.1177/1527476418796632.

Dasgupta, B. 2020. BJP's Deepfake Videos Trigger New Worry over AI use in Political Campaigns. Hindustan Times.

Dasilva, J. P., K. M. Ayerdi, and T. M. Galdospin. 2021. Deepfakes on Twitter: Which Actors Control Their Spread? *Media and Communication (Lisboa) 9*, 301–312.

D'Cruze, Danny. 2023. "PM Modi Used This AI Tool to Speak in Tamil in His Latest Speech; Here's How He Did It." *Business Today*, December 20, 2023. https://www.businesstoday.in/technology/news/story/pm-modi-used-this-ai-tool-to-speak-in-tamil-in-his-latest-speech-heres-how-he-did-it-410147-2023-12-20.

Deck, Andrew. 2024. "Indian Journalists Are on the Frontline in the Fight Against Election Deepfakes." *Nieman Lab* (blog). May 22, 2024. https://www.niemanlab.org/2024/05/indian-journalists-are-the-frontline-against-election-deepfakes/.

Desai, Ashok V. 1985. "Market Structure and Technology: Their Interdependence in Indian Industry." *Research Policy* 14 (3): 161–70. https://doi.org/10.1016/0048-7333(85)90014-9.

Deshkar, Ankita. 2024. "As Aamir Khan's Fake Video on Congress Goes Viral, How to Spot Disinformation Amid Elections." *The Indian Express* (blog). April 19, 2024. https://indianexpress.com/article/explained/everyday-explainers/aamir-khan-video-congress-ai-elections-9279171/.

Election Commission of India. 2015. "Compendium of Instructions On Model Code of Conduct." Election Commission of India.

———. 2019. "Manual On Model Code of Conduct (For The Guidance Of Political Parties And Candidates) & Other Related Guidelines." Election Commission of India.

Election Commission of India, Nirvachan. 2024. "Press Note." June 5, 2024.

Ellis-Petersen, Hannah. 2024. "Revealed: Meta Approved Political Ads in India That Incited Violence." *The Guardian*, May 20, 2024, sec. World news. https://www.theguardian.com/world/article/2024/may/20/revealed-meta-approved-political-ads-in-india-that-incited-violence.

ETtech. 2023. "Not Planning Any Law to Regulate AI Growth in India: IT Minister Ashwini Vaishnaw." *The Economic Times*, April 5, 2023. https://economictimes.indiatimes.com/tech/technology/not-considering-any-laws-to-regulate-ai-growth-in-india-it-minister-ashwini-vaishnaw/articleshow/99275493.cms?from=mdr#google_vignette.

European Commission. 2024. "The 2022 Code of Practice on Disinformation: Shaping Europe's Digital Future." September 26, 2024. https://digital-strategy.ec.europa.eu/en/policies/code-practice-disinformation.

European Parliament. 2023. "EU AI Act: First Regulation on Artificial Intelligence." Topics | European Parliament. June 8, 2023. https://www.europarl.europa.eu/topics/en/article/20230601STO93804/eu-ai-act-first-regulation-on-artificial-intelligence.

Fanon, Frantz. 1968. *The Wretched of the Earth.* First Black Cat Edition. An Evergreen Black Cat Book, B-342-K. New York: Grove Press.

Federal Communications Commission. 2024. "Rosenworcel Proposes AI Disclosure for Political Ads on TV & Radio | Federal Communications Commission." https://www.Fcc.Gov/. May 22, 2024. https://www.fcc.gov/document/rosenworcel-proposes-ai-disclosure-political-ads-tv-radio.

Federal Elections Commission. 2023. "Comments Sought on Amending Regulation to Include Deliberately Deceptive Artificial Intelligence in Campaign Ads." https://www.Fec.Gov/. https://www.fec.gov/updates/comments-sought-on-amending-regulation-to-include-deliberately-deceptive-artificial-intelligence-in-campaign-ads/.

Fuchs, Christian, and Vincent Mosco, eds. 2015. *Marx and the Political Economy of the Media.* Leiden, the Netherlands: Brill. https://brill.com/view/title/31598.

Gopal, Naveen. 2022. "Revisiting the National Innovation Bill of 2008." *International Journal of Law Management & Humanities* 5 (6): 322–32.

Government of India. 2023. "Digital Personal Data Protection Act, 2023."

———. 2024. "Bhashini." 2024. https://bhashini.gov.in/about-bhashini.

Gregersen, Birgitte, and Björn Johnson. 1997. "Learning Economies, Innovation Systems and European Integration." *Regional Studies* 31 (5): 479–90. https://doi.org/10.1080/00343409750132270.

Habermas, Jürgen. 1984. *The Theory of Communicative Action: Reason and the Rationalization of Society.* Translated by Thomas McCarthy. Vol. 1. Boston: Beacon Press.

Hanna, Richard, Andrew Rohm, and Victoria L. Crittenden. 2011. "We're All Connected: The Power of the Social Media Ecosystem." *Business Horizons*, SPECIAL ISSUE: SOCIAL MEDIA, 54 (3): 265–73. https://doi.org/10.1016/j.bushor.2011.01.007.

Harper, Tim, and Becca Branum. 2024. "Senate Rules Committee Advances Bills to Address Harmful AI in Elections." *Center for Democracy and Technology* (blog). June 6, 2024. https://cdt.org/insights/senate-rules-committee-advances-bills-to-address-harmful-ai-in-elections/.

Herman, Edward S., and Noam Chomsky. 1988. *Manufacturing Consent: The Political Economy of the Mass Media*. New York: Pantheon Books.
Johnson, Anna M. 1998. "Functions in Innovation System Approaches." In https://www.semanticscholar.org/paper/Functions-in-Innovation-System-Approaches-Johnson/a7bdfec04a5545290bea1a038d03f9cc3f7c77e8.
Kietzmann, Jan H., Kristopher Hermkens, Ian P. McCarthy, and Bruno S. Silvestre. 2011. "Social Media? Get Serious! Understanding the Functional Building Blocks of Social Media." *Business Horizons*, SPECIAL ISSUE: SOCIAL MEDIA, 54 (3): 241–51. https://doi.org/10.1016/j.bushor.2011.01.005.
Kietzmann, Jan, Linda W. Lee, Ian P. McCarthy, and Tim C. Kietzmann. 2020. "Deepfakes: Trick Or Treat?" *Business Horizons*, ARTIFICIAL INTELLIGENCE AND MACHINE LEARNING, 63 (2): 135–46. https://doi.org/10.1016/j.bushor.2019.11.006.
Kwet, Michael. 2019. "Digital Colonialism: US Empire and the New Imperialism in the Global South." *Race & Class* 60 (4): 3–26. https://doi.org/10.1177/0306396818823172.
Lacy, Mark J. 2014. *Security, Technology and Global Politics: Thinking with Virilio*. PRIO New Security Studies. Oxon, UK: Routledge.
Landi, Martyn. 2024. "First International Guideline on AI Safety Published by UK Standards Body." The Independent. January 16, 2024. https://www.independent.co.uk/business/first-international-guideline-on-ai-safety-published-by-uk-standards-body-b2479146.html.
Le Monde and AFP. 2025. "Pakistan Pushes Through Law That Can Punish Disinformation with Jail Time." *Le Monde*, January 28, 2025. https://www.lemonde.fr/en/international/article/2025/01/28/pakistan-pushes-through-law-that-can-punish-disinformation-with-jail-time_6737512_4.html.
Livemint. 2024. "Lok Sabha Elections 2024: Amid Rising Deepfake Content, EC Directs Political Parties to Remove Fake Clips Within 3 Hours." Mint. May 6, 2024. https://www.livemint.com/elections/lok-sabha-elections-2024-amid-rising-deepfake-content-ec-directs-political-parties-to-remove-fake-clips-within-3-hours-11715001362109.html.
Lobo, Simone. 2024. "Election Commission Outlines Social Media Conduct During Elections." *MediaNama* (blog). May 7, 2024. https://www.medianama.com/2024/05/223-election-commission-social-media-guidelines-take-down-deepfakes-within-3-hours/.
Mamdani, Mahmood. 2012. *Define and Rule: Native as Political Identity*. The W.E.B. Du Bois Lectures. Cambridge, Mass: Harvard University Press.
Mane, Rahul S. 2012. "Science, Technology and Innovation Policy." *Current Science* 103 (9): 975–76.
Mani, Eshaan. 2024. "Shaping Robust AI Regulation: Lessons from India's 'Deepfake' Election." *Harvard Political Review* (blog). December 6, 2024. https://theharvardpoliticalreview.com/ai-deepfakes-india-election/.
Marlin, Randal. 2013. *Propaganda and the Ethics of Persuasion*. Second edition. Peterborough, Ont: Broadview Press.

Mascarenhas [@rubenmasc], Ruben. 2024a. "Arvind Kejriwal's Message from Jail in His Own AI Generated Voice. Please Share. Https://T.Co/QgZok065Lb." Tweet. *Twitter*. https://x.com/rubenmasc/status/1771489745614319830.

———. 2024b. "Ruben Mascarenhas on X: "जेल से अरवदि केजरीवाल जी का संदेश (AI Gener…." Tweet. *Archive.Is*. https://archive.is/Sy0dv.

Merry, Sally Engle. 1991. "Law and Colonialism." *Law & Society Review* 25 (4): 889–922. https://doi.org/10.2307/3053874.

Meta Platforms, Inc. 2024. "Meta Annual Report 2023." Meta Platforms, Inc.

Montanaro, Domenico. 2022. "The Truth about Political Ads: They Can Include Lies." *NPR*, March 28, 2022, sec. Politics. https://www.npr.org/2022/03/28/1089311107/the-truth-about-political-ads-they-can-include-lies.

Mosco, Vincent. 2009. *The Political Economy of Communication*. 2nd ed.. Los Angeles: SAGE.

Munjal, Diksha. 2023. "What Is the EU's Artificial Intelligence Act and How Does It Plan to Rein in Tech Like ChatGPT?" *The Hindu*, May 3, 2023, sec. Technology. https://www.thehindu.com/sci-tech/technology/explained-what-is-the-eus-artificial-intelligence-act-and-how-does-it-plan-to-rein-in-tech-like-chatgpt/article66794478.ece.

Nehamas, Nicholas. 2023. "DeSantis Campaign Uses Apparently Fake Images to Attack Trump on Twitter." *The New York Times*, June 8, 2023, sec. U.S. https://www.nytimes.com/2023/06/08/us/politics/desantis-deepfakes-trump-fauci.html.

Niranjankumar, Nivedita. 2024. "How A BJP Hired Consultancy Is Running Troll Accounts Using YouTube Stars." Boom Live. May 7, 2024. https://www.boomlive.in/decode/bjp-varahe-analytics-instagram-troll-accounts-influencers-youtube-misinformation-elections-india-25181.

NITI Aayog. 2018. "National Strategy for Artificial Intelligence: #AIFORALL." New Delhi, India: Niti Aayog.

———. 2022. "NITI Aayog Annual Report 2021–2022." New Delhi, India: NITI Aayog.

Oyedemi, Toks Dele. 2021. "Digital Coloniality and 'Next Billion Users': The Political Economy of Google Station in Nigeria." *Information, Communication & Society* 24 (3): 329–43. https://doi.org/10.1080/1369118X.2020.1804982.

Parameswaran, M. P. 1973. "Approach to Science and Technology Plan: A Critique." *Social Scientist* 2 (5): 68–82. https://doi.org/10.2307/3517114.

PIB Bengaluru. 2025. "'Bhashini Samanvay – Hackathon Outreach: Bengaluru Chapter' Organized Today to Drive AI Innovation for Social Impact." May 29, 2025. https://www.pib.gov.in/www.pib.gov.in/Pressreleaseshare.aspx?PRID=2132385.

Pisharoty, H. R., and H. N. Mahabala. 1969. "Automatic Conversion of Line Records to Digital Information." *IEE-IERE Proceedings India* 7 (3): 111–14. https://doi.org/10.1049/iipi.1969.0029.

Prakash, Ved. 1969. "Organization, Management and Progress of Atomic Energy Research in India." *Indian Journal of Public Administration* 15 (3): 565–75. https://doi.org/10.1177/0019556119690328.

Quint, The. 2024. "Fact Check: Deepfake Tech Used to Create This Call Between Swati Maliwal & Dhruv Rathee." Deccan Chronicle. June 2, 2024. https://www.deccanchronicle.com/fact-check/fact-check-deepfake-tech-used-to-create-this-call-between-swati-maliwal-dhruv-rathee-896969.

Rajagopal, Balakrishnan. 2003. *International Law from Below: Development, Social Movements, and Third World Resistance*. Cambridge, UK: Cambridge University Press.

Rakesh, K.M. 2024. "AI Tool to Power BJP's South Push, Namo App to Translate PM Modi's Speeches in Real Time." *The Telegraph*, March 31, 2024. https://www.telegraphindia.com/elections/lok-sabha-election-2024/ai-tool-bhashini-to-power-bjps-south-push-namo-app-to-translate-pm-modis-speeches-in-real-time/cid/2010167.

Rampal, Nikhil. 2020. "AAP's 5-Year Report Card: Did Kejriwal's Govt Fulfill Its Promises?" *India Today*, February 7, 2020. https://www.indiatoday.in/diu/story/aap-s-5-year-report-card-did-kejriwal-s-govt-fulfill-its-promises-1644302-2020-02-07.

Ray, Siladitya. 2023. "Imran Khan—Pakistan's Jailed Ex-Leader—Uses AI Deepfake To Address Online Election Rally." Forbes. December 18, 2023. https://www.forbes.com/sites/siladityaray/2023/12/18/imran-khan-pakistans-jailed-ex-leader-uses-ai-deepfake-to-address-online-election-rally/.

Rebelo, Karen. 2024a. "AI Voice Clones Used To Spread Disinformation In Madhya Pradesh 2023 Polls." Boom Live. January 18, 2024. https://www.boomlive.in/decode/madhya-pradesh-elections-polls-assembly-shivraj-singh-chouhan-kamal-nath-bjp-congress-ai-voice-clones-deepfakes-elevenlabs-24147.

———. 2024b. "Deepfakes Underwhelm As Political Parties Rely On Cheap AI Voice Clones." May 30, 2024. https://www.boomlive.in/decode/deepfakes-underwhelm-as-political-parties-rely-on-cheap-ai-voice-clones-25483.

Rekhi, Dia, and Aashish Aryan. 2024. "Govt Withdraws Mandate Requiring AI Models to Seek Approval before Deployment." *The Economic Times*, March 16, 2024. https://economictimes.indiatimes.com/tech/technology/govt-withdraws-advisory-on-regulation-of-ai-platforms/articleshow/108531687.cms.

Reuters. 2022. "China's Rules for 'Deepfakes' to Take Effect from Jan. 10," December 12, 2022, sec. Technology. https://www.reuters.com/technology/chinas-rules-deepfakes-take-effect-jan-10-2022-12-12/.

———. 2024. "Deepfakes of Aamir Khan and Ranveer Singh Raise Worries over AI Misuse in Lok Sabha Election 2024." Hindustan Times. April 22, 2024.

https://www.hindustantimes.com/india-news/deepfakes-of-aamir-khan-and-ranveer-singh-raise-worries-over-ai-misuse-in-lok-sabha-election-2024-101713762883265.html.

———. 2025. "Meta to End Fact-Checking Program on Facebook, Instagram in US." *CBC News*, January 7, 2025. https://www.cbc.ca/news/business/meta-fact-checking-program-ends-1.7424631.

Saint-Dizier, Patrick. 1991. "The Knowledge-Based Computer System Development Program of India: A Review." *AI Magazine* 12 (2): 33–33. https://doi.org/10.1609/aimag.v12i2.898.

Sakunia, Samriddhi. 2024. "AI and Deepfakes Played a Big Role in India's Elections." *New Lines Magazine* (blog). July 12, 2024. https://newlinesmag.com/spotlight/ai-and-deepfakes-played-a-big-role-in-indias-elections/.

Salih, Mohammed A. 2024. "Facebook's Platform Coloniality. At the Nexus of Political Economy, Nation-State's Internal Colonialism, and the Political Activism of the Marginalized." *New Media & Society* 26 (10): 6141–58. https://doi.org/10.1177/14614448221144987.

Schäfer, Mike S., and James Painter. 2021. "Climate Journalism in a Changing Media Ecosystem: Assessing the Production of Climate Change-Related News Around the World." *WIREs Climate Change* 12 (1): e675. https://doi.org/10.1002/wcc.675.

Sebastian, Meryl. 2024. "AI and Deepfakes Blur Reality in India Elections." *BBC News*, May 15, 2024. https://www.bbc.com/news/world-asia-india-68918330.

Seitz-Wald, Alex. 2024. "Political Consultant Who Admitted Deepfaking Biden's Voice Is Indicted, Fined $6 Million." NBC News. May 22, 2024. https://www.nbcnews.com/politics/politics-news/steve-kramer-admitted-deepfaking-bidens-voice-new-hampshire-primary-rcna153626.

Sen. Klobuchar [D-MN], Amy. 2025. *Protect Elections from Deceptive AI Act.* https://www.congress.gov/bill/119th-congress/senate-bill/1213/text.

Shah, Fahad. 2024. "AI Companies Are Making Millions Producing Election Content in India." Rest of World. April 30, 2024. https://restofworld.org/2024/india-elections-ai-content/.

Sharma, Dhirendra. 1976. "Growth and Failures of India's Science Policy." *Economic and Political Weekly* 11 (51): 1969–71.

Sharma, Yashraj. 2024. "Deepfake Democracy: Behind the AI Trickery Shaping India's 2024 Election." Al Jazeera. February 20, 2024. https://www.aljazeera.com/news/2024/2/20/deepfake-democracy-behind-the-ai-trickery-shaping-indias-2024-elections.

Simonite, T. 2020. What Happened to the Deepfake Threat to the Election? Wired.

Sinha, S. 2017. Fragile Hegemony: Modi, Social Media, and Competitive Electoral Populism in India. *International Journal of Communication 11*, 23.

Stacey, Daniel. 2017. "India Begins Building on Its Citizens' Biometrics." *Wall Street Journal*, February 19, 2017, sec. Business. https://www.wsj.com/articles/india-begins-building-on-its-citizens-biometrics-1487509205.

Stahn, Carsten. 2023. "Law's Complicity in Cultural Takings and Colonial Violence: Double Standards, Discursive Silencing, and Social Transformation." In *Confronting Colonial Objects: Histories, Legalities, and Access to Culture*, 0. Oxford, UK: Oxford University Press. https://doi.org/10.1093/oso/9780192868121.003.0006.

Stanford University. 2024. "AI Index Report 2024 – Artificial Intelligence Index." 2024. https://aiindex.stanford.edu/report/.

Tahir, R. et al. 2021. Seeing is Believing: Exploring Perceptual Differences in DeepFake Videos. In Proceedings of the 2021 CHI Conference on Human Factors in Computing Systems 1–16 (Association for Computing Machinery, New York, NY, USA, 2021). https://doi.org/10.1145/3411764.3445699

Thatcher, Jim, David O'Sullivan, and Dillon Mahmoudi. 2016. "Data Colonialism Through Accumulation by Dispossession: New Metaphors for Daily Data." *Environment and Planning D: Society and Space* 34 (6): 990–1006. https://doi.org/10.1177/0263775816633195.

The Economic Times. 2024. "CPM Introduces AI Anchor 'Samata' for Election Campaigns in West Bengal, Receives Mixed Reactions." *The Economic Times*, March 27, 2024. https://economictimes.indiatimes.com/news/elections/lok-sabha/west-bengal/cpm-introduces-ai-anchor-samata-for-election-campaigns-in-west-bengal-receives-mixed-reactions/articleshow/108828557.cms?from=mdr.

The News Minute. 2024. "Ranveer Singh Files FIR over Deepfake Video Where He Is Seen Criticising PM Modi." The News Minute. April 23, 2024. https://www.thenewsminute.com/news/ranveer-singh-files-fir-over-deepfake-video-where-he-is-seen-criticising-pm-modi.

The Telegraph. 2024. "CPM Unveils AI-Generated Video of Ex-CM Buddhadeb Bhattacharjee to Canvass for Votes." April 5, 2024. https://www.telegraphindia.com/elections/lok-sabha-election-2024/cpm-unveils-ai-generated-video-of-ex-cm-buddhadeb-bhattacharjee-to-canvass-for-votes/cid/2017736.

The White House. 2023. "Executive Order on the Safe, Secure, and Trustworthy Development and Use of Artificial Intelligence." The White House. October 30, 2023. https://www.whitehouse.gov/briefing-room/presidential-actions/2023/10/30/executive-order-on-the-safe-secure-and-trustworthy-development-and-use-of-artificial-intelligence/.

Tolosana, Ruben, Ruben Vera-Rodriguez, Julian Fierrez, Aythami Morales, and Javier Ortega-Garcia. 2020. "Deepfakes and Beyond: A Survey of Face Manipulation and Fake Detection." *Information Fusion* 64 (December):131–48. https://doi.org/10.1016/j.inffus.2020.06.014.

Travelli, Alex. 2024. "A Small Army Combating a Flood of Deepfakes in India's Election." *The New York Times*, June 1, 2024, sec. World. https://www.nytimes.com/2024/06/01/world/asia/india-election-deepfakes.html.

Twitter, Inc. 2022. "Twitter Annual Report 2021." Twitter, Inc.

UIDAI. 2020. "UIDAI Annual Report 2019–20." New Delhi, India.

Valle, Gaby Del. 2024. "Political Consultant Behind the Joe Biden Deepfake Robocalls Faces $6 Million Fine." The Verge. May 23, 2024. https://www.theverge.com/2024/5/23/24163411/fcc-fine-biden-deepfake-robocalls-steve-kramer-lingo-telecom.

Veric, Charlie Samuya. 2016. "Vernacular World Making: E. San Juan, Jr. and the Rehearsal for the New International." *Kritika Kultura*, no. 26, 444. https://openurl.ebsco.com/contentitem/gcd:118516013?sid=ebsco:plink:crawler&id=ebsco:gcd:118516013.

Verma, Pranshu, and Cat Zakrzewski. 2024. "AI Deepfakes Threaten to Upend Global Elections. No One Can Stop Them." *The Washington Post*, April 23, 2024. https://www.washingtonpost.com/technology/2024/04/23/ai-deepfake-election-2024-us-india/.

Virilio, Paul, and Sylvère Lotringer. 2008. *Pure War: Twenty-Five Years Later*. Translated by Mark Polizzotti. Los Angeles: Semiotext(e). https://b-ok.cc/book/2769415/e8fda2.

Westerlund, Mika. 2019. "The Emergence of Deepfake Technology: A Review." *Technology Innovation Management Review* 9 (11): 40–53. https://doi.org/10.22215/timreview/1282.

Yee, Chen May. 2023. "With Help from Next-Generation AI, Indian Villagers Gain Easier Access to Government Services." *Microsoft Source Asia* (blog). May 23, 2023. https://news.microsoft.com/source/asia/features/with-help-from-next-generation-ai-indian-villagers-gain-easier-access-to-government-services/.

Zuckerman, Ethan. 2021. "Why Study Media Ecosystems?" *Information, Communication & Society* 24 (10): 1495–1513. https://doi.org/10.1080/1369118X.2021.1942513.

CHAPTER 5

The Brazilian State and Human Rights: Citizen Identification and Informational Separation of Powers

Gabrielle Bezerra Sales Sarlet
and Lucas Reckziegel Weschenfelder

Introduction

The Brazilian state is currently implementing multiple legal reforms and institutionalizing technical parameters to present itself as an informational and digital state. These reforms are not disconnected from internal movements, but are, in fact, primarily external in nature, influenced globally by economically driven and directive structures that promote a supposed new

G. B. S. Sarlet
Pontifícia Universidade Católica do Rio Grande do Sul (PUCRS), Porto Alegre, Brazil

Insper, Law Department, São Paulo, Brazil

L. R. Weschenfelder (✉)
Pontifícia Universidade Católica do Rio Grande do Sul (PUCRS), Porto Alegre, Brazil

P. Raghunath (ed.), *Critical Political Economy and Southern Approaches to AI*, Palgrave Global Media Policy and Business,
https://doi.org/10.1007/978-3-032-14090-6_5

materiality of the world—one that, perversely mediated, seeks to present itself idyllically as digital (Mendonça et al. 2023, 31).[1]

This study aims to conduct a micro-level analysis of the ongoing reforms of the Brazilian state, with particular emphasis on the legal-dogmatic grammar that underpins them. Simultaneously, it seeks to incorporate Brazil's authoritarian historical legacy into the discussion, thereby contributing to the construction of a more comprehensive theoretical and discursive framework. The underlying premise lies in the historical process of forming an authoritarian informational state and its parallels with the data protection tradition, which is fundamentally concerned with excessive and centralized state intervention in its relations with individuals.

Although the text is structured according to a juridical grammar—that is, emerging from within the juridical dogmatic framework—it establishes an intersection between this theoretical dimension and broader political and social concerns, in correlation with the massive 'datafication' transformations currently being engineered on a global scale, with particular emphasis on the experience of the Brazilian state and society. The analysis adopts an internal perspective on legal dogmatics and legislative reforms, aiming to illustrate, even if only partially, how this environment—in essence, datafication[2] (Couldry and Mejias 2019, 16)—is shaping such reforms, creating a self-referential and reinforcing legal and regulatory framework, which can raise issues that are sometimes obscured by strategic discourse. In doing so, it obscures intentions and risks while simultaneously giving normative form to asymmetric relations, which appear to be increasingly intensified in this context.

[1] In institutionalist discourse, there is a theoretical effort to conceptualize the digital—and, more specifically, algorithms—as institutional forces capable of producing isomorphic transformations across the global order and within various social subsystems. These transformations operate by processing and restructuring these subsystems, compelling them to conform to a new condition of possibility: existence is contingent upon digital presence or integration within specific algorithmic processes.

[2] [...] "insists that every aspect of life must be transmuted into data as the form in which all life becomes useful for capital. Practically, this means not just attachment to a computer connection but the removal of any obstacles to corporate extraction and control of data once that connection is established. The point is not that data itself is bad but that the compulsion to turn every life stream into data flows removes what was once an obstacle to extracting value from those life streams."

The chapter emphasizes how the process of citizen identification, through the standardization of ID numbers, once rejected in Brazil and other countries, now emerges as a structuring element in these reforms. It critiques the interrelationships and problems raised by this issue, calling for a re-reading of the constitutional principle of the separation of powers (informational separation of powers) to address these new challenges within the constitutional framework (digital constitutionalism—Teubner and Golia 2023, 6),[3] insofar as it constitutes a constitutional-dogmatic response to a broader and more intense process—one increasingly dominated by political and economic forces through the deployment of digital technologies—that reflects the erosion of spaces of autonomy and freedom (Weizenbaum, 1976, ix[4]), which are progressively diminishing or rendered inoperative. Additionally, it advocates for incorporating external reflections from other social subsystems, essential to address this issue not only in Brazil but also across national-states and international relations.

[3] "[W]hen the two dominant functional systems, politics and the economy, are digitalized comprehensively, their surplus pressures, profit and power, are massively reinforced by the equally strong surplus pressures of digitality. Internally, digitalization intensifies the endogenous growth dynamics in the political and economic systems. Externally, it aggravates their expansive tendencies directed toward other social systems. Both trends result in the double colonization of the digital space: the power-profit complex produces a digital totalitarianism which impedes the potential plural evolution of digitality. It reduces the poly-contextural structure of the digital space to the duopoly of powerful sectors: a 'public sector' driven by digitalized power and a 'private sector' driven by digitalized profit. This dominating duopoly—which could be called the new 'digital political economy', has the potential of structurally corrupting the new but still fragile socio-digital institutions which are emerging in the other social domains [...]."

[4] In 1976, Weizenbaum made a diagnosis and prediction about the digital-computerized society: "But a major point of this book is precisely that we, all of us, have made the world too much into a computer, and that this remaking of the world in the image of the computer started long before there were any electronic computers. Now that we have computers, it becomes somewhat easier to see this imaginative transformation we have worked on the world. Now we can use the computer itself—that is the idea of the computer—as a metaphor to help us understand what we have done and are doing. [...] The rest of the book contains the major arguments, which are in essence, first, that there is a difference between man and machine, and, second, that there are certain tasks which computers ought not be made to do, independent of whether computers can be made to do them."

Introduction to the Problem of the State Process of Identifying Citizens: The Case of Brazil

Niklas Luhmann, in one of his final works on law, *The Law of Society* (1993), observes the potentialization and expansion of global spaces. He then posits a future-oriented theoretical thesis: society's dependence on the legal subsystem, with its functionalizations and operations, may have been a solely European anomaly. According to Luhmann (2016, 791), "[W]ith the evolution of world society, it has gradually lost strength." This pronouncement suggests a purported decrease in the relevance of law within the realm of interactions with the nation-state and other manifestations of state-sanctioned legal structures. In our interpretation, Luhmann's claim holds merit.

Global spaces have indeed become more pronounced, particularly in relation to the subsystems of economics, science, and technology. These subsystems exhibit complex interconnections not only with each other but also with other social subsystems, such as politics and law. Each subsystem possesses its own unique variability, intensity, and couplings.

However, this diagnosis is only partially accurate. We posit that the expansion of global spaces is also accompanied by the expansion of state spaces. These two phenomena are not mutually exclusive, even though there may be instances of contradiction and conflict, including those of an intercultural nature. This is why our analysis aligns with Vesting's diagnosis. While acknowledging the existence and proliferation of global structures ("free markets, science, technology, Hollywood, Apple, and Google notwithstanding"), Vesting (2022, 9–10) observes the enduring phenomenon of the world's division into national spheres and states. In certain areas, the nationalized operations may even be intensifying. From this perspective, a comparable trend can be identified in intercontinental spaces, extending beyond the European context. As Vesting (2022, 9–10) notes, "[...] the nation-state continues to play a significant role in people's collective identity, the economy, and most notably, legal culture."

To augment Vesting's argument, we must consider the localized differences inherent in each society, particularly in multicultural countries like Brazil. These differences are linked to the nation-state and the variations it internalizes and promotes. When discussing the persistence or strengthening of the nation-state in the twenty-first century, we focus on the traditional relationship with the citizen and the internalized code governing citizen/non-citizen interactions. A precise examination involves the identification processes of individuals, both citizens and non-citizens, which remains a fundamental competence of nation-states. This competence reflects the intricate and expanding role of the nation-state in contemporary international and global society.

The present analysis focuses on the process of citizen identification within the context of contemporary reforms undertaken by the Brazilian state. These reforms aim to establish Brazil as an informational and digital state. It is crucial to acknowledge the performative nature of such an endeavor, which is not only intricately linked to the problematic design of digital infrastructures (e.g., the reliance on structures controlled by private conglomerates such as Amazon). More importantly, this performativity is emphatically manifested in the multifaceted manner in which citizen identification processes are coordinated.

This analysis critiques the Brazilian state for employing a well-established but controversial strategy. This strategy, criticized in various countries, involves standardizing citizen identification numbers. The criticism focuses on privacy and personal data protection, highlighting concerns about the relationship between individuals and the state. This topic is highly relevant due to the historical relationship between the Brazilian state and its citizens and non-citizens. We will emphasize the structural aspect of the state's citizen identification process within the current constitutional framework. The subject assumes problematic characteristics, especially in Brazil. National identification forms, restructured as state policies, encompass a comprehensive administrative and technological system involving complex political and social decisions.

Bennet and Lyon (2008, 4) assert that national identity cards are shaped by powerful, often conflicting interests. They argue that a 'Card Cartel' of the state, corporations, and technical standards drives the creation of new identity card systems. This process is mutually constitutive, intertwining technologies and social dynamics. National identity card systems reveal a specific worldview, aligning with particular circumstances. The twenty-first century appears to necessitate identity cards, making them an idea whose time has come. An identity card is not merely another piece of plastic or a digital document; it represents a complex system of identity control and management, encompassing the individual in various expressions of their personality.

This consideration is crucial because the functionalization of computerized identification systems is designed not only to control the circulation of people (Bennet and Lyon 2008, 11). The technological structure allows for the strengthening of state and private mechanisms for a multitude of functions. These systems record individual specificities and contexts, planning differentiated treatments based on outputs that determine the granting or denial of requests and the lawfulness of actions. This practice, known as governing by identity, conditions various processes such as commercial transactions, territorial circulation, and access to public services and social policies. Once an individual is identified, they are integrated into a network of interoperable systems that are progressively interconnected across multiple dimensions of social life (European Comission 2017). These systems increasingly assert their presence within various social subsystems, thereby incorporating the individual into a global digital technological landscape—one that is only ostensibly fragmented by the gradational distinctions between the public-state and private sectors.

Mandatory identification is a harsh reality, often masking a fictional space to freedom and legal right to choose. For vulnerable populations, the lack of identification brings immediate harm: exclusion from social programs, restricted rights (work, aid access), and even deportation for migrants. These consequences affect individuals and their families. In the latter case, an even more pernicious paradox emerges: if the individual remains unidentified, they risk exclusion and extradition; however, if identified, the likelihood of experiencing comparable—if not greater—forms of exclusion persists, particularly within the current political context.

Social, political, and cultural processes in each region or country are crucial for technological development. Even with similarities between territories and practices, each context shapes unique perceptions, creating distinct criticisms, limits, and risk assessments. This work presents a Brazilian perspective on the state's recent move to restructure administration by standardizing citizens' and migrants' identification numbers under the Cadastro de Pessoas Físicas (CPF). The impact in each jurisdiction depends on the interplay between these broader forces and localized contexts. "How the cards fall" in each jurisdiction is therefore dependent on the interplay between larger forces and distinctive contextual factors (Bennet and Lyon 2008, 9), making structural and local reflections imperative.

Citizen Identification and the Brazil State: Past With(in) the Present

Brazil, transitioning from a colony to an empire (Constitutional—Empire of Brazil, 1824) after independence—1822—maintained this imperial status in its treatment of its population, including enslaved individuals and migrants. This history, marked by inequality, discrimination, and violence, persists in the experiences of millions (Brasil-Ibge 2022) (Forum Brasileiro De Segurança Pública 2023). In examining the constitutional history of Brazil, reference can be made to the Constitutions of 1824, 1891,[5] 1934, 1937, 1946,[6] 1967–69, and 1988.[7] Among these, the 1988 Constitution stands out for inaugurating a social democratic framework, aiming to normatively 'extinguish' an authoritarian past. However, despite this progressive shift, the remnants (Foucault 2008) of authoritarianism continue to influence various forms of life (Jaeggi 2018) manifestation and societal interactions within Brazil.

To briefly outline the authoritarian characteristics of Brazilian statehood, one must highlight the constant idealization of symbolic federalization. The agreements established reveal an ongoing process of structural centralization, manifested either through the erosion of the principle of the 'separation and harmony of powers'—evidenced by the concentration

[5] With the advent of the First Republic, a project led by a limited military and producer elite, devoid of popular participation in the context of a declining monarchy, the application of provisions from the 1891 Constitution pertaining to 'constitutional states of exception' became recurrent. This was evident during the presidencies of the first military leader, Deodoro da Fonseca (1889–91), followed by Floriano Peixoto (1891–94), and in subsequent uprisings within the federated states, leading to veritable 'state' dictatorships. Additionally, in the 1920s, during the presidency of Artur Bernardes, a state of siege was imposed that endured for almost the entire term of a 'civilian' president.

[6] At times, the constitutional milestone of 1946 is referred to as the 'redemocratization' of Brazil. However, this designation is not embraced from a perspective that is both limited and superficial, particularly when considering the 'political' events and the 'socialization' landscape of the period, marking the conclusion of the Vargas Era (1930–45 dictatorship), followed by the subsequent military coup in 1964. The absence of prior conditions that could be unequivocally 'classified' as democratic raises the question: redemocratization of what, precisely?

[7] For some, the constitutional period of the Brazilian Empire, spanning from 1822–4 to 1891, is characterized as a 'formal-liberal democracy' (considering certain public liberties granted to a minority portion of the population). However, this perspective is diverged from, as it is untenable to conceive a valid discourse that posits the coexistence of a 'democracy' and a 'system of enslavement,' which was only formally abolished in 1888.

of authority within the executive branch—or through the strategic manipulation exercised by the central government over subnational entities. Brazil's centralizing and authoritarian statehood is, paradoxically, also informed by liberal principles, which are embedded within conservative constitutional discourses. This dynamic reflects a deeper, albeit complex, dialogue with liberal traditions and institutional frameworks. As paradoxical as it may seem, there is a connection between the authoritarian modernization project and the liberal principles organizing society and the state (Rosenfield 2021, 275). This perception continually resurfaces in Brazil's socio-political landscape, even in the twenty-first century, manifesting in recent articulations as 'expressed and unexpressed feelings,' part of a history that remains ever-present.

Particularly concerning the topic of the article, inevitably, its traditional contours are expressions of historical contexts. The 1930s (Vargas era) saw the beginning of the idealization of a centralized and integrated system, which preserved the conception of a national body that would relate to the Civil Registry of Natural Persons and Civil Identification, with an additional architecture of a broad database and which would be portrayed again during the 1970s, with the National Registry of Natural Persons (RENAPE) (Doneda 2021, 39) (Vianna 2014). Initiatives of 'state intelligence' from the same period began projecting a 'modern' image of surveillance, targeting groups and individuals opposed to the Vargas regime. As the administration expanded, its focus shifted toward systematic population monitoring.

This authoritarian root solidifies and evolves with the military coup of 1964. With Law No. 4,341/1964, the National Information Service (SNI) was established, which, with new 'cybernetic mechanisms,' was able to create a coordinated surveillance system centralized in the federal executive power. Its foundations lay in producing 'information and counter-information' and informational capture of social contexts to provide an 'adequate estimate of the national situation.' The entire administrative apparatus was governed by the 'doctrine of national security' (Zanatta 2022, 44), expressing itself as regional and national policy, as well as international, inseparable from the geopolitical circumstances of the Cold War and the country's alliances with the United States.

The authoritarian use of information drew attention for its constant and diffuse potential to limit public freedoms. In subsequent processes, still under the yoke of military dictatorship in the 1970s, the first debates emerged with a dogmatic language strictly concerned with a data protection approach. It was precisely with the resurgence of a centralizing project, namely the National Registry of Natural Persons (RENAPE), during the military dictatorship of the 1970s, that the first data protection bill (No. 4,365/1977) in Brazil came to life, authored by federal deputy Roberto Faria Lima. In summary, this initiative represented a counterpoint to the intentions of the dictatorial state, which aimed to forge a database fueled by materials collected from citizens, characterized by being a centralized *system with a unique identification number* (Zanatta 2022, 48).

In general terms, in Brazil, especially considering the above-outlined bill, there was greater communication and influence from/to Portugal and Spain (Doneda 2020, 273), both experiencing 'similar situations (dictatorship-redemocratization)' and possessing strictly constitutional initiatives concerned with new scenarios of 'information rights and freedoms.' Especially in relation to the prohibition of the institution of a single identification number for citizens, in the case of Portugal (Article 35.3 of the 1976 Constitution—Portugal, 1976), subsequently provided for in the Cape Verdean Constitution, in the 1992 reform (Article 42.4—Cabo Verde, 1992).

Other influences, such as those from North America (Fuster 2014, 33–35)[8] and Europe (Doneda 2020, 192), are also integrated into this social and constitutional environment. Notably, the German experience stands out, having inaugurated a conceptual and normative differentiation related to privacy and intimacy, including the protection of personal data and the related concept of informational self-determination. The dogmatic conception regarding informational self-determination (*Informationelles Selbstbestimmungsrecht*) in the German context began to

[8] In the United States, since the 1960s, with the formal inquiry of the Special Committee on Science and Law of the Association of the Bar of the City of New York (1962) and the subsequent formation of a subcommittee on Invasion of Privacy in Congress, concerns about privacy and computerization of the state and private apparatus took shape. With reciprocal communications, involving actors such as Alan F. Westin and Cornelius E. Gallagher, these movements laid the groundwork for the formation, in 1972, of a broad report at the Secretary of the US Department of Health, Education and Welfare, whose committee included Arthur R. Miller and Willis H. Ware. This report established the basic principle called 'fair information practice (FAIR),' which still influences regulatory projects on the subject today and paved the way for the establishment of the US Privacy Act of 1974.

develop, influencing many legal initiatives in Germany itself, as well as in Europe and beyond[9] (Martins 2016, 58).

There is a consolidation of an expanded scope of personal data protection, moving further the traditional notions of privacy, intimacy, or secrecy as the protection of personality. In modern automated data processing, no data is considered insignificant, the German Constitutional Court ruled in 1983. Initially, the normative dimension that fostered linguistic sophistication regarding informational self-determination focused on the citizen-state relationship.

Given the technological development stage of the time, the massive collection and centralization of personal and non-personal data and information by a state influenced by authoritarian movements reflected one of the main concerns in Brazil and the Iberian region, latent to the historically commonality regarding the data protection tradition.

In Brazil, efforts were made to distance the consolidation of such state projects through technical indicators of their difficulties, and with demonstrations by epistemic communities in the field of law, but also by social movements. Toward the end of the 1970s and the beginning of the 1980s, as the military bases of the regime began to weaken, legislative processes within the state apparatus moved toward a protective environment strategically designed to hinder the excessive control exerted by the National Security apparatus, under the Special Secretariat for Informatics. Examples include proposals by Maria Cristina Tavares (Bill 4,810/1981).

[9] Although it was officially recognized in the famous census decision of 1983, pronounced in the German Constitutional Court (BVerfGE 65, 1, Census), the notion of informational self-determination underwent a gradual process of formation. It was present in the opinion (drafted by Steinmüller) presented in the German Parliament in 1971, in the context of the early discussions for the enactment of the Federal Data Protection Act, and in an interpretative 'progress' by courts and legal scholars on Article 2, § 1 of the German Basic Law, which guarantees everyone the right to the free development of their personality (among the various conceptual developments of this provision, one can mention: *Recht der Selbstbestimmung*—right to self-determination—*Recht der Selbstbewahrung*—right to self-preservation—*Recht der Selbstdarstellung*—right to self-presentation). In the mentioned decision of 1983, the Constitutional Court expressed one of the main contours of emerging informational self-determination: "Who cannot determine with sufficient certainty which information about themselves is known in certain areas of their social environment, and who cannot assess more or less the knowledge of possible communication partners, may be substantially inhibited in their freedom to plan or decide with self-determination. A social order and a legal order that supports it, in which citizens no longer knew who, what, when, and on what occasion is known about them, would no longer be compatible with informational self-determination."

From 1977 to 1985, during the authoritarian regime, embryonic ideas emerged for a legal-normative structure focused on data protection. These ideas centered on citizens' rights, administrative control charts, database operation licenses (influenced by Sweden), supervisory authorities, transparency mechanisms, prevention of automated decisions, basic rights of access and rectification, social control over databases, and a principled system emphasizing normative parameters for purpose and data minimization. None of these proposals were approved in parliament,[10] but they can be interpreted as institutional and social brakes that produced their respective results.

In Brazil there exists a tradition linked to data protection, distinct from occasional assertions suggesting otherwise (such as the misconception that Brazil merely 'imported' ideas and models, e.g., in relation to the most recent general data protection law—Lei Geral de Proteção de Dados, LGPD). This tradition is an expression of a time inevitably marked by various social, political, cultural, economic, and legal nuances, as well as the tradition of the constitutional action *Habeas Data* (Mendes 2018, 198).[11] This historical context demands recognition to understand the ongoing replication of past processes that ignore its lessons.

This analysis emphasizes the value of examining recent state reforms within the context of Brazil's ongoing efforts to establish itself as an informational and digital state. A key element of this proposal involves the interoperability of the state structure in its interactions with citizens. This interoperability would be facilitated by the implementation of a single citizen identification number. It is noteworthy that such a system was previously rejected during Brazil's authoritarian past. However, the current proposal suggests a resurgence, and even a potential normalization, of this approach.

[10] For a systematic analysis of these legislative movements—Bills (PL): José Roberto Faria Lima (Bill 4,365/1977); Maria Cristina Tavares (Bill 2,796/1980—Bill 4,810/1981—Bill 4,646/1984); José Freitas Nobre (Bill 4,856/1984); Jose Eudes (Bill 5,732/1985).

[11] It is important to consider the Latin American initiative similar to the Brazilian one, as outlined in the 1985 Constitution of Guatemala. Article 31 of the Constitution preserves the right to access state archives and records. Every person has the right to know about the information concerning them in state archives, files, or any other form of records, including the purpose for which the information is used, as well as the right to correction, rectification, and updating. Registration and files related to political affiliation are prohibited, except those conducted by electoral authorities and political parties (Guatemala 1985).

Contemporary Legal Initiatives in Brazil: Centralization and the Unification of Citizen Identification

The aim of this section is to highlight the risks of current initiatives which, initially in an uncoordinated manner and through isolated, piecemeal reforms, brought about changes at structural levels that today amount to a comprehensive transformation—or at least claim to do so—in the relationship between the state and the citizen (Laws Nos. 7,116 1983; 13,444 2017; 14,129 2021; 14,534 2023; and Decrees No. 10,046 2019; No. 11,266 2022; No. 11,574 2023; No. 11,797 2023; and No. 12,069 2024). A central government program proposes a comprehensive citizen data collection system with a unique identifier (Cadastro de Pessoas Físicas—CPF number). This initiative, with connections across branches and levels of government, raises concerns about its origins and potential impact.

It is imperative to note that the objective is not to identify a definitive solution to the outlined problem but rather to highlight certain nuances that can be envisioned in light of the General Data Protection Law. Furthermore, the approval of Constitutional Amendment 115/2022, which explicitly enshrines the right to data protection as a fundamental right in the constitutional text, and decisions rendered by the Supreme Federal Court (STF—Brazilian Constitutional Court), which recognize the right to data protection as fundamental, including a limited specific decision on the matter discussed in the jointly judged constitutional actions numbered 6649 (ADI) and 695 (ADPF), further underscore this complexity.

Historically, data protection in Brazil has shown significant concern over state treatment of personal and non-personal data in a power-concentrated environment. Risks associated with using a unique citizen identification within centralized state databases managed by the Executive Branch have been noted. Influences from Portugal, Spain, the United States, Sweden, Germany, Norway, France, Austria, and Luxembourg highlight a common concern shared in social, political, and legal movements in these countries.

Nevertheless, it seems that Brazil, as is sometimes the case, forgets its own history. With Laws and Decrees mentioned above, new architectures are envisioned, some already implemented, others in the process of development. The legal-juridical and dogmatic language of the current reforms—briefly addressed in this analysis—may also be perceived as presenting notable contrasts. This notion of contrast arises from the observation that, as previously discussed, there appears to have been a greater awareness of the technical, political, and legal risks associated with a highly centralized model of data governance, which was exponentially reinforced by an emerging epistemic community during the military dictatorship (1964–85). Such awareness seems to be lacking in the present context, in which the epistemic community is already consolidated, widely disseminated across the national territory, and internationally articulated. This contrast may stem from an excessive confidence in the constitutional-democratic environment which, despite its limitations, continues to impose constraints on the Brazilian State and society—particularly in those sectors that still bear the imprint of the militarized arbitrariness of the past. It is worth recalling, in this regard, the attempted coup d'état that reached its peak in January 2023, following the 2022 elections.

This reality must also be understood as inseparable from a broader historical and contemporary context of socialization processes, and thus of the creation and reproduction of political and legal normativities. These normativities, while revealing emancipatory potential, simultaneously carry within their internal paradoxes the legacies of both internal and external forms of domination that continue to manifest concretely in the present. Within the juridical and political spheres of a multiethnic country, the dynamics of (the code) exclusion and inclusion assume distinctive contours, often exploited as loopholes or facilitators for the intensification of new forms of domination—particularly those rooted in an economically driven and pervasive globalism. This globalism, when allied with politics in increasingly innovative configurations and mediated by digital technologies, seeks to project upon the legal and state apparatus standardized legal-engineering frameworks. Such frameworks tend to distance themselves from concerns with human and fundamental rights, fostering a model of legality that privileges technical-rational uniformity over democratic and inclusive principles. Thus, they appear to mimic a constitutional disregard for the lived experiences of individuals—their practices, desires, and subjective hopes (*qualia*)—aligning with Gayatri Spivak's (2013, 1–2) prescient warning that "globalization takes place only in capital and data. Everything else is damage control." This suggests a normative framework increasingly detached from the concrete realities of human life, privileging abstract systems of economic and informational governance over the protection and promotion of human dignity and constitutional guarantees.

It is not possible to exhaustively analyze each piece of legislation and fully expose their correlations. However, it is important to emphasize that they collectively establish a comprehensive legal-normative framework for the organization and production of an informational state. This section undertakes an examination of the (apparently) surface of the legal-state regulatory network, which, however, must not be analyzed solely within its textual boundaries. Rather, it should be situated within the broader legal-political context in which it operates—representing, reinforcing, facilitating, and authorizing the existence, materialization, and functioning of such structures.

This framework appears to have 'decentralized' structures with thematic specificities and controls for access and sharing, yet, in principle, it is interoperable through a unique identification number for citizens, specifically the Cadastro de Pessoas Físicas (CPF). To illustrate, without going into the details, the latest decree, from 2024, consolidates the process inaugurated by the previous initiatives, with The National Digital Government Strategy For The Period 2024 to 2027, emphasizing, in art. 9, item III, that the specific objective of the new strategy is III—to implement and maintain a structuring solution for single, national identification, associated with the National Identity Card, with security, wide availability, and validity for all federal entities.

Although 'unique identification' of citizens does not initially appear central to the technical-legal systems, it is an essential functional structure. It 'decentralizes' the federated environment, with subnational entities required to use this unified identification. The CPF is crucial for system interoperability, notably impacting the 'Cadastro Base do Cidadão' and its thematic bases. The centralization of the system is achieved precisely through the dispersion of citizen data collection via the use of a single identification number, while the system appears fragmented to 'functionalize' itself as a composition of informational individualities. It should be noted that there is not a broad debate, transparency, and public disclosure about such initiatives by the Brazilian state. A profuse data infrastructure (Karaboga et al. 2016, 32)[12] is established without presenting the real

[12] KARABOGA, Murat.; MATZNER, Tobias.; OBERSTELLER, Hannah.; OCHS, Carsten. Is There a Right to Offline Alternatives in a Digital World? In: LEENES, Ronald et al. (org.). Data Protection and Privacy: (In)visibilities and Infrastructures. Cham: Springer 2016, p. 32.

or approximate forms and scopes that a database, or the various interoperationalized databases with a unique identifier, may achieve.

To bring the subject in a concise and systematic manner, it is important to mention Law No. 7,116/1983, which, at the time, aimed to establish national parameters regarding organizational procedures for issuing Identity Cards. These identification cards were issued by subnational entities (States, Federal District, and Territories) and were valid throughout the national territory. Without delving into points preceding the mentioned Law, since 2017, with Law No. 13,444/2017 (which establishes the National Civil Identification—ICN), the Brazilian state has been gradually reforming its statute toward centralizing the citizen's identification structure for unification using the CPF number (which, with initiatives through Laws and Decrees in the years 2019, 2020, 2021, 2022, 2023, and 2024, shows that this path was being paved with these initiatives). Anticipating in Article 1 of Law 13,444/2017, the creation of the National Civil Identification (ICN) is outlined with the aim of identifying Brazilians in their relations with society and government and private entities. Article 2 states that the ICN will initially be populated by the biometric databases of the Electoral Court (one of the branches of the Judiciary in Brazil, exclusively focused on electoral matters) (Article 2, I), the database of the National Civil Registration Information System (Sirc), National Civil Registration Information Center (CRC Nacional) (Article 2, II), as well as identification databases of subnational entities, States, and the Federal District, or even the National Identification Institute, or provided by other agencies (Article 2, III). It emphasized the need to take measures to ensure the integrity, availability, authenticity, confidentiality of content, and *interoperability* between government electronic systems (Article 2, § 1). Article 3, § 1, authorizes the Executive Power of other federative entities to integrate the information from the ICN database into their own databases, with the exception of biometric data.

The National Identity Document (DNI) is created (Article 8) valid and legally binding throughout the national territory. Precisely in Article 8, § 6, the identification number is shifted toward a standardization process: in the issuance of new DNIs, the CPF number will be adopted as the unique number, a change introduced by Law No. 14,534, 2023. This measure is reinforced, even with the original 2017 text, in which a duty is imposed on the public authorities to provide mechanisms that enable the cross-referencing of information from official databases. Another important initiative anticipated in Law No. 14.129/21, which leads to a reform of the

Identity Card, is the delegation to the authorities of the Tax Federal Agency to establish a CPF registration whenever possible by means of other documentation, or the obligation to assign a CPF number to the person applying for an Identity Card, even without their consent. The same legislation establishes the principles and guidelines for the Digital Government project, with Article 3 highlighting the interoperability of the system and an open data design (item XIV). Chapter II of the law contains many proposals, although there is programming for cooperation between the institutions of the federal public administration (Article 15) and authorizing the other federal entities to organize their strategies, while respecting constitutional competences and compatibility with the federal plan (Article 16). The intention is to platformize the issue by instituting Digital Government Platforms, formally allowing citizens to exercise the rights provided in Law No. 13,709/2018 (LGPD). A dialogue with the National Data Protection Authority (ANPD) is sought, stating that the named authority may issue complementary rules to regulate the matter (Article 25, caput, I, II, § 2).

The central aspect, not only due to the material of the text under development but also of the regulatory framework itself, lies in Chapter III, where, once again, the aim is to standardize the informational identification of citizens (and, in this regard, legal entities) using the CPF number. Article 28 explicitly preserves that the registration number in the CPF is established as a sufficient identification number for citizens, as appropriate, in public service databases, with the free registration and changes in these registries guaranteed. In § 1, there is an intention to broaden the incidence and obligation of using the CPF number in State-Citizen relations, stating that the CPF number must appear in the registries and documents of public entities, natural persons' civil registry, identification documents, and professional councils.[13]

[13](i) Birth certificate; (ii) marriage certificate; (iii) death certificate; (iv) National Identification Document (DNI); (v) Worker Identification Number (NIT); (vi) registration in the Social Integration Program (PIS) or in the Public Servant Patrimony Formation Program (PASEP); (vii) National Health Card; (viii) voter registration card; (ix) Work and Social Security Document (CTPS); (x) National Driver's License (CNH) or Driving Permit; (xi) military certificate; (xii) professional card issued by councils overseeing regulated professions; (xiii) passport; (xiv) identity cards regulated by Law No. 7,116/1983; (xv) and other registration certificates and identification numbers existing in federal, state, and municipal public databases.

Article 39 schedules the establishment of an interoperability mechanism, which aims to enhance the management of public policies (Article 39, I), facilitate the creation of unified means of citizen identification for the provision of public services (Article 39, III), and facilitate data interoperability among government agencies (Article 39, IV), ultimately processing information from databases based on the citizen's CPF registration number, as provided in Article 11 of Law No. 13,444, dated May 11, 2017. With Law No. 14,534, this legislative movement was ratified, reinforcing unification, and the obligation to use and register citizens in the CPF. The same legislation also sent a message to other entities and agencies, inducing actions to regularize themselves with the standardized identification of citizens with CPF (Article 9, I, II).

In this context, it is essential to consider administrative productions guided by a decree from the Federal Executive Power, which extensively expands the possible data and information constituted/constitutable through the use of a unique identifier for citizens. With Decree No. 10,046, dated October 9, 2019,[14] the governance of data sharing within the scope of the federal public administration is addressed, expanding the scope to include the other branches of the Union (Legislative and Judiciary) (Article 1, last part). The Citizen Base Registry and the Central Data Governance Committee are instituted. In Article 1 of the Decree, it is stated that the rules within aim to regulate data sharing among agencies and entities of the federal public administration (Article 1, I), guide the formulation, implementation, evaluation, and monitoring of public policies (Article 1, II), as well as other purposes connected to the data structure of the state and its other federated entities. Article 2 of the decree defines certain categories of data and personal information intended to be organized in state databases. It refers to *biographical* attributes, *biometric* attributes, and *registration data*, each with a different legal classification,

[14]The named Decree replaces Decree No. 8,789/2016, which was also designed to expand correlations among state databases, without much consideration for the protection of personal data, and limited to the federal Public Administration, unlike what is stated in Decree No. 10,046/2019, which anticipates, at the end of the caput of Article 1, the following wording: "This Decree establishes the rules and guidelines for data sharing among the bodies and entities of the direct federal public administration, autarchic and foundational, and the other Powers of the Union [...] (potential violation of the separation—informational—of powers, as well as interconnecting and aligning with other initiatives at subnational levels).

although encompassing countless interrelated and excessive personal data and information.[15]

The sole paragraph of this article was amended on November 25, 2022, after the judgment of constitutional action No. 6,649/22 on September 15, 2022. Its wording is as follows: the use of the Citizen Base Registry, or its cross-referencing with other databases, is prohibited for data processing aimed at mapping or exploring individual or collective behaviors of citizens, without the express, prior, and specific consent of the affected individuals and without the proper transparency of motivation and purpose. The text reveals an inconsistency, prohibiting while authorizing initiatives with such characteristics, and employing the legal basis of 'consent,' which is extremely problematic in citizen-state relationships, with no provision for measures in the event of withdrawal of consent or the periodicity of data flows used in various opportunities (data processing ad infinitum?). Moreover, there is no specific concern about the successive possibility of creating thematic databases with citizens' data and information, which, in principle, can be articulated with past data and with datafied and developed congruences in the future (seemingly weakening informational self-determination in this aspect).

In Article 18 of the aforementioned Decree, the so-called integrating base is regulated, which will initially be made available with the biographical data contained in the thematic base of the CPF. However, successively, an evolutionary association is established, alluding that the biographical and registration attributes that will initially compose the integrating base will be composed of an excessive amount of personal data.[16] Similarly, only

[15] (i) Biographical attributes are physical person data related to facts of their life, such as civil or social name, date of birth, parentage, birthplace, nationality, gender, marital status, family group, address, and employment links (Article 2, I); (ii) biometric attributes are linked to measurable biological and behavioral characteristics of the individual that can be collected for automated recognition, such as palm prints, fingerprints, eye retina or iris, facial features, voice, and walking style (Article 2, II); and (iii) registration data, identifying information in public agency registries, with a movement for all existing data to have CPF as the unique and uniform number (Article 2, III and sub-items). In addition to other purposes, the sharing of citizens'/migrants' personal data between state agencies is reinforced, as is the cross-referencing of information between official databases, based on the unique identification number—CPF (Article 16, V, VI).

[16] the following: (i) CPF registration number; (ii) CPF registration status; (iii) full name; (iv) social name; (v) date of birth; (vi) gender; (vii) parentage; (viii) nationality; (ix) place of birth; (x) death indicator; (xi) date of death; (xii) date of registration or last modification in the CPF. Simultaneously, the creation of other thematic bases is authorized, which will par-

with Decree No. 11,266, dated November 25, 2022 (after the mentioned constitutional action was judged), a timid 'limitation' to initiatives was foreseen: the inclusion of new personal data in the integrating base and the selection of new thematic bases will be preceded by a detailed formal justification, in line with the principles of proportionality, reasonableness, and the protection of personal data (Article 18, § 7th).

It is important to conclude the present reading with Article 19 of Decree No. 10,046/2019, a space where an assignment is given to the Secretariat of Digital Government of the Ministry of Public Services, with the text provided by the subsequent Decree No. 11,574, dated June 20, 2023. The named Secretariat is granted the authority to take necessary measures to enable the implementation, operation, and monitoring of the Citizen Base Registry (Article 19, I), propose to the Central Data Governance Committee the data governance policy of the Citizen Base Registry (Article 19, II), as well as guide the entities responsible for thematic bases in the process of updating data from the Citizen Base Registry[17] (Article 19, III). Recently, the federal government proposed a new program, named the Citizen Identification Service, with Decree No. 11,797/2023. This follows a legal communication with the previously mentioned decrees. In addition to encompassing and interoperating with other systems and entities (Article 19, 20, 21 22), it regulates its own Federal Executive Chamber of Citizen Identification (CEFIC), which aims to act in federal governance—with strong connections to subnational entities—related to citizen identification. The system is notable for being authorized for use in criminal identification (Article 3, I, 'a') and for secret identification procedures carried out in systems related to "national defense and state security" (Article 3, I, 'b'), indicating it as mandatory for 'all other cases' (Article 3, II).

ticipate in the integrating base. There will be the addition "through the CPF registration number, a key attribute for the unequivocal consolidation of biographical, biometric, and registration attributes" (Article 18, § 1st, § 2nd). It is anticipated that the thematic bases will be constantly updated, including attributes from other bases with which it integrates or may integrate, and periodically sent to the integrating base (Article 18, § 4th and 5th). The only exception expressly provided for in this regard is the addition of genetic attributes to the integrating base (Article 18, § 6th).

[17] Right after, in Article 21, § 4, a level of optionality is anticipated in such dialogue: The Digital Government Secretariat of the Ministry of Management and Innovation in Public Services *may consult* the Central Data Governance Committee on issues related to data governance policies and guidelines for the direct, autarkic, and foundational public administration.

There are still other[18] procedural initiatives conceived by Decree; however, they will not be the subject of this text, as it would greatly expand its content and deviate from its purpose.

Informational Separation of Powers: An Essential Constitutional Approach to New Challenges

A doctrinal-constitutional approach to these processes is imperative, one that is open to "[…] the insertion of the constitution into its spatial context, as well as the complex relationship between constitution and time," precisely because the digital reality is not limited to replicating physical reality but transforms it. Thus, the constitutional culture, fundamental rights, the idea of democracy, the Rule of Law, and the characteristics of the legal system end up acquiring different dimensions (Callejón 2023).

In light of these assertions, a re-examination of the separation of powers is inspired through the concept of informational separation of powers, which "consists of a logical and necessary reinterpretation of the semantics of the principle of the division of powers (Article 2 of the Brazilian Constitution) in the light of digital constitutionalism, considering the current state of data sharing within the Brazilian state" (Sarlet and Sarlet Sales 2022, 28). It is precisely for this reason that a broad normative incorporation of data protection into the culture of principles and fundamental rights (including a rethinking of the separation of powers) must be embraced by the State, especially the Brazilian state, establishing "[…] through the use of action parameters forged based on the principle of separation of powers, an organizational regime guided by division of

[18] In the aforementioned Decree, a distinct legal framework is provided for equally distinct classifications of data and information in Chapter II—Data Sharing Levels. Data sharing is categorized, associating it with three levels, according to the 'confidentiality level' (Article 4). Broad sharing is connected to public data not subject to any access restrictions, the disclosure of which must be public and guaranteed to anyone interested, in accordance with the law (Article 4, I); restricted sharing applies to data protected by secrecy, as provided by the law, with access granted to all organs and entities referred to in Article 1 for the execution of public policies, with the sharing mechanism and rules simplified and established by the Central Data Governance Committee (Article 4, II); specific sharing applies to data protected by secrecy, as provided by the law, with access granted to specific organs and entities, in the cases and for the purposes provided by law, with the sharing mechanism and rules defined by the data manager (Article 4, III). It is stated that the categorization of the sharing level will be determined by the data manager, based on the law (Article 4, § 1), in addition to other specificities.

competencies, making every effort to avoid abusive, disproportionate, unrestricted, and therefore unconstitutional sharing of personal data."

An informational state can enhance policy formulation and public service implementation, improving social rights in an unequal country. However, these benefits come with significant risks to human and fundamental rights, necessitating vigilant oversight to prevent violations in a centralized informational state. The dogmatic-constitutional conception of informational separation of powers is adaptable to both traditional and contemporary social communications, focusing on the concentration and diffusion of power. In its state-informational form, power is creatively accumulated. Human Rights and Fundamental Rights, while byproducts of power, also transform it by delineating its limits, purposes, and scope. This framework supports a digital notion of democracy, which is unfolding through three horizons: Online Politics, Digital Democracy, and the Digital State (Gomes 2016, 39–50).

The Brazilian state's push to reorganize the federal powers and federated administrative apparatus and standardize citizen identification numbers conflicts with informational separation of powers and data protection rights. This approach undermines data protection by enabling constant interventions in citizens' digital identities. It results in a juridicalized power asymmetry (Döhmann 2023, 79) in the State-citizen relationship, as a condition for the functioning of the state apparatus traditionally related to 'public interest.'

The decentralized layers characterizing each individual are subject to presumed datafication, excluding genetic data, creating an environment capable of identifying individuals across various intersectionalities (Crenshaw 1991). This introduces another dimension: the inadequate treatment of identity risks that individuals and groups may face over time. The standardization of citizens' identification numbers results in the uniformity and neutralization of the informational apparatus, potentially leading to interconnected data processing without explicit safeguards for individuals' data and information.

A concern related to cybersecurity cannot be overlooked. With the centralization of the system and its interoperability based on the unique identification number (CPF), citizens, in principle, are prone to greater risks such as unauthorized access, hacking, leakage of sensitive and non-sensitive data and information (including metadata), and the common theft of informational identity. This calls for specific state protection duties in the informational and digital environment.[19,20]

Brazil's history of authoritarian movements, with more dictatorships than democracies in the twentieth century, serves as a significant warning. Recent political movements have led to the election of popular figures associated with authoritarian, nationalist, and discriminatory proposals. These processes are termed "autocratic legalism," using constitutional-democratic legal instruments to undermine the very democratic architecture that supports them (Scheppele 2018).

In fact, constitutional action No. 722 was judged by the Supreme Federal Court in 2022 (Supremo Tribunal Federal 2022a), and in this case, it was decided that the acts (at the time) of the Ministry of Justice and Public Security, related to the production or sharing of information about the personal life, political choices, civic practices of citizens and public servants identified as members of an anti-fascist political movement, within the bounds of legality, exercise their rights to freely express themselves, assemble, and associate, were unconstitutional.[21] This constitutional action, beyond communicating with others, unfolds as a symbolic, social, and constitutional event,[22] representing the tone in which

[19] In the constitutional dogmatics of German influence (*Schutzplifcht des Staates*) to configure a prohibition of insufficient protection (*Untermaßverbot*) aligned with the prohibition of excess (*Übermaßverbot*). This would mean an active pursuit of a cybersecurity perception attentive to existing risks, as well as an informational reordering capable of mitigating them, and, furthermore, objective proposals in which related subjective rights can be exercised independently or in conjunction with the state apparatus.

[20] On December 26, 2023, in Brazil, the National Cybersecurity Policy and the National Cybersecurity Committee were established, unfolding into the National Cybersecurity Strategy (Article 4, I) and the National Cybersecurity Plan (Article 4, II). Still in a nascent stage, it represents a primary legal milestone in the realm of digitization, aiming to coordinate cyber concerns among the Union, States, Federal District, and Municipalities, across the three branches, in the private sector, and in 'society at large' (Article 3, IX, a, b, c, d), placing the issue on the Brazilian agenda.

[21] The winning vote, delivered by Justice Carmen Lúcia, had the opportunity to state the obvious (which represents an act of courage by the Constitutional Court in the context of judging the action): "Intelligence activities, therefore, must respect the democratic regime, in which the persecution of opponents and political takeover of the State are not allowed. Moreover, the history of reported abuses regarding intelligence services emphasizes the imperative need for effective control of this activity."

[22] One speaks of a symbolic event, from one of its angles, that effectively permeates the constitutional political-legal environment of a particular state and society. At this juncture, a warning about the symbolic power of Law is recalled, or brought forth: the naturalization of

concerns about Human and Fundamental Rights in contemporary Brazil inevitably arise, along with their associations with the authoritarian past-present-future that invariably affects its citizens.

This constitutional action represents only the visible surface of a broader set of state practices implemented during the previous administration, grounded in the legal framework established by the aforementioned Decree (Citizen Base Register). These actions were directed against civil servants, professionals, and ordinary citizens, which recover a latency of forms of sociability in Brazil, that existed before, and still persist, regardless of such processes and after the 2022 election.

In a society as deeply stratified as Brazil's, the targeting of these groups is already cause for concern; it is even more alarming to consider the potential uses and consequences of such 'intelligent' systems across a wide range of sectors—particularly in criminal prosecution[23] and in decisions regarding the granting of social security benefits. It is important to note that these systems operate in conjunction with private infrastructures and interests (in the consumer market and beyond), including national and international corporations seeking large public contracts. These contracts may cover software operation, system maintenance and development, and data migration to external data centers—data which may ultimately be repurposed for undisclosed objectives, beyond the reach of existing accountability and oversight mechanisms.

the institution of the State, of Law, and its 'institutions,' which, when successful, makes one forget that to 'be,' it managed to impose itself at the expense of other alternatives. It exists in objectivity and subjectivity, in 'things' and in 'brains,' until it ceases to be an institution, forgetting itself as an institution that had a birth, a beginning, and a specific development (Bourdieu 2012).

[23] Criticism and scholarly analyses frequently address the power asymmetry between the state's surveillance capacities in the criminal sphere and the deployment of overt surveillance technologies, such as facial recognition systems—widely implemented across Brazil in both large and small cities, industrial urban centers, and even rural areas. Brazil has increasingly functioned as a testing ground for surveillance technologies, particularly biometric surveillance, facilitated by substantial public contracts that integrate both national and international technologies into the apparatus of state-citizen interaction. The recent report ***Mapping Biometric Surveillance*** documents this landscape. However, it also reveals one of the cognitive limitations that this article seeks to highlight: the lack of transparency on the part of the Brazilian state, which appears to operate as a strategic mechanism for assembling a diffuse and interoperable surveillance structure—one that often manifests only through fragmentary and indirect indications.

The arguments presented in the chapter are limited to specific and identified administrative reforms which, despite their ostensibly superficial and bureaucratic nature, in fact bring about a substantial transformation of the constitutional pact established in Brazil since 1988. This process has occurred without the effective participation of citizens and, arguably, even of Parliament itself. These reforms typically embody governmental policy measures initiated by the Executive Branch and are implemented through executive decrees. Parliamentary involvement in these processes is markedly limited, as is citizen participation, which is often confined to internal committees that appear equally disengaged from the broader implications of the scenario briefly outlined here.

The interpretative approach adopted here is also constrained by both dogmatic limitations and spatial considerations. Nonetheless, it is inspired by theoretical fragments drawn from systems-based social theory, as well as by critical perspectives concerned with generating insights from within the internal environment of the juridico-political discourse of the state. This orientation deliberately avoids self-congratulatory moralism disguised as theory, and instead embraces a posture of confrontation—of exposing and naming the wound—drawing inspiration from Krenak (2024),[24] who argues for a stance that is not merely decolonial or postcolonial, but *counter-colonial*. Such a stance entails the elevation of epistemological and normative criteria that differ from those established by the so-called core countries. These countries, despite presenting themselves as avant-garde in the context of the relationship between state law and digital technologies—often through narratives and symbols such as the well-known 'Brussels effect' within the European Union—appear to be charting a pre-formatted legal-normative path heavily influenced by global corporations. These corporations, to a considerable extent, wield more legislative influence than European citizens themselves within the European Parliament and Commission.

The central point is as follows: Brazil neither possesses nor requires the need to look toward the juridico-political and regulatory framework of the European Union (or another country or international organization in the Global North) in order to develop its own legal self-reference and self-reflection. The Brazilian regulatory scenario is profoundly deficient, and this deficit appears to be exacerbated precisely when it attempts to emulate

[24] Ailton Krenak: "We don't need to engage in decolonial criticism, but rather countercolonial criticism."

regulatory measures from core countries—measures that fail to respond to Brazil's regional particularities and differentiated challenges, which demand specific and localized regulatory responses. This is not to suggest that foreign experiences should be disregarded; quite the contrary. Observing differences can provide the conceptual material necessary to creatively distance oneself from inadequate models and to construct autonomous and contextually grounded legal structures.

Brazil's laws and Constitution deserve the same degree of respect and protection as those of the so-called core countries. This applies equally to the subjective relationship between the state and its citizens with regard to rights and guarantees. However, such recognition must be accompanied by an internally driven, self-referential critical process, one committed to the ongoing development necessary for the country to live up to the (constitutional) standards it has set for itself.

Although this overview—only briefly addressed in this chapter—reveals global dimensions, its manifestation in Brazil incorporates the country's own normative practices and productions, as well as its internal differentiations. Drawing from a Luhmannian systems-theoretical perspective, it is important to recall that modernity, and its complex process of differentiation, presents regional particularities—especially within the center-periphery dynamic—that challenge the very premise of functional differentiation. As Neves (1992) warned as early as the 1990s (conducting an internal critique of systems theory, based on the Brazilian experience), the functional differentiation of modern society presupposes a level of inclusion that countries in the Global South are still striving to achieve. This does not imply that countries of the north do not face serious problems comparable to those found in the South, particularly in Brazil. However, the nature of these challenges assumes distinct contours and is expressed through experiences that, once again, reveal features of modern societies in which exclusion is normalized and embedded within systemic operations. In theoretical terms, this implies an acknowledgment of its own geopolitical positioning—that of being situated in the Global North—and, consequently, an awareness of its corresponding epistemological limitations. It engages in a process of self-learning—or, to adopt Luhmann's terminology, theoretical autopoiesis—grounded in the experiential and epistemic contributions of the Global South. It is not only functional differentiation that characterizes modern societies, but precisely the code of inclusion-exclusion that underlies them.

The societal project envisioned by the 1988 Brazilian Federal Constitution aims to generate contingencies that disrupt this normalization of exclusion, while also defending itself against internal and external forces of colonization. This dynamic is once again illustrated by the attempted coup that reached its peak in January 2023. The persistent disregard for the democratic constitutional framework—both in the failure to institutionalize social-state practices in accordance with constitutional principles and in episodes such as the one cited, which reproduce the coup-driven ethos characteristic of Brazil's twentieth-century authoritarian period—represents two facets of the same structural dynamic.

However, these events have not occurred in isolation from the democratic constitutional and social resistance present in Brazil, which therefore warrants attention both within the national context and as a point of reference for other experiences in the Global South—and, indeed, in the Global North as well. Although affected in distinct ways, these regions are also undergoing troubling socio-normative developments, within which digital technologies—through their co-productions and intersections between state and private actors—occupy a central role.

Attention must be paid to juridical-state models of normativity, while also considering their interaction with normative frameworks originating from other social subsystems. It is equally important to examine how digital technologies operate within these contexts—both in micro and in macro structures—which may only appear separable under an ontological, non-polycontextural perspective (Günther 2018). A polycontextural analysis reveals the multiplicity of normative orders and the differentiated roles that digital technologies assume across distinct institutional environments. These roles manifest within various social systems and their couplings, as well as in instances of disproportionate infiltration or dominance of certain systems over others.

Conclusion

The implementation of an apparently decentralized but highly interoperable system, with the use of standardizing citizens' identification numbers (CPF registration), is notable for designing a centralized system that is overly interventionist in the lives of citizens and their relationship with the state and in private relations. In addition to the Brazilian historical approach, which is concerned with the matter, and also with the suggested re-reading of the—informational—separation of powers, there is a message from one of the first institutional documents related to the protection of personal data, which were established in Europe at the same time that Brazil was criticizing dictatorial reforms, with concerns about the excess of data and centralization that a project to unify citizens' identification numbers would bring. The Resolution 74 (public databases—Council of Europe 1974) and Convention 108 of the Council of Europe (1981): these historical documents provide guidelines related to data treatment (still in an embryonic stage, not only in Europe but in other regions as well), emphasizing the prohibition of collecting excessive data and information for specific purposes (Article 5, 'c'), and the preservation of the principle that the identification of individuals should only be possible if strictly necessary is also highlighted. This concern was likewise present in the early technical and political movements that addressed the asymmetry of informational power between the state and its citizens—a dynamic that significantly influenced the emergence of data protection as a legal and political field in Brazil during the 1970s.

We must examine our history, contemporaneity, and experiences, as well as those of others, to avoid possible mistakes (Deutsche Welle 2023). Some of them have already been avoided in worse contexts. The analysis proposed in this text adopts a general approach and emerges from within the Brazilian state legal subsystem, particularly its historical-dogmatic nuances and legislative reforms, which, in synthesis, reveal inherent contrasts. This scenario—briefly addressed herein—does not disregard its broader political and social context, which transcends micro- and macro-level relations and incorporates a dynamic that extends into and reproduces itself within global society. States and global private entities appear more as collaborative actors than as drivers of divergent processes. Recent elections in the United States and developments within the European Union—such as the fragility of certain regulations aimed at digital technologies—serve as evidence of this phenomenon.

Nevertheless, these pre-institutionalized normative spaces are also arenas of contestation. Although Law may appear to be losing its structural centrality in the global context, it continues to serve as a mechanism through which society expresses itself and exerts influence over both institutional and non-institutional spheres. It creates grammars, practices, and avenues of political resistance that, under the banner of human and fundamental rights, are capable of constraining technopolitical and economic movements unaccustomed to limitations.

Countries in the Global South—often shaped by global forces and their state partners in the Global North, acting through public-private coalitions—remain focal points within global society, indicating the possibility of alternative trajectories. Attending to the intersection of law and technology at the micro level—as this text seeks to do—is part of this broader process. Its aim is to reveal, to bring to light, the developments currently unfolding within Brazilian society and the state, as well as the risks inherent in such movements. One must not overlook that exposing a scenario—even if only partially—is one of the ways through which it may become subject to public contestation, thereby challenging the deterministic character ascribed to it by those who benefit from such structures and who craft their strategic narratives accordingly.

One of the central objectives of this study was to elucidate how these structures operate within the intricate dynamics—or 'alchemy'—of juridical-administrative processes, often concealed beneath ostensibly bureaucratic procedures and dichotomous logics. By making these operations visible, the study seeks to draw attention to the broader normative and political issues at stake. The analysis developed here may be extrapolated for broader theoretical applications or serve as a conceptual foundation for further inquiry within the specific thematic scope under examination.

References

Bennet, Colin J.; Lyon, David. (2008). *Playing the identity card: surveillance, security and identification in global perspective*. Oxon/New York: Routledge.

Bourdieu, Pierre. (2012). *Sobre o Estado: Cursos no Collége de France (1989–92)*. São Paulo: Companhia das Letras.

Brasil. *Censo IBGE*. (2022–3). Brasília. https://cidades.ibge.gov.br/.

Couldry, Nick; Mejias, Ulises A. (2019). *The costs of connection: how data is colonizing human life and appropriating it for capitalism*. Stanford: Standford University Press.

Callejón, Francisco Balaguer. (2023). Inteligencia artificial y cultura constitucional. In: Sarlet, Ingo Wolfgang; Callejón, Francisco Balaguer (Ed.). *Derechos Fundamentales y Democracia en el constitucionalismo digital*. Cizur Menor: Aranzadi/Reuters.

Council of Europe. Committee of Ministers. (1974). *Resolution (74) 29. On the protection of the privacy of individuals vis-a-vis electronic data banks in the public sector*. Adopted on 20 September.

Council of Europe. (1981) *Convention for the Protection of Individuals with regard to Automatic Processing of Personal Data. European Treaty n° 108*. Strasbourg.

Crenshaw, Kimberle. (1991). Mapping the Margins: Intersectionality, Identity Politics, and Violence against Women of Color. *Stanford Law Review*, vol. 43, n. 6, pp. 1241–1299.

Decree n° 10.046, de 9 de outubro de 2019. Dispõe sobre a governança no compartilhamento de dados no âmbito da administração pública federal e institui o Cadastro Base do Cidadão e o Comitê Central de Governança de Dados. Brasília, 2019. Recuperado em 19 ago. 2023, de https://www.planalto.gov.br/ccivil_03/_ato2019-2022/2019/decreto/D10046.htm.

Decree n° 11.266, de 25 de novembro de 2022. Altera o Decreto n° 10.046, de 9 de outubro de 2019, que dispõe sobre a governança no compartilhamento de dados no âmbito de administração pública federal e institui o Cadastro Base do Cidadão e o Comitê Central de Governança de Dados. Brasília, 2023. Recuperado em 19 ago. 2023, de http://www.planalto.gov.br/ccivil_03/_ato2019-2022/2022/decreto/D11266.htm.

Decree n° 11.574, de 20 de junho de 2023. Altera o Decreto n° 10.046, de 9 de outubro de 2019, que dispõe sobre a governança no compartilhamento de dados no âmbito da administração pública federal e institui o Cadastro Base do Cidadão e o Comitê Central de Governança de Dados. Brasília, 2023. Recuperado em 19 ago. 2023, de http://www.planalto.gov.br/ccivil_03/_ato2023-2026/2023/decreto/D11574.htm.

Decree No. 11,856, of December 26, 2023. Establishes the National Cybersecurity Policy and the National Cybersecurity Committee. Brasília, 2023. Recuperado em 27 dez., 2023, de https://www.planalto.gov.br/ccivil_03/_ato2023-2026/2023/decreto/D11856.htm.

Decree n° 12.069, de 21 de junho de 2024. Dispõe sobre a Estratégia Nacional de Governo Digital e a Rede Nacional de Governo Digital—Rede Gov.br e Institui a Estratégia Nacional de Governo Digital para o período de 2024 a 2027. Brasília, 2024. Recuperado em 4 jul. 2024, de https://www.planalto.gov.br/ccivil_03/_ato2023-2026/2024/decreto/d12069.htm.

Deutsche Welle. (2023). Atos Golpistas em Brasília, 13 dez. 2023. Disponível em: https://www.dw.com/pt-br/atos-golpistas-em-bras%C3%ADlia/t-64326231.

Döhmann, Indra Spiecker gen. (2023). The more the merrier: a dynamic approach learning from prior misgovernance in EU data protection law. In: Kettemann, Matthias C.; Peukert, Alexander.; Döhmann, Indra Spiecker gen. (Ed.) *The law of global digitality*. New York: Routledge.

Doneda, Danilo. (2020). *Da privacidade à proteção de dados pessoais*. São Paulo: Thomson Reuters Brasil.

Doneda, Danilo. (2021). Panorama Histórico da Proteção de Dados Pessoais. In: Mendes, Laura; Doneda, Danilo; Sarlet, Ingo Wolfgang; Rodriguez Jr., Otavio Luiz (Ed.). *Tratado de proteção de dados pessoais*. Rio de Janeiro: Forense, 2021.

European Commission. (2017). New European Interoperability Framework: promoting seamless services and data flows for European public administrations. Luxembourg: Publications Office of the European Union.

Foucault, Michel (2008). *A arqueologia do saber*. Rio de Janeiro: Forense Universitária, 2008.

Forum Brasileiro De Segurança Pública (2023). *Anuário Brasileiro de Segurança Pública*. https://forumseguranca.org.br/wp-content/uploads/2023/07/anuario-2023.pdf.

Fuster, Gloria González. (2014). *The emergence of personal data protection as a fundamental right of the EU*. Heidelberg/New York/Dordrecht/London: Springer.

Gomes, Wilson. (2016). 20 anos de política, Estado e democracia digitais: uma cartografia do campo. In: SILVA, Sivaldo Pereira et al. (Ed.). *Democracia digital, comunicação política e redes: teoria e prática*. Rio de Janeiro: Letra e Imagem.

Guatemala. (1985). Constituición Política de la República de Guatemala. Available: https://siteal.iiep.unesco.org/sites/default/files/sit_accion_files/siteal_guatemala_4000.pdf. Accessed: 24 ago. 2023.

Günther, Gotthard. (2018). Life as Poly-Contexturality, *Vordenker.*

Jaeggi, Rahel. (2018). *Critique of Forms of Life*. Cambridge: Belknap Press of Harvard University Press.

Karaboga, Murat.; Matzner, Tobias.; Obersteller, Hannah.; Ochs, Carsten. (2016). Is There a Right to Offline Alternatives in a Digital World? In: Leenes, Ronald et al. (Ed.). *Data Protection and Privacy: (In)visibilities and Infrastructures*. Cham: Springer.

Krenak, Ailton. (2024). *Não temos de fazer crítica decolonial, e sim, contracolonial*: pensador indígena ministrou uma das conferências de inauguração da cátedra Darcy Ribeiro, do leat, nesta segunda-feira. Universidade Federal de Minas Gerais, 2 dez. 2024. Available: https://ufmg.br/comunicacao/noticias/ailton-krenak-nao-temos-de-fazer-critica-decolonial-e-sim-contracolonial.

Law n° 7.116, de 29 de agosto de 1983. (1983). Assegura validade nacional as Carteiras de Identidade regula sua expedição e dá outras providências. Brasília, 1983. Recuperado em 18 ago. 2023, de https://www.planalto.gov.br/ccivil_03/leis/1980-1988/l7116.htm.

Law n° 13.444, de 11 de maio de 2017. Dispõe sobre a Identificação Civil Nacional (ICN). Brasília, 2017. Recuperado em 18 ago. 2023, de https://www.planalto.gov.br/ccivil_03/_ato2015-2018/2017/lei/l13444.htm.

Law n° 14.129, de 29 de março de 2021. Dispõe sobre princípios, regras e instrumentos para o Governo Digital e para o aumento da eficiência pública e altera a Lei n° 7.166, de 29 de agosto de 1983, a Lei n° 12.527, de 18 de novembro de 2011 (Lei de Acesso à Informação), a Lei n° 12.682, de 9 de julho de 2012, e a Lei n° 13.460, de 26 de junho de 2017. Brasília, 2021. Recuperado em 18 ago. 2023, de https://www.planalto.gov.br/ccivil_03/_ato2019-2022/2021/lei/l14129.

Law n° 14.534, de 11 de janeiro de 2023. Altera as Leis n°s 7.116, de 29 de agosto de 1983, 9.454, de 7 de abril de 1997, 13.444, de 11 de maio de 2017, e 13.460, de 26 de junho de 2017, para adotar número único para os documentos que especifica e para estabelecer o Cadastro de Pessoas Físicas (CPF) como número suficiente para identificação do cidadão nos bancos de dados de serviços públicos. Brasília, 2023. Recuperado em 19 ago. 2023, de https://www.planalto.gov.br/ccivil_03/_ato2023-2026/2023/lei/l14534.htm.

Luhmann, Niklas. (2016). *O direito da sociedade.* São Paulo: Martins Fontes.

Martins, Leonardo. (2016). *Tribunal Constitucional Federal Alemão: decisões anotadas sobre direitos fundamentais. Volume 1: Dignidade humana, livre desenvolvimento da personalidade, direito fundamental à vida e à integridade física, igualdade.* São Paulo: Konrad-Adenauer Stiftung—Kas.

Mendes, Laura Schertel Ferreira. (2018). Habeas data e autodeterminação informativa: os dois lados da mesma moeda. *Direitos Fundamentais & Justiça*, 39, 185–216.

Mendonça, Ricardo F, Filgueiras, Fernando, Almeida, Virgílio. (2023). *Algorithmic institutionalism: the changing rules of social + political life.* Oxford: Oxford University Press.

Neves, Marcelo. (1992). *Verfassung und Positivität des Rechts in der peripheren Moderne: eine theoretische Betrachtung und eine Interpretation des Falls Brasilien.* Berlin: Duncker und Humblot.

Rosenfield, Luis. (2021). *Revolução Conservadora: genealogia do constitucionalismo autoritário brasileiro (1930–1945).* Porto Alegre: ediPUCRS.

Regulation (EU) 2023/2854. (2023). European Parliament and of the Council of 13 December 2023 on harmonised rules on fair access to and use of data and amending Regulation (EU) 2017/2394 and Directive (EU) 2020/1828 (Data Act). Recuperado em 26 dez. 2023, de https://eur-lex.europa.eu/eli/reg/2023/2854.

Sarlet, Ingo Wolfgang; Sarlet Sales, Gabrielle. (2022). *Separação Informacional de Poderes no Direito Constitucional Brasileiro.* São Paulo: Associação Data Privacy Brasil de Pesquisa, 2022.

Scheppele, Kim Lane. (2018). Autocratic Legalism. *The University of Chicago Law Review*, 85 (2), 545–583.

Spivak, Gayatri Chakravorty. (2013). *An Aesthetic Education in the Era of Globalization.* Cambridge: Harvard University Press.

Supremo Tribunal Federal (Tribunal Pleno), 13 de maio de 2022a. Arguição de Descumprimento de Preceito Fundamental (ADPF) n° 722 (Brasil). https://redir.stf.jus.br/estfvisualizadorpub/jsp/consultarprocessoeletronico/ConsultarProcessoEletronico.jsf?seqobjetoincidente=5967354.

Supremo Tribunal Federal (Tribunal Pleno), 15 de setembro de 2022b. Ação Direta de Inconstitucionalidade n° 6695 (Brasil). https://portal.stf.jus.br/processos/downloadPeca.asp?id=15358978491&ext=.pdf.
Teubner, Gunther; Golia, Angelo Jr. (2023). Societal constitutionalism in the Digital World: An Introduction. *MPIL Research Paper Series No. 2023-11.*
Vesting, Thomas. (2022). *State theory and the law: an introduction.* Northampton: Edward Elgar Publishing.
Vianna, Marcelo. Um novo "1984"? O projeto RENAPE e as discussões tecnopolíticas do campo da informática brasileira durante os governos militares na década de 1970. (2014). *Oficina do Historiador*, 1, 1148–1171.
Weizenbaum, Joseph. (1976). *Computer power and human reason: from judgment to calculation.* New York: W.H. Freeman and Company.
Zanatta, Rafael Augusto Ferreira. (2022). *A proteção coletiva dos dados pessoais no Brasil: a defesa de direitos entre autoritarismo e democracia.* Universidade de São Paulo, São Paulo.

CHAPTER 6

Caste Bias in Indian Prison Datasets: A Data Feminism Study on Kaggle.com

Nishanshi Shukla

Introduction

Data is a non-neutral, subjective, and political entity that serves as one of the reasons for bias in AI systems and ways in which these systems exercise power. In Geoffrey Bowker's words as quoted and argued for by Lisa Gitelman and Virginia Jackson, "'raw data' is both an oxymoron and a bad idea" (Gitelman 2013, 1). Data is the subjective abstraction and aggregation of contextual information (Gitelman 2013). It is a cultural entity curated by the socio-technical system through which it is produced and in which it is stored. So, it mimics the socio-cultural biases of and around that system and exerts power. Along with numbers and scores, data also consists of texts, images, sounds, and videos. The correlations of these various elements of data are established in the way data are stored. From classification systems to tables to datasets to databases to algorithms to AI systems, data live a life of continuous analysis, guided and framed by the very socio-technical system producing and storing data.

The biases and power exerted by data are reflected either *through* or *because of* the process of analytical interpretation. The politics of data are

N. Shukla (✉)
The University of Texas, Dallas, TX, USA
e-mail: Nishanshi.Shukla@utdallas.edu

P. Raghunath (ed.), *Critical Political Economy and Southern Approaches to AI*, Palgrave Global Media Policy and Business,
https://doi.org/10.1007/978-3-032-14090-6_6

encoded in the choices made during this process, including collecting data, recording data, labeling data, classifying data, storing data, rendering data legible, making data accessible, performing statistical analysis on data, and implementing actions based on such data analysis and insights (Bowker and Star 1999; Merry 2016). The biases of data as encoded through this process are further supported by the AI systems. Along with fully developed AI applications, the techno-cultural and often techno-solutionist aspects of data in AI systems include: the need for the data, the cultural context of data collection, categorization, and use, and the platforms that make data available and ready for use. These are the steps that data goes through from inception to being used to train models. If data, its classification, and its storage are political, then by extension, practicing data science, the field of statistically analyzing and extracting insights from data, is a political project. These political performances of data are executed by various practices in the field of data science. One such political performance is the issue of datafication, which is the collection of data about everything and converting everything into data.

A political performance of data, in the context of Indian sub-continent, is datafication of caste. The datafication of caste system is a postcolonial project built on existing caste discriminations, along with lack of voice and data literacy of the subaltern publics. The analysis of this chapter joins with other work in critical AI studies to expose data as non-neutral and subjective entities that support the existing power structures in society by analyzing publicly available tabular data on caste. To do so, I turn to one of the most popular collections of publicly available data wherein I undertake reading of specific datasets around caste, crime, and the carceral system in India. These datasets are chosen because crime and carcerality provide points of visibility to politics of caste data. While news around caste-based crimes and atrocities is common, caste data is also becoming a common denominator in training carceral predictive systems. An example of such a system is JARVIS, an AI warden employed in prisons of Uttar Pradesh for increased surveillance, monitoring and actionable insights on any suspicious activity from prisoners or visitors. To understand the influence of caste-based data on such predictive systems, it is important to unpack the politics of caste data itself.

In this chapter, I investigate the politics of caste data and digital infrastructures surrounding them. I study a dataset file titled "Caste.csv" shared on Kaggle (n.d.), a Google-owned online data repository for the machine learning and data science community. "Caste.csv" is a file first uploaded by a Kaggle user profile in the "Indian Prison Statistics" dataset (Ilangovan 2017) and later reuploaded by another Kaggle user profile in the "Prison Inmates in India" dataset (The Devastator 2022). Containing only tabular text data, the Kaggle users frame the file "Caste.csv" as containing accurate caste-based statistical information about Indian prison inmates. This file was uploaded and shared by these Kaggle users on Kaggle Datasets (n.d.) for the larger Kaggle community to use in data science projects and experiments with machine learning algorithms. Through examining this case, I argue that systems of structural classification and social stratification are often encoded in data, but seldom questioned in their use and analysis. Questioning the power dynamics of this Kaggle dataset and its corresponding file on "Caste.csv" reveals the politics of ignorance in the digital infrastructures surrounding the data, and politics of use embedded within the data science processes through which such data is engaged with.

Caste Data and Social Stratification

Caste data is a prime example by which data, its classification, and its storage are political. The caste system today is a form of social stratification that codifies graded social inequality. It has been written about in the *Manusmriti*, a discourse that sets out the socio-legal apparatus that forms a part of Hinduism, indicating the caste system as one of its intrinsic properties. It lays down a social hierarchy that comprises social stratification into community groups (varnas) named *Brahmins*, *Kshatriyas*, *Vaishnavas* and *Shudras*, followed by communities who were spatially segregated from the four, called the *Dalits* and *Adivasis* today. *Varnas* and *Jatis* (social identities drawing on one's occupation and handed down by birth) combine social identity that is passed down through the patrilineal system, on the basis of one's birth. The term Dalit is a political term given to the communities by Dr. B. R. Ambedkar, social reformer and head of India's Constituent Assembly during the process of formal decolonization. Even as these categories of social stratification existed for centuries across South Asia, the colonial encounter brought in newer nomenclatures. Affirmation action in the form of reservation often draws on these nomenclatures. Therefore, caste is not recorded in the terms mentioned above. Rather, it is recorded as the following categories: (1) Other (unofficially known as "general"), which consists of higher castes like *Brahmins*, *Kshatriyas* and *Vaishnavas*; (2) Scheduled Caste (SC), which consists of *Shudras* and

Dalits; (3) Scheduled Tribe (ST), which consists of *Adivasis*; and (4) Other Backward Classes (OBC), which consists of people from higher castes but belonging to backgrounds deemed socially, educationally, and economically backward. Regardless of an individual's religion, each Indian citizen is classified into a caste category upon birth. In other words, despite its origin Hindu religion, the caste categories, as part of the aggregated demographic data of India, also consist of people from all other religions. This classification is guided by the Constitution of India and contingent upon the political history of different sections of people in different states of India. The strategic use of these castes and their categories for electoral and political benefit of political party leaders is a well-discussed postcolonial phenomenon (Ahuja 1999; Arora 2019; Ayyathurai 2021; Beteille 1990; Dirks 1989; Ketkar 2018; Kumar 2000; Singh 2005; Spivak 2015; Sundar 2000; Visvanathan 2001).

Even though demographic numbers for India's caste system are not publicly and individually published, all public databases of Indians include the caste category as a shown or hidden column. This system follows what Ruha Benjamin calls "coded exposure" (Benjamin 2019). As a form of coded exposure, this system overexposes the weaker castes by explicitly recording them in various specified categories but masks the upper castes by putting all of them together in a category titled "general/ other." This nomenclature itself begins with the political nature of caste-based data, which can be easily perpetuated in the AI systems trained on it.

This chapter considers the politics of datasets that include caste. These are publicly available datasets or data collection mechanisms that have caste as a column or label, and which can be used to train AI systems. The data about crime is centered in this chapter because of the emergence of AI systems to monitor and control crime. All classifications are political, and the reasons why certain decisions were made to include or elide certain information are forgotten after the classification system is in place (Bowker and Star 1999). It is important to study the AI and data science practices behind use and analysis of easily and publicly accessible data.

Building on this understanding, the following section discusses the methodological tools used in this chapter to analyze caste data. This includes three ways of reading data as given by Lindsay Proirier (2021) and the principles and framework of Data Feminism illustrated by Catherine D'Ignazio and Lauren Klein (D'Ignazio and Klein 2020).

Data Feminism

I analyze caste datasets and its surrounding discourses using a humanities model of reading denotative, connotative, and deconstructive meanings (Proirier 2021). The denotative reading is literal and highlights the technical aspects. Connotative reading is genealogical; it employs hermeneutic methods to contextualize cultural meaning. The deconstructive reading employs critical analysis to question what and who are absent, and why (Proirier 2021). These three types of readings are done simultaneously to raise questions about the politics of these datasets and the discourses about them. Specifically, I question the caste-based discriminatory politics of data and AI and their relationship to crime and carcerality in India. To do so, I engage with the lens of Data Feminism presented by D'Ignazio and Klein (2020) as a tool of wielding back the power of data.

A data feminism lens, as presented by D'Ignazio and Klein (2020), is a form of intersectional feminism that takes the inequities of the present moment as its starting point and begins its work by asking questions around the process of world making undertaken by data. Intersectional feminism is the concept of acknowledging and challenging all the overlapping systems of power working together in a society to form an intertwined network of privileges and oppressions (Crenshaw 1989). Data feminism is committed to action about uses and limits of data. Its objectives are to unpack how existing inequalities are reinforced by usual practices in data science, and to not only challenge but also change the unequal distribution of power using data science. I engage through this data feminism as a lens to unpack caste data and discourses about caste data in order to shift the narrative (and flip the paradigm) on how this data is understood. This critique reveals that this data masks the inequalities on which it was built and argues that AI systems built on such data are bound to inherit those inequalities. Before delving deeper into the analysis, let me describe and discuss the background of Kaggle Datasets, the Indian Prison Datasets and the file "Caste.csv" present in them.

Indian Prison Datasets and "Caste.csv" on Kaggle

Kaggle Datasets

To examine the politics of caste data in AI systems, I delve into one of the most famous dataset banks, Kaggle (n.d.), in this section. Kaggle is an online platform that has built an online community around data science. Specifically, Kaggle is a dataset platform that performs as a hub for all publicly available data; it is a place to upload, find, and collaborate on datasets for various machine learning tasks. With large chunks of data and datasets available, Kaggle is regarded as easy to use for training prototypes of data science and ML/AI projects by data scientists and engineers; Kaggle is known for hosting large sets of freely available datasets and codes to build and run machine learning models.

Most of the publicly available resources on Kaggle are published by the users of this platform. According to the website Kaggle Datasets (n.d.), Kaggle is a place to "explore, analyze, and share quality data" that is non-proprietary, and in many cases open access, and thus mostly made available to the public. However, not all datasets uploaded to and shared on Kaggle are drawn from public databases, and not all datasets uploaded to and shared on Kaggle are made accessible to the public. The platform also has an option of uploading private datasets and notebooks. These can be accessed only after receiving permission from their publisher ("How to Use Kaggle | Datasets" n.d.).

Kaggle situates itself as an AI and ML community of "Kagglers" to increase participation and establish its importance in the field. It hosts competitions, datasets, models, code, discussions, and courses around different aspects of data science and machine learning. Kaggle uses this sense of community building as a promotion of leveling up in the field of AI and ML. Each dataset is also framed as a community project where data and various techniques of working on it can be discussed and deliberated on with online peers (Banachewicz and Massaron 2022).

Kaggle promotes datasets ("Kaggle | Datasets" n.d.) based on not only their categories but also their popularity, their usability, and their relationship to recent trending activities. The datasets are grouped into categories based on topics tags, which include, among others, sports, health, travel, food, software, computer-science, biology, history, cancer, covid, crime, arts and entertainment, education, investing, and NLP. These tags are often defined by the publishers or users of the dataset. Thus, the power to define datasets lies with the people that collect, upload, and publish data. Kaggle focuses on having a huge collection of "high-quality public datasets" but in spite of its focus on community building, it does not clarify who is included in this community, and who is the intended public for these high-quality datasets. Kaggle ignores the fact that many publics whose data might be present on Kaggle are not equipped with the data literacy to contribute to the community analyzing it nor able to validate the quality of the data. Also, the way the dataset is viewed and interacted with by the Kagglers is highly influenced by the publisher of the database and not the people whose data is being represented. Thus, the power to define and use this data clearly does not reside with the people to which this data belongs.

India Prison Datasets

"Indian Prison Statistics: Details of Inmates Are Classified According to 35+ factors Dataset" (Ilangovan 2017) and "Prison Inmates in India: Demographics, Age, Education, Caste, Wages, Rehabilitation, Technical Info Dataset" (The Devastator 2022) are two datasets uploaded by two different user profile on Kaggle. These two datasets have similar data, both datasets link their publishing source to National Crime Records Bureau of India's (n.d.-a) website, and the second dataset cites the first dataset as the original. A denotative reading shows that both the datasets consist of the same 37 csv files with identical file names and information. The only difference is that the "Indian Prison Statistics" dataset has all tables upfront. The "Prison Inmates in India" dataset only has tables related to prison inmates upfront, and the rest are inside a folder named Other Prison Data. To contextualize the data further, along with using MS Excel's features like pivot tables to compare the data in these datasets, I also undertook a connotative reading. Each of these tables represents different demographics and information about prison inmates or prisons in India over the same timeframe. "Indian Prison Statistics" dataset has collaborators working on the data. There are eight computer codes written to perform some analysis or visualization on its data. The analyses of the results from these programs are also discussed in one discussion section of the "Indian Prison Statistics" dataset; while "Prison Inmates in India" dataset does not contain any codes or discussions.

Caste.csv

"Caste.csv" is a file found in both "Indian Prison Statistics" dataset and "Prison Inmates in India" dataset. A deductive reading of this file shows the technical details of this file. For example, it contains the following column headings: "state_name," containing rows regarding the names of Indian state; "is_state," containing value 1 for state or 0 for union territory; "year," containing values from 2001 to 2013; "gender," containing values as male or female; "caste," containing values as SC, ST, OBC, or Others (the General Category); "convicts," "under_trial," "detenues" [detainees], and "others," containing values representing the count. Upon examining these data via a pivot table in MS Excel, it is clear that on an average 65%, that is the majority of the prisoners are from SC, ST, and OBC categories.

The news publication The Wire (The Wire Staff 2019) and the newspaper *Mint* (PTI 2021) have also published about the trend of majority of prisoners in Indian prisons being from SC, ST, and OBC castes. In the 2011 census of India, the Office of the Registrar General, and Census Commissioner, India (2011) only released the population distribution of the SC and the ST categories in the Indian subcontinent, but it did not release the population distribution for the OBC and the Other categories. While there are existing surveys that estimate the percentage population for the OBC and the Other categories, they are not entirely useful here as they are sample surveys. The sample surveys do not explain how they are establishing samples and sub-groups for "ease of calculation," and to what extent regional and geographical policies, politics and population distribution are considered in estimating percentage of people in OBC and Other categories. The quantifications and classifications done by the indicators in a few of these columns signify the political nature of data. The data is presented as objective truth and the narrative behind the data is untold (Merry 2016). Thus, a deconstructive reading shows that the question is not whether the prison data mimics the population percentage of categories; the question is what happens when a crime prediction or surveillance AI is trained on such data and/ or its data labels? The next section uses tools of Data Feminism (D'Ignazio and Klein 2020), ways of reading datasets (Proirier 2021), and theories of critical data studies to explore such questions in detail.

Analysis Using Data Feminism

Power and discrimination are not evenly distributed, but they are in fact layered. One group can experience both power and discrimination based on their positionality in the dominant and minority groups to which they belong (D'Ignazio and Klein 2020). Understanding this is important to acknowledge the hidden power, privilege, oppression, and discrimination hidden in data. Examining how power is routed (D'Ignazio and Klein

2020) in the digital infrastructure around "Caste.csv" includes examining technological power embedded in Kaggle and its datasets, socio-technical power held by the collectors and publishers of datasets, and cultural power held by the higher caste groups, especially in sociotechnical assemblages like caste data within prisons where caste-based discrimination is a recognized norm.

Undertaking a deconstructive reading of "Caste.csv" and the datasets that contain this data, as stated by D'Ignazio and Klein (2020), is examining power by asking the "Who questions:" "who does the work," "who benefits," and "whose priorities get turned into products" to understand the privilege hazard happening within the data. The privilege hazard is defined as the idea that the privileged individuals and groups in society occupying the decision-making positions are not sufficiently equipped to identify the nuances of oppression around them. Privilege hazard hampers the systems of power from recognizing the extent of discrimination happening within them. In the case of data science, privilege hazard happens when oppressive systems and biases like racism, sexism, ableism, and casteism are coded within the digital ecosystems and are barely questioned (D'Ignazio and Klein 2020).

These two Kaggle datasets that contain "Caste.csv," a dataset file around caste (varnas as literally translated to practices of labor), never ask the question of "who does the work?". The work here refers to the work of collecting data. Even the original source of data on National Crime Records Bureau of India's (NCRB) (n.d.-a) website available under the Crime in India (National Crime Records Bureau n.d.-b) and Prison Statistics India (National Crime Records Bureau n.d.-c) webpages, does not clarify who, exactly, collected this data. So, we can only infer that NCRB as a whole, a biopolitical bureaucracy, that supports carceral systems did the work. The dataset also does not provide any transparency around data collection. It lacks information about the data inputs taken from the prisoners when they become a part of the carceral system, and thus, by extension a quantified object in this data. For the data on caste, it does not contain the caste and caste-based beliefs of the people who recorded this data. In absence of the history and context of individual sources of these data and its indicators, caste-based data clearly occludes the labor involved behind this dataset.

The answer to who benefits from this data is in accordance with who uses it and why. The description of the dataset provided by its publishers suggests using this data to understand India's criminal justice system, highlight frequency of different crimes in different states, and uncover different crime trends. As this data has the capability of training crime prediction or surveillance AI systems, this data benefits the surveillors of the criminal justice system. It benefits the technochauvinist logic of quantifying and categorizing the prisoners to predict their next illegal move. Technochauvinist logic is the technocentric bias where people believe that computers are superior to humans and do the work more effectively (Broussard 2019, 7). It benefits the institutionally manufactured need of predicting crime with technology. It helps them in showing that certain crimes are being undertaken by certain groups of people. It enables the automatic predicting systems to tag certain crimes to certain groups, and label likelihood of their criminality. Thus, the carceral system benefits. Those who profit off of prisons benefit. Systems of oppression that are built on the manufactured need to imprison people benefit. This analysis of the political economy of prisons and its data shows that the people (prisoners) represented in these Kaggle datasets do not benefit at all.

As publishers write the descriptions of datasets, the power to define perspectives about the possible use and need of the data lies with them. The context section in the description of the "Indian Prison Statistics" dataset states that "This dataset contains the complete detail about the Prison and various characteristics of inmates. This will help to understand better about the prison system in India" (Ilangovan 2017). The description of the "Prison Inmates in India" dataset states that "This dataset not only sheds light on India's criminal justice system but also highlights prevalence [sic] of crimes in different states and union territories as well as providing insight into crime trends across Indian states over time" (The Devastator 2022). It also claims that this data is from the year 2001 to 2013 or 2019. This discrepancy in years is because while the description states that this data "includes information on inmates from all states/union territories for the year 2019," the highest value in the "year" column of the first table Age_Group.csv is 2013. Thus, there is lack of clarity around what it means for a dataset to be deemed "complete." The way the datasets are presented and the tone that is set for the datasets depends on the description in the dataset documentation that their publisher writes for them. Also, Kaggle's infrastructure indicates that to be high on usability score, the source and authenticity of the data is not important, as long as it ranks high on the usability score; it just needs to be deemed useful to do or practice data science work and to be uploaded by a profile assessed credible on the platform. Thus, there is also an aspirational value assigned to the numbers in this dataset to provide understanding and insights about prisons and crime trends in India. By aspirational value, I mean the rhetoric that advocates for "complete information" and "high usability" to increase that data's visibility and use.

These datasets are used, or recommended to be used, to do various types of descriptive and predictive statistical analysis. They frame the dataset for users and instruct users to think about the dataset in very specific ways. "Indian Prison Statistics" Dataset states that it can be used to answer many questions about Indian prisons (Ilangovan 2017). These questions include:

> Percentage of jails overcrowded. Is there any change in percentage over time? How many percentage of inmates re-arrested? Which state/u.t pay more wages to the inmates? Which state/u.t has more capital punishment/life imprisonment inmates? Inmates gender ratio per state [sic]. (Ilangovan 2017)

This dataset also has codes attached to it. These attached codes show that other users have performed different kinds of statistical analysis by running Python scripts on this dataset and combining this dataset with other datasets. "Prison Inmates in India" dataset states that this data can provide insight about crime trends in India, and this dataset is recommended to be used toward building machine learning models (The Devastator 2022). It states that:

> This dataset can be used to understand the demographic composition of the prison population in India as well as the types of crimes committed. It can also be used to gain insight into any changes or trends related to sentencing patterns in India over time. Furthermore, this data can provide valuable insight into potential correlations between different demographic factors (such as gender and caste) and specific types of crimes or length of sentences handed out. (The Devastator 2022)

The recommended research ideas stated in the description of this dataset include:

> i. Using the age and gender information to develop targeted outreach strategies for prisons in order to reduce recidivism rates; ii. Creating an AI-based predictive model to predict crime trends by analyzing crime head data from a particular region/state and correlating it with population demographics,

economic activity, etc.; iii. Analyzing the caste of inmates across different states in India to understand patterns of discrimination within the criminal justice system. (The Devastator 2022)

Given that Kaggle as a platform encourages data science projects like analyzing data, creating data visualizations, and making models from data, these usage and research ideas are usually followed. But it is worth questioning what it means to use this dataset for predictive data analysis and the societal implications of using this dataset for such analysis.

The groups whose priorities have the highest visibility are turned into products. In most obvious cases, these groups are the government and the carceral system. But other groups whose priorities are turned into products also include institutions and people working in AI and ML. This is because these groups have access to open access data on Kaggle. Also, these groups with special technical access and knowledge are the narrators of how technical discourses and uses of data are shaped. They are the people with the vocabulary to understand the data and code the data into algorithms and software that get turned into products. It is the groups that accept caste-based categorization as an integral part of products. It is not the people whose data this is.

Except for the user profiles of the people who uploaded these datasets and credited them to the NCRB, no other labor around this data is made visible. The dataset on Kaggle does not state who the people that originally collected the data are. It also does not describe the process of gathering and uploading these datasets on the platform. It shows data only as a collection of numbers about a prison system and not as the work undertaken by various humans at different levels. Kaggle as a platform attempts to make the work of its users visible by showing their names and display-picture beside the datasets they uploaded, code they wrote, models they created, and comments they uploaded. But that is where the definition of labor ends. It does not show the work of all the people and technologies who work in creating and maintaining this platform.

Thus, the power here lies not directly with the upper caste, but with the people who believe in the caste-based system and ignore the privilege of the upper class inherently coded within the system. The reservation quota provided for the lower castes, which is the basis of their argument in favor of caste-based classification as a demographic information, works in favor of the non-privileged categories to give them opportunities, but it also exposes them to more social discrimination by the upper castes. The resulting systems and data like "Caste.csv" in prison datasets ignore the perspectives and identities linked with lack of power by being at the lower strata in social classification. Postcolonial feminist theorist Gayatri Spivak (2015) has outlined the violence emerging from the "codification of [caste-based] Hindu law" to highlight the lack of power and stature that rests the lower castes. Spivak (2015) states that due to this lack of structural privilege, the voice of the lower castes goes unheard, unconsidered, and uncatered to. This lack of voice in the SC, ST, and OBC groups in these datasets is the result of privilege hazard within the dataset. It leads to data that overexpose these groups, in a system already discriminating against them, being used to further predict potential crimes and criminals. Also, there is no conversation about whether the people whose data this represents have the data literacy to recognize the valence of this data and are able to give consent over the derivative use of their data.

Processing data reduces its historical and contextual ground, and governments and corporations often use this reduction in context as management technique and as a means of control. As such, data feminism (D'Ignazio and Klein 2020) argues that it is important to keep in mind that people come before data, and they are involved in every step, from data collection to its use. But, in most cases, the ownership of the data is retained by the publisher of the dataset with the power to modify, repurpose, and describe data. Thus, the people who are represented by the data lose the original ownership of their own data. For example, in "Digital Natives," Joanna Radin (2017) examines the PIDD dataset that was collected from the people of the Gila River Indian Community Reservation in 1990. Owing to its size and simplicity/ complexity, that is simple as compared to bigger datasets, but complex compared to small datasets, this dataset has been over-used much beyond its original reason and context while propagating the logics of settler colonialism. Due to this continuous re-use of data, the Akimel O'odham people have been subjected to repeated questioning and data collection, such that they have refused to participate further and have appealed to take down the data (Radin 2017). Even after that, this dataset is still publicly available on websites such as Kaggle. This raises questions about ownership of data and the right to ensure data in/visibility. Such questions become more pertinent in dataset containing sensitive information like crime, criminality, prison inmates, and prison conditions.

Kaggle's digital infrastructure and the Indian Prison datasets in question are devoid of context and pluralism. Kaggle's digital infrastructure, the Indian Prison datasets in question, and the process through which they set up the use of these data take socio-cultural and structural hierarchical, like caste, for granted. Kaggle's digital infrastructure and the Indian Prison datasets in question neither question the binaries present in the data, nor critically rethink any hierarchies present within (D'Ignazio and Klein 2020). It does not question systems of counting and classification while evaluating assumptions and beliefs behind the database. The gender column just has two values, male and female. There is no place for any non-binaries. There is also no information about how and whether non-binary genders are considered. The caste column has just four values. One of these four is the category named "others," which obfuscates the general category as it groups the three upper castes into a single categorical classification. It also does not give any information on provision for people who do not wish to adhere to the classification system of the caste or do not wish to disclose the information. It also does not give any information on provision for people who do not wish to adhere to the classification system of the caste or do not wish to disclose the information. In doing so, it sets-up "Caste.csv" data to propagate the existing classification systems and their biases and power dynamics. Thus, Kaggle's digital infrastructure, Indian Prison datasets and the users of this data in question also take data as is because of the process through which they are set up to use this complex data laden with complexities of intersectionality.

The data in caste.csv and the two Kaggle datasets does not challenge the beliefs and assumptions that were used while formulating the gender and caste classification systems. This data just accepts those beliefs as objective truth for creating further systems. The systems made using this data, like the data visualizations made by writing scripts on this data as mentioned in the earlier point, show the continuous propagation of gender and caste binaries in them. The visualized pie charts can only have the classification that exists in data, which would also be true for the AI trained on this data. By not questioning the binaries and hierarchies, Kaggle supports their presence in the data.

Connotative reading of Indian Prison datasets shows that even before considering context, it negates the importance of authentic data. Both the datasets have a Creative Commons (n.d.) license CC BY-SA 4.0 Attribution-ShareAlike 4.0 International. CC BY-SA 4.0 license allows the user to share and adapt the data as long as you "give appropriate credit" and "indicate what changes were made" (Creative Commons n.d.). If these are the terms of reusing, does the license check if these terms were followed when the data was originally published? The license seems like merely a way to not get into any legal troubles regarding the copyright usage of data by original collectors of data, people whose data it is, or future users of the data. It shifts the responsibility of checking the authenticity of the data from the publisher to the user of the data, and thus establishes the leeway for data fabrication.

A method of contextualizing data is by acknowledging that it comes from living bodies with both emotion and reason and using those humane experiences in the resulting data visualizations and visceralizations. In D'Ignazio and Klein's (2020) principle, it involves checking if the data elevates emotion and embodiment. A deconstructive reading of the Indian Prison datasets showcases that there is no emotion and embodiment captured in the data nor in the data visualizations attached to the codes of "Indian Prison Statistics" Dataset. These data visualizations comprise graphs on various statistical analysis. It includes a notebook titled "Indian Prison System Analysis" (Sugandh 2020). This notebook is a set of data processing code and data visualizations graphs on sub-topics like: gender distribution, religious distribution, education of prisoners, crimes committed, "number of convicts and under trial per year," "year-wise trends and top ten states in capital punishments," life imprisonments, murder, crimes against women, violent crimes, robbery, and white-collar crimes (non-violent crimes that include cheating, counter-feiting, and breach of trust) (Sugandh 2020). It also has a pie chart on caste distribution in convicts and under trial prisoners i.e., the percentage of people from SC, ST, OBC, and Others in the prison system. These visualizations treat people as numbers and do not distinguish between the representations of crime data and people data. It does not capture the plight behind crimes and lives of people in prison. It does not capture the difference in treatment and surveillance of prisoners.

A denotative reading of the tabular data of "Caste.csv" just shows the state-wise, year-wise, and caste-wise data of "number of convicts," "under trials," "detenues" [detainees], and "others." It does not capture anything beyond these counts. It has no acknowledgment of the experiences of these people. Thus, the data and its visualization do not use emotion in their representation. It includes the vision of the people and ideology that consider people as just countable objects and classification systems like caste as neutral, objective, powerless social structures. It considers the technochauvinist view (Broussard 2019) in such data to suggest its usage to predict crime patterns without analyzing its relation to caste discriminations and reasons. It excludes the vision of the people who would be at the losing end when crime prediction AI systems are trained on this emotionless data. Kaggle, and thus by extension the Kagglers, do not consider the importance of experience, emotion and embodiment in data collection, representation, and use.

Considering the context of data entails analyzing them as objects emerging from unequal societal structures and being subjective. Deconstructive reading of the data in "Caste.csv" is devoid of any context. It does not give context about the structural system behind differences in caste dynamics. It does not consider the overexposure of certain groups and obfuscation of others. One of the two datasets states the source of this data as reports from a government website, but there is no information on the methods used to collect this data, and no context regarding whose data was collected. It does not question the difference in data recording and treatment of different groups of society in different states. It does not represent the power dynamics of caste as a backdrop of the way this data is recorded, structured, and suggested to be used. The datasets and thus by extension Kaggle make data seem to be some objective truth lifted out of history or culture or society.

Context is not considered an important factor in working with or promoting a dataset on Kaggle. For instance, the usability score of these datasets also does not consider context. It does not question the use of data by whom, for whom, and for which purpose. It concentrates on completeness of documentation as being higher in the usability rating but does not consider the need and understanding of local knowledge, especially in utilizing this dataset to make machine learning models. By not questioning the context, it secludes the data from its subjectivity.

A way to challenge and redistribute this power is collecting counter data and practicing pluralism (D'Ignazio and Klein 2020) by considering and integrating multiple perspectives to develop complete knowledges while giving priority to knowledges that are local and based on experience. The counter data cannot be constructed by simply erasing caste from the data recording system. That erasure would simply ensure that the structural oppression based on caste continues without questions. A deconstructive reading of the dataset and the codes run on it do not reflect on the possible existence of pluralism in this data. There is no information about whether multiple sources and groups were engaged in collecting and reporting this data. The datasets also lack transparency in terms of whose decisions were considered in collecting these data. It does not question the need for data from the prisoners. It does not envision the existence of a participatory process that would have data from the people whose data this is. While Kaggle supports collaboration on its platform, it does not embrace pluralism. The platform urges Kagglers to work together on data to produce data visualizations and machine learning models to create more predictions (and knowledges?) but does not establish the need for integrating multiple perspectives of thinking through data and using it. It does not give priority for local and experience-based knowledges that introduce data-based subjectivity in these data science discussions and processes.

Discussion and Conclusion

Thus, a data feminist critique of these datasets on Kaggle reveals that data needs to be examined before being used to make AI systems. The data is heavily influenced and biased, and the platforms collecting and hosting it support that by ignoring its subjectivities. It also establishes the need for collaboration with people from non-privileged groups devoid of any cultural power. This first part of the chapter has established that the politics of AI is not just a result of politics of data, but all the systems that surround this data. Examining power dimensions in popular data platforms which turn into sources for catering to the need and use of the datasets with rigid structural classifications has established that while it is important to understand what the data system can do and represent, it is also necessary to question what is missing and not questioned because of the normalized world view of the dominant group being reflected in the data.

Throughout the chapter, I engage with critical data and caste studies literature to showcase the politics of caste data and how it gets presented, accessed, and used in its digital form. Digital datafication of caste is a complex project that is further convoluted when that caste data is used for purposes of training AI systems and prediction models.

To repurpose the principles of data feminism for analyzing caste-based data includes questioning and addressing the history of caste, not just caste categories, within AI datasets. This chapter has pointed out that loss of context and history is usually equivalent to loss of power by the historically under-privileged. Thus, one of the ways of addressing history is going beyond the quantified caste-based category distribution, and questioning why individuals from specific social backgrounds and locations are being represented in a certain way. While there are demands for caste census in

India, my argument is not around it, in fact it is a juxtaposition against that. The arguments in this chapter do not advocate for more or less data in terms of caste-wise population records. Instead, the arguments presented in this chapter establish the need to move beyond quantification of caste and tap into caste data that is rich in history and context. Just the imagination of the data that does not exist points the ahistoricity embedded within the current caste data. For now, all caste-based data needs to be seen with questions like "who does it not consider?", "whose lived experiences does it not tell?", and then include those people, groups, and experiences within the dataset to establish a non-hegemonic counter narrative and reduce the current obfuscation of upper castes and overexposure of lower castes. AI would be able to recognize casteism and make it visible only when the datasets it is trained on represent caste for what it is, rather than how institutional powers and structures see it.

References

Ahuja, R. (1999). *Society in India: Concepts, Theories and Changing Trends*. Rawat Publication.

Arora, P. (2019). "Politics of Algorithms, Indian Citizenship, and the Colonial Legacy." *Global Digital Cultures: Perspectives from South Asia* (A. Punathambekar and S. Mohan, Ed.). University of Michigan Press.

Ayyathurai, G. (2021). "Colonialism, Caste, and Gender: The Emergence of Critical Caste Feminism in Modern South India." Journal of Women's History, 33(3), 133–156.

Banachewicz, K., & Massaron, L. (2022). *The Kaggle Book: Data Analytics and Machine Learning for Competitive Data Science*. Packt Publishing.

Benjamin, R. (2019). *Race After Technology: Abolitionist Tools for the New Jim Code*. Polity Press.

Beteille, A. (1990). "Race, Caste and Gender." *Man, New Series*, 25(3), 489–504.

Bowker, G. C., & Star, S. L. (1999). *Sorting Things Out: Classification and its Consequences*. The MIT Press.

Broussard, M. (2019). *Artificial Unintelligence: How Computers Misunderstand the World*. The MIT Press.

Creative Commons. (n.d.). Creative Commons — Attribution-ShareAlike 4.0 International — CC BY-SA 4.0. Creativecommons.org. Retrieved on September 25, 2024, from https://creativecommons.org/licenses/by-sa/4.0/.

Crenshaw, K. (1989). "Demarginalizing the Intersection of Race and Sex: A Black Feminist Critique of Antidiscrimination Doctrine, Feminist Theory, and Antiracist Politics." *University of Chicago Legal Forum*, 1(8), 139–167.

The Devastator. (2022). *Prison Inmates in India*. Kaggle | Datasets. Retrieved on September 25, 2024, from https://www.kaggle.com/datasets/thedevastator/prison-inmates-in-india-demographics-crimes-and.

D'Ignazio, C., & Klein, L. F. (2020). *Data Feminism*. The MIT Press.

Dirks, N. B. (1989). "The Original Caste: Power, History and Hierarchy in South Asia." *Contributions in Indian Sociology*, 23(1), 59–77.

Gitelman, L. (Ed.). (2013). *Raw Data is an Oxymoron*. The MIT Press.

How to Use Kaggle | Datasets. (n.d.). Retrieved on September 25, 2024, from https://www.kaggle.com/docs/datasets.

Ilangovan, R. (2017). Indian Prison Statistics. Kaggle | Datsets. Retrieved on September 25, 2024, from https://www.kaggle.com/datasets/rajanand/prison-in-india.

Kaggle. (n.d.). Retrieved on September 25, 2024, from https://www.kaggle.com/.

Kaggle | Datasets. (n.d.). Retrieved on September 25, 2024, from https://www.kaggle.com/datasets.

Ketkar, S. V. (2018). *History of Caste in India*. Rawat Publications.

Kumar, R. (2000). "Caste Enumeration in Census: Constitutional Imperative." *Economic and Political Weekly*, 35(35/36), 3100–3102.

Merry, S. E. (2016). *The Seductions of Quantification: Measuring Human Rights, Gender Violence, and Sex Trafficking*. University of Chicago Press.

National Crime Records Bureau. (n.d.-a). Retrieved on September 25, 2024, from https://www.ncrb.gov.in/.

National Crime Records Bureau. (n.d.-b). *Crime in India*. Ministry of Home Affairs, Government of India. Retrieved on September 25, 2024, from https://www.ncrb.gov.in/crime-in-India.html and https://www.ncrb.gov.in/crime-in-india-all-previous-publications.html.

National Crime Records Bureau. (n.d.-c). *Prison Statistics India*. Ministry of Home Affairs, Government of India. Retrieved on September 25, 2024, from https://www.ncrb.gov.in/prison-statistics-India.html and https://www.ncrb.gov.in/psi-all-previous-publications.html.

Office of the Registrar General & Census Commissioner, India. (2011). *Basic Population Figures of India/State/District/Sub-District/Village – 2011*. Ministry of Home Affairs, Government of India. Retrieved on September 25, 2024, from https://censusindia.gov.in/nada/index.php/catalog/42555.

Proirier, L. (2021). "Reading Datasets: Strategies for Interpreting the Politics of Data Signification." *Big Data and Society*, SAGE Publications, 1–19.

PTI. (2021, February 10). *65.90% prison inmates are from SC, ST and OBC categories, NCRB data says*. Mint. Retrieved on September 25, 2024, from https://www.livemint.com/news/india/6590-prison-inmates-are-from-sc-st-and-obc-categories-ncrb-data-says-11612951470742.html.

Radin, J. (2017). ""Digital Natives": How Medical and Indigenous Histories Matter for Big Data." *OSIRIS*, 32, 43–64.

Singh, E. (2005). *Caste System in India: A Historical Perspective*. Kalpaz Publications.

Spivak, G. C. (2015). "Can the Subaltern Speak?" *Colonial Discourse and Post-Colonial Theory: A Reader* (P. Williams, & L. Chrisman, Ed.). Columbia University Press, Routledge, 66–111.

Sugandh. (2020). *Indian Prison System Analysis*. Kaggle | Code. Retrieved on September 25, 2024, from https://www.kaggle.com/code/sugandhkhobragade/indian-prison-system-analysis.

Sundar, N. (2000). "Caste as Census Category: Implications for Sociology." *Current Sociology*, 48(3), 111–126.

Visvanathan, S. (2001). "The Race for Caste: Prolegomena to the Durban Conference." *Economic and Political Weekly*, 36(27), 2512–2516.

The Wire Staff. (2019, January 20). *One in Every Three Under-Trial Prisoners in India Is Either SC or ST: Study*. The Wire. Retrieved on September 25, 2024, from https://thewire.in/rights/one-in-every-three-under-trial-prisoners-in-india-is-either-sc-or-st-study.

CHAPTER 7

Epilogue: From Frontier Technologies to Frontier Lives

Preeti Raghunath

The chapters in this short edited collection explored *some* Southern perspectives and experiences with Artificial Intelligence technologies and data, with a view to explore questions that emanate from the Critical Political Economy theorising as well as Southern theoretical and empirical traditions. By placing them in dialogue, the introductory chapter presented common concerns as well as dissonances between the two. The chapters that followed looked at situated experiences and lenses to socio-legal, techno-political as well as socio-economic questions around these technologies, their machines and machinations. These included research on financial mobile apps, legal provisions around digital IDs and data, the colonial underpinnings associated with AI deepfake technologies as well as gig work, and empirical studies of how caste and social stratification and discrimination get codified in datasets used to train AI systems. These rich explorations allow us to understand a range of concerns that connect to the larger premise of this edited book collection, which is the recurrence and codification of older power hierarchies discrimination, larger

P. Raghunath (✉)
University of Sheffield, Sheffield, UK
e-mail: p.raghunath@sheffield.ac.uk

P. Raghunath (ed.), *Critical Political Economy and Southern Approaches to AI*, Palgrave Global Media Policy and Business,
https://doi.org/10.1007/978-3-032-14090-6_7

transnational economic and national legal structures that enable current and newer modes of identification, categorisation and control, and finally, the discrepancies inherent in how AI technologies get made. We started this collection with the recognition that 'critical' in Critical Political Economy does not allude to 'criticism' alone. Critique, as the introductory chapter explained, is an inquiry into truth claims, how they get naturalised and how they may be unsettled. Similarly, the introductory chapter presents Southern approaches as an umbrella and as a starting point to bring to the fore marginalised, situated experiences, without relegating them as relativist.

The chapters in this short edited collection have each engaged with ideas that showcase this dialogue and cross-pollination between Critical Political Economy and Southern approaches, These range from showcasing historical underpinnings to current experiences of multiple techno-modernities, with each chapter offering grounded experiences and accompanying critique of universalised stories, policies and practices of the global AI and the data economy.

Resource Economy Around Digital Infrastructures and Sociality

The prevailing narrative of the AI and data economy focuses myopically on proprietary algorithms, platform scale, and the capital expenditure of technology corporations and national governments globally. This collection, however, brings to the fore a more rigorous, grounded view of the resource base that sustains this global infrastructure—a base founded on both invisible human labour and captured sociality.

The introductory chapter began with a passage about Sheela, a data annotator. Her labour, involving the meticulous cleaning, labelling, and tagging of datasets, is the invisible backbone of the global data annotation industry, an industry worth hundreds of millions of dollars. Sheela's job role, while seen as low-skilled low-paid work, is essentially knowledge work replete with her interpretation, engagement and decision-making in the absence of specific real-world scenarios that are pre-determined as guidelines provided to data annotators. People like Sheela bring to their jobs skills that are in effect unrecognised. This necessary knowledge work is, ironically, destined for automation, illustrating how the data worker is structurally required but ultimately disposable.

The chapter by Prince introduces the conceptual terrain to understand this value extraction in the data economy through the idea of the surplus value of sociality, derived from the anthropological critique of computational data. This analysis fundamentally challenges the notion that data is a neutral, finite resource, arguing that "social interaction as such, insofar as it is recorded as data, is an excess that has value in itself". This excess, which cannot be contained in a priori frames, is the raw material that is continuously captured and capitalised upon by platforms. This excess converts human sociality that is produced and reproduced through structured interactions in digital infrastructural circuits to a quantified resource that generates value. This argument that data-is-not-raw is reinforced by Shukla's chapter that speaks of that data as a 'cultural entity', meaning its very collection and storage are embedded in socio-cultural biases. The resource economy of digital infrastructures is thus revealed not as a mere transfer of information, but as a continuous process of epistemic and economic capture that transforms human social existence into a persistent commodity. These instances showcase how the metrics of value creation and extraction are being fundamentally altered in the AI and data economy.

Long-Distance Governance of Labour and Trusteeship

An important aspect that chapters in this collection draw attention to is the cartography and power invested in long-distance governance of digital systems. Harking back to colonial long-distance governance of entire populations in colonies, the authors point us to the ability of Big Tech corporations as well as governance structures that incentivise them to maximise power while strategically minimising accountability, leading to a deliberate and structural evasion of Trusteeship.

Lestari chapter's concept of "AI colonialism" provides empirical evidence for this governance model. It details how multinational platform capital enforces a new governance regime that intensifies the "dual burden" faced by female gig workers. Algorithmic management acts as the instrument of this long-distance control, dictating wages, working hours, and standards across continents, all the while evading the liabilities of a traditional employer or the social protections mandated by local labour laws. The governance is algorithmic, gendered, and extractive, successfully externalising risk onto the precarious frontier lives of these women. The control is precise and immediate, yet the responsibility for welfare, safety and security remains conveniently remote.

Crucially, this structural failure of Trusteeship is not limited to the market; it is mirrored in the state's domain. Sahoo's analysis of deepfakes in Indian elections reveals that the state's governance power is not neutrally applied; it is entangled in a "co-constitutive ecosystem" with political parties and transnational tech platforms. The state, instead of acting as a steadfast trustee of democratic integrity, is part of a nexus that facilitates, or critically fails to regulate, the spread of politically manipulative synthetic media—a phenomenon described by Sahoo as creating "fake language intimacy" to subvert democratic processes. This entanglement means that the state is either complicit in, or institutionally overwhelmed by, the governance challenge, leading to a profound erosion of the social contract. The chapters argue that trusteeship is systematically undermined in the digital age when neither the platform (the de facto employer and governor of labour) nor the state (the legal sovereign and guardian of democracy) acts as an accountable guardian of public interest. Rebuilding trusteeship requires confronting this long-distance governance that allows power without corresponding accountability.

Internal Colonisation

This collection's focus on Southern theorising insists on the principle of genealogical critique, demanding that we treat technology not as an exceptional event, but as a historically situated phenomenon. This principle reveals that the digital age is defined not by a simplistic external imposition, but by a complex, multi-layered process of internal colonisation, where global AI power leverages and deepens pre-existing, localised power hierarchies. The political baggage of the past is encoded into the socio-technical systems of the present. Shukla's chapter on caste bias in Indian prison datasets provides powerful evidence of this internal colonisation. Shukla argues compellingly that the creation of digital infrastructure is inseparable from the historical, structural violence of caste. The biases found in AI training data are not errors; they are encoded histories, translated from social stratification into computational logic. The technology becomes a new, highly efficient medium for internal colonisation, reinforcing the historical exclusion of so-called lower caste groups in the criminal justice system through algorithmic injustice. The data pipeline, starting from the initial decision to collect certain types of data, to how it is labelled, classified, and stored, is shown to be steeped in the practice of caste and technologises this discrimination.

Similarly, Sarlet and Weschenfelder's chapter on the unification of citizen identification numbers highlights the internal colonisation of information by the state itself. The authors meticulously link the push for a digital and informational state to the country's political history. The proposal for federated interoperability and the massive consolidation of citizens' data is viewed through the lens of a historical context where the state has often treated its citizens as subjects to be controlled. The authors reiterate the continuities in legal-administrative systems that predispose the digital ID system not as a neutral administrative tool but a potential instrument for reviving and streamlining historical patterns of surveillance and control. These continuities exist in various forms. Sahoo's writing on vernacular forms of colonialism is again revelatory of how the source of colonial power is now the state and the manifestation of this vernacular form of colonialism is in the public. Sahoo's idea of how "local practices of governance manifest colonial tendencies" locates colonialism and colonisation in the hands and minds of everyday people, the amorphous public and in an interiority rather than external sources.

What follows is a brief exploration of possible pathways to think through and undertake action-oriented efforts towards emancipatory politics in times of artificial intelligence, for pathways for future research and praxis:

1. ***Acknowledging Business and Technology Histories***: Scholars of anti-colonial practice as well as decolonisation have stressed the importance of *acknowledgement* when it comes to longer histories of categorisation and discrimination of people on the basis of race, class, gender, religion, caste and ableism. Placing technology and associated infrastructures in the longue durée allows us to recognise recurrent patterns, structures and practices that essentially continue this categorisation and discrimination of people. Understanding the governing logics of technologies and their infrastructures historically can enable us to make sense of motivations and imperial logics in current technology regimes. For instance, the logics that allowed technology to become embedded in European imperial projects and in advancing missions of colonial powers are as important to study as the current geopolitics of technology control. The role of IBM in enabling Holocaust organisers has been well-documented, in this context. Similarly, radio's role in Nazi and Cold War propaganda makes for case studies in propagandist usage

of technology. Scholars have written about how technology has been part of international development and aid efforts since the 1950s, oftentimes creating newer structures of domination and alienation. It is imperative to locate imperialism and colonial practices in not just transnational systems, but also the missions of modern nation-states. National governments have used technology to surveil and curb expression across generations, including through present-day manifestations of internet shutdowns or facial recognition technologies. Acknowledging these longer, repetitive histories of how technology gets intertwined with dominant structures of power and control is perhaps the first step in bringing the lens onto historical continuities and inequities that get compounded along intersectional lines. Such an effort can be facilitated through cross-epochal studies to recognise continuous patterns and logics, across physical as well as political and administrative geographies.

2. ***Going beyond global bipolar contests:*** Going a step beyond acknowledging imperial histories and technology, progressive scholars seek to critique the emergence of a global bipolar geopolitical contest in contemporary technology building, expansion and discourse. The setting up of global value chains of the technology and data infrastructures, labour as well as policies is an extension of this centricity, influencing the manner in which the building blocks and processes that enable the profitable functioning of the global technology industries are organised and extracted from. This is seen in the way technology corporations operating out of the United States' Silicon Valley have sought to control, overtly or through backdoor negotiations, entire governments, homegrown industries and their infrastructures in countries of the Global South. From the Cambridge Analytica scandal which revealed the influence of political data on elections in various countries to influencing the technology and foreign investment policies of countries, we see the power of Big Tech corporations incorporated in one region and the long-distance governance of their infrastructures and technologies.

In addition to gig and contractual labour for data annotation work, content moderation and call centre jobs, we see these global supply chains becoming prominent today in the realm of rare earth and critical minerals extraction. These minerals are crucial for the development of chips, undersea cables and other infrastructures that enable the functioning of emerging technologies. Geopolitical contests between the United States and China in this realm of minerals are influential in the global reorganisation of power and interests. In addition to this, we have and continue to witness incongruencies between the Silicon Valley and European legal systems, especially with numerous instances of antitrust cases against American Big Tech companies. While this creates yet another global bipolar contest to reign in the overreach of these companies, we also witness the Brussels Effect with the European Union assuming de facto world leadership in data governance laws and externalising these legal frameworks related to technology beyond its jurisdiction. These contemporary developments map onto older patterns of carving out the world, erasing the importance of the 'human' on the geopolitical map.

3. ***Recognising 'Frontier Lives'***: The third consideration before us is to then bring to focus a different referent object in the global AI order—from the frontier technologies of AI and machine learning to 'frontier lives'. 'Frontier lives' refer to those individuals and communities that interface with, enable and bear the adverse repercussions of these technologies, even while contributing to filling private coffers and remaining amiss in the grand story of frontier technology. This would essentially mean that the remit of critical scholarship on AI/ML technologies and the data economy should take cognisance of the lives and livelihood conditions for those doing the maintenance work of subsea cables, bring the lens onto miners and those processing minerals to build critical internet and AI infrastructures, those engaged in factory work to bring chips to enable the massive training needs of Generative AI systems, and the knowledge work of data annotators who experience deskilling and socio-economic immobility upon their jobs being automated. These instances are only a tiny dent on the surface of conversations on global divisions of labour, control over intellectual property and geopolitics of technology transfers today.

In recognising 'frontier lives' through public research and engagement efforts, we in the academy have a chance to communicate across regions, disciplinary specialisms and the perceived incommensurables of theoretical and praxeological traditions alike.

Index

P. Raghunath (ed.), *Critical Political Economy and Southern Approaches to AI*, Palgrave Global Media Policy and Business,
https://doi.org/10.1007/978-3-032-14090-6

The manufacturer's authorised representative in the EU is Springer Nature Customer Service Centre GmbH, Europaplatz 3, 69115 Heidelberg, Germany. If you have any concerns regarding our products, please contact ProductSafety@springernature.com

Printed and bound by CPI Group (UK) Ltd, Croydon, CR0 4YY
16/09/2026
02217786-0001